Peter Matthiessen

For Edna Nagle and in memory of William Nagle
and for Bill Nagle and Bruce & Lurelda Nagle

Peter Matthiessen

An Annotated Bibliography

by WILLIAM H. ROBERSON

McFarland & Company, Inc., Publishers
Jefferson, North Carolina, and London

Acknowledgments: I am grateful to a number of people who assisted me in ways large and small during the time I have worked on this book. They should in no way be held accountable for any errors or omissions I have made. My thanks to Robert Gerbereux, Dan Giancola, Charisse Loder, Peter Matthiessen, Robert Pattison, and Jane Schillie. Special thanks to Elizabeth Herbert for her extraordinary helpfulness in obtaining items through interlibrary loan and for her general interest and good cheer. Thanks to Tim Roberson and Jean Roberson, both of who seem to know a great deal more about computers than I do. My work was made easier because of them.

ISBN 0-7864-1055-8 (softcover : 50# alkaline paper)

Library of Congress cataloguing data are available

British Library cataloguing data are available

Manufactured in the United States of America

*McFarland & Company, Inc., Publishers
Box 611, Jefferson, North Carolina 28640
www.mcfarlandpub.com*

Contents

Preface

Although Peter Matthiessen has had one of the most distinguished careers in American literature since the publication of his first novel, *Race Rock*, in 1954 — publishing since that time seven additional novels, one short story collection, and over fifteen works of nonfiction — he remains one of the most under-recognized and under-appreciated writers of our time. For his work to have generated but one monograph devoted to it, after a career of almost fifty years, is an embarrassment to the academic community. Clearly, he and his work have not received the commensurate amount of attention and popularity they deserve.

In part, this has been a result of Matthiessen's own reticence in talking about his work or himself, but more importantly, he has been victimized by the very diversity of his interests and work. He can not be neatly identified or easily categorized by critics. He is an environmentalist, explorer, naturalist, social activist, Zen priest, journalist, travel writer, nature writer, and novelist. At any time, these roles and more may merge and overlap to produce both fiction and nonfiction of a sensitivity and lyricism unmatched by most other writers. As his Zen name, Muryo, suggests, he is without boundaries, and critics and readers find it difficult to anticipate where his myriad interests will next take him.

This bibliography is offered in recognition of Matthiessen's accomplishments thus far and in an effort to facilitate the start of a correction to the critical oversight regarding his work. It is the first attempt to present a complete and accurate annotated record of all English language materials by and about Peter Matthiessen.

All bibliographic work concerning Matthiessen owes a debt of gratitude to D. Nicholas's brief enumerative primary and secondary bibliography, *Peter Matthiessen: A Bibliography: 1951-1979* and, to a lesser extent, James Dean Young's "A Peter Matthiessen Checklist" which appeared in *Critique* in 1979. Both of these works were used as the starting points for my own research. I have not accepted the accuracy of any previous entry, however. This bibliography seeks to correct all earlier omissions and errors while adding over twenty years of primary and secondary material to the previous works. I have attempted to personally verify all entries either in the original or by photocopies. The one area where it was not possible for me to examine each entry was the foreign language editions of Matthiessen's books. I relied upon the *Index Translationum: International Bibliography of Translations* (UNESCO), the OCLC WorldCat database, and the various national union catalogs available through the Internet. For those other entries that I have not been able to personally verify, I have cited the source for the entry.

The intent of this bibliography was to be inclusive rather than exclusive in the selection of material. Works that mention Matthiessen only in passing or within a larger group of representative writers, however, have not been included.

The first part of the bibliography, "Works by Peter Matthiessen," is divided into individual sections for "Books and Broadsides," subdivided into "Fiction," "Nonfiction," and "Edited Works"; "Short Fiction"; "Articles and Essays," "Sound Recordings"; "Video Recordings"; "Adaptations"; and "Miscellany." The entries within each section are arranged chronologically, and same year entries are arranged alphabetically. In the "Books and Broadsides" section, physical descriptions of United States trade first editions are given. Annotations and content notes are provided where appropriate.

Part II, "Works About Peter Matthiessen," is an annotated listing of secondary material containing sections for "Books and Articles," "Book Reviews," "Dissertations," "Reviews of Sound Recordings," "Reviews of Videos," and "Miscellany." The entries are arranged chronologically by year of publication, and entries within each year are arranged alphabetically. The sections of reviews are arranged chronologically according to the publication of the Matthiessen work. The arrangement of the reviews for each title is then alphabetical.

The annotations attempt to provide an indication of the central and significant points of each piece through description, summary, and/or quotation. In some cases, an evaluation is made about the relative merit of the work. In those instances where Matthiessen is treated in only part of the article or essay, the pages cited are those that are particularly relevant to him. The pages for the entire article or review are given in brackets.

The "Index" provides name, title, and subject access to the material presented in both Part I and Part II.

Bibliographies are always ongoing, especially those dealing with a living, working author. The purpose of this work is to provide as accurate and comprehensive a beginning as possible for those readers, researchers, and critics who want to pursue and study Matthiessen's work. I hope they will add to it, revise it, and benefit from it.

Chronology

1927	Born in New York City on May 22nd to Erard A. Matthiessen and Elizabeth Bleecker Carey
1932–1945	Attends St. Bernard's School in Manhattan and Hotchkiss School in Connecticut
1945–1946	Serves in the U. S. Navy; stationed at Pearl Harbor
1947	Enters Yale University
1948–1949	Attends the New School for Social Research at the Sorbonne, Paris
1950	Graduates from Yale with a B.A. in English
1950–1951	Creative writing instructor at Yale
1951	Receives the *Atlantic* Prize for best first story for "Sadie"
	Marries Patricia Southgate
	Moves to Paris
	Founds *The Paris Review* with Harold Hume
1953	Son, Lucas, is born
1954	Daughter, Sara Carey, is born
	Moves to Long Island, New York
	Race Rock is published
1954–1956	Works as a commercial fisherman and as captain of a deep-sea charter fishing boat out of Montauk, Long Island
1955	*Partisans* is published
1957	Conducts research on North American wildlife
1958	Divorced
1959	*Wildlife in America* is published

"The real act of discovery consists not in finding
new lands but in seeing with new eyes."
— Marcel Proust

"I believe in grit and passion; if you don't get mad
and put feelings into things, those things are
dead."
— Peter Matthiessen

"...connect the prose and the passion, and both
will be exalted..."
— E. M. Forster

Introduction

Peter Matthiessen was born May 22, 1927, at Le Roy Hospital in Manhattan. He was the second of three children born to Erard A. Matthiessen and the former Elizabeth B. Carey; his sister Mary was the oldest child, his brother, George, the youngest. His father was a noted architect who established his own firm, Matthiessen, Johnson & Green, in Manhattan and Stamford, Connecticut. The family, affluent and socially prominent, was "well insulated" from the effects of the Depression. They had an apartment on Fifth Avenue overlooking Central Park and a country home with a view of the Hudson River before settling in Stamford, and they maintained a summer home on Fishers Island.

Matthiessen attended St. Bernard's School in New York City which, as he wrote, "offered an all–British faculty and strong Old World ideas about corporal punishment, first grade Latin and other such enlightenments."[1] After the family moved to Connecticut, he attended the Greenwich Country Day School before entering The Hotchkiss School in Lakeview, Connecticut, preparatory to entering Yale, as his father had done before him.

Matthiessen was a bit wild when young. He says he was "immensely difficult" and that his parents went through a lot. He was enough of a troublemaker at Hotchkiss to be "banished to a penitential corridor" at the beginning of his second year. He admits that his "formative years left me unformed; despite kind family, superior schooling, and all the orderly advantages, I remained disorderly."[2] The rebelliousness and antagonism finally led his father to tell him he wasn't welcome at home — fearing, perhaps, that he would be a bad influence on his younger brother.

While he admits to "a lot of rich-boy fun," by the age of ten Matthiessen began to develop "a lifelong uneasiness about unearned privilege that was to become an important factor in [his] life."[3] He came to repudiate much of what he refers to as WASP or Establishment values. His writing would come to reflect an

1

obligation to write on behalf of those people who didn't have the advantages he had.

Matthiessen was seventeen and in his third year at Hotchkiss when he lied about his age and joined the U. S. Coast Guard Temporary Service. His parents had no idea where he was for a number of months during 1944. Finally, his father, who was serving in the United States Naval Reserves, was able to locate him and informed the Coast Guard that he was under age. Matthiessen returned to Hotchkiss to finish his last year. Upon graduation, he enlisted in the Navy.

As a result of poor eyesight, Matthiessen was assigned shore duty and stationed at Pearl Harbor during 1945–46. He served as a Ships Service Laundryman Third Class before being broken back to Seaman First Class as a result of an altercation with the Shore Patrol. He also served as the manager for the Navy Golden Gloves team and wrote sports articles for the Honolulu *Advertiser*.

As early as fifteen or sixteen, Matthiessen knew he wanted to write. He had written for various school publications, and after he was discharged from the Navy in 1946, he eventually entered Yale in 1947 as an English major. While there he co-wrote a hunting and fishing column for the *Yale Daily News* entitled "Two in the Bush" and continued to write short stories. During his senior year his story, "Sadie," won the *Atlantic* Prize. After graduation in 1950, he spent another year at Yale as a creative writing instructor.

While at Yale Matthiessen had participated in the first class of the Smith-Yale junior year aboard program, studying at the New School for Social Research at the Sorbonne. While there he met Patricia Southgate. Her father worked for the State Department and had been Chief of Protocol at the White House for Franklin Roosevelt. Following a tempestuous engagement, they married in 1951. After briefly living in New York, they decided to move to Paris.

Their apartment in Paris became the center for a group of young expatriate American writers, including James Baldwin, Terry Southern, and William Styron, as well as a few older, established writers like Irwin Shaw and Richard Wright. It was during this time that Matthiessen conceived of the idea for a literary journal that would become *The Paris Review*. With Harold (Doc) Humes, the journal was begun in 1951 with an investment of $1000. Matthiessen asked his old childhood friend from St. Bernard's, George Plimpton, to come from Cambridge University to be editor of the journal. According to Matthiessen the purpose of starting a new journal "was really to give some kind of exposure to young writers who weren't well known. And we hit upon the idea of interviewing well known writers, which we knew would sell a magazine."[4]

While in Paris he completed his first published novel. By the time *Race Rock* appeared in 1954, he and his family, which now included a son, Lucas, had returned to the United States settling in the Springs in East Hampton on Long Island.

Matthiessen's second novel, *Partisans*, was published the next year. Neither work, he believes, is very good. He agrees with William Styron's assessment that *Partisans* isn't a novel; "it's a short story that goes on too long."[5] Matthiessen says that a novel should have "a sense of shambling looseness, unpredictability; it shouldn't be taut." *Partisans* is "too pared down, too cut away." Six years later he published *Raditzer*, the first novel that "showed signs of a little hope." Yet, it too, in Matthiessen's view, is "a little bit too tight, too neat."[6]

Taken together, despite Matthiessen's own assessment, the first three novels should not simply be dismissed as apprentice work. The books were widely reviewed and generally well received, in some cases, quite extravagantly so. The consensus of the reviewers was that Matthiessen showed a great deal of promise, particularly in the clarity and precision of his prose, but if there was an obvious failure in the works, it was to be found in their structure. More than one critic noted the Conradian influence within the works. The books suffer from a deadly seriousness that is not yet lightened by the humor that is to be consistently found in Matthiessen's later works but which is rarely ever acknowledged by reviewers.

While the books may have been politely received, they were not financial successes. Needing to support his family, which now also included a daughter, Sara, Matthiessen began to work as a commercial fisherman in 1954. During the spring and fall he would clam and scallop and work on a haul-seining crew; in the summer he captained a charter fishing boat out of Montauk. This schedule left him the winter and days of bad weather to write. For Matthiessen the experience of fishing and writing was a happy combination. "I had plenty of writing time, and when I was outdoors, working with my hands, I was in good shape, and off and on I made good money."[7]

But the amount of time he devoted to his various activities took a toll on his marriage, and by the end of the summer of 1956 Matthiessen and his wife had split up and he decided to give up the charter boat business. Matthiessen acknowledges that the split freed him to do the traveling he should have done before marrying and becoming a father. For the next five years he traveled the world.

In late 1956 he began to drive around the North American continent in his Ford convertible doing research for a survey of the effects of civilization on the wildlife of North America. *Sports Illustrated* had agreed to publish three articles on the vanishing wildlife of America but then decided that they would publish only two.[8] Matthiessen did not want the research he had done to be wasted, and he realized that there was no book available on the subject. From his six months of visiting the continent's wildlife refuges, he produced his first nonfiction work, *Wildlife in America*, which was published in 1959.

When Matthiessen decided that he needed to write nonfiction to earn money to support his family, there were two subjects he thought he knew something about: boats and wildlife. His knowledge of boats he had gained from his practical experience in the Navy and as a commercial fisherman. His interest in wildlife was a lifelong passion, influenced by both his mother and father. His father was active in conservation work, founding the Nature Centers for Young America, and later serving as a trustee of the National Audubon Society, the Nature Conservancy, and the American Museum of Natural History. He had shared his mother's interest in birds since he was a child, and he and his brother caught snakes on their property in Connecticut. While at Yale he took courses in zoology and ornithology. But he acknowledges that he doesn't deserve the labels of anthropologist and naturalist that he is sometimes given. He refers to himself as an informed amateur and generalist in the natural sciences, a person with "a lot of slack information" who brings more curiosity than expertise to his research.

Wildlife in America was published to considerable critical acclaim and popular success. It is a seminal book on North American wildlife and for the conservation movement in the United States. Roger Tory Peterson said it was necessary reading for any ethical person, and more than one reviewer suggested that every member of Congress read it. The book established Matthiessen as a nature writer of stature.

After his trip across the United States, Matthiessen traveled to South America for five months in 1959 and 1960. This trip was sponsored by the *New Yorker* after Matthiessen suggested to its editor, William Shawn, a series of trips around the world studying and reporting on the last remaining wild places, enabling him to satisfy his own interest in what he terms "wildlife, and wild places, and wild people." The trip resulted in his second work of nonfiction, *The Cloud Forest: A Chronicle of the South American Wilderness.* It also provided him with the material for his next novel and the one that would prove to be his breakthrough work of fiction, both critically and commercially.

At Play in the Fields of the Lord was published in 1965; it was nominated for the National Book Award and optioned by Metro-Goldwyn-Mayer. Here Matthiessen was finally able to produce a novel that had the requisite "sense of shambling looseness [and] unpredictability" that he found lacking in his earlier works. It is, as William Styron has stated, "the fully realized work of a novelist at white heat and at the peak of his powers: a dense, rich, musical book, filled with tragic and comic resonances, it is fiction of genuine stature."[9]

Prior to the publication of *At Play in the Fields of the Lord*, Matthiessen had continued with his world travels, joining the Harvard-Peabody expedition of 1961 to study the Kurelu, a tribe of Stone Age warriors in the Baliem Valley of New Guinea. His resulting book, *Under the Mountain Wall: A Chronicle of Two Seasons in the Stone Age*, provided Matthiessen with his third successful work of nonfiction. The book makes clear what had become a standard for Matthiessen's nonfiction — his scrupulous and discerning observations. His ability as a novelist benefits his reportage in his ability to set scene and character succinctly and well. By this third book, one adjective has become almost de rigueur in describing Matthiessen's prose — evocative.

Matthiessen followed the successes of *Under the Mountain Wall* and *At Play in the Fields of the Lord* with a period of continued travel, resulting in essays for the *New Yorker* and subsequent books. These works reinforced his position as a nature and travel writer of the first order.

In 1967 he published *Oomingmak: The Expedition to the Musk Ox Island in the Bering Sea*, a narrative of his participation in an expedition to Nunivak Island to capture musk oxen calves. The same year he contributed the text for *The Shorebirds of North America*, which would later be published as *The Wind Birds*. It was also in 1967 that he traveled to the Grand Cayman islands to sail on a converted schooner to hunt green turtles. This trip provided him with the material for "A Reporter at Large: To the Miskito Bank," one of his best *New Yorker* articles, and was also the inspiration for *Far Tortuga*.

During the same year he also participated in and reported on Peter Gimbel's attempt to film the great white shark for his documentary, *Blue Water, White Death*. Published in 1971, *Blue Meridian* is Matthiessen's account of the expedition's search for what has been referred to as the most dangerous fish in the sea.

In the midst of this world travel, Matthiessen found the time to visit Delano, California and meet with Cesar Chavez in the summer of 1968. He was profoundly affected by Chavez and has referred to him as the most impressive man he has ever known. He returned a year later during the national boycott of table grapes and following Chavez's hunger strike. *Sal Si Puedes*, published in 1970 and based on his experiences with Chavez, is often referred to as Matthiessen's first book of advocacy journalism, which he would later continue with works on Leonard Peltier, the American Indians, and the baymen of eastern Long Island. But this is a narrow view of both advocacy journalism and of Matthiessen's work. Much, if not all, of his nonfiction has always been advocacy journalism of one kind or another. While one may narrowly define his work on Chavez and the Indians as social advocacy, his earlier works are examples of environmental advocacy. They are eulogies and warnings for the impending loss of eco-systems and indigenous peoples.

Matthiessen's next book is one of his best works of nonfiction, *The Tree Where Man Was Born*, his first book on Africa. Published in 1972, it presents a melange of observations and impressions from his travels in East Africa in 1961, 1969, and 1970. With his two later works on Africa—*Sand Rivers* (1981), an account of "the last safari into the last wilderness," a trip into the Selous Game Reserve of Tanzania, and *African Silences* (1991)—this work forms a moving trilogy eulogizing the African landscape and people.

The Tree Where Man Was Born was nominated for a National Book Award and solidified Matthiessen's reputation as one of the premier nature writers in America. His nonfiction work was consistently praised for the grace and clarity of his prose style as well as the sensitivity of his observations and impressions.

This presented a problem for Matthiessen. He had begun his career as a journalist for a simple reason—he needed the money to support his family. He has repeatedly made the analogy between writing nonfiction and cabinet-making:

Nonfiction may be extremely skillful, it may be cabinetwork rather than carpentry, but it's still assembled from facts, from research, from observation; it comes from outside, not from within. It may be well made or badly made, but it's still assemblage. If you're an honest journalist, you're inevitably confined by the facts; you can't use your imagination beyond a certain point.[10]

Each new work of nonfiction added to his prominence as a nature writer, and each nonfiction book put another year between his last piece of fiction and his next. Yet fiction remained his passion. Whereas nonfiction wears him out, he says that fiction writing is exhilarating: "your battery is constantly being recharged with the excitement of it."[11] Matthiessen's next two works would accentuate the problem in the perception and recognition of him as a writer.

It had been ten years since *At Play in the Fields of the Lord* when Matthiessen's next novel, *Far Tortuga*, was published in 1975. The novel, based on his trip to the Grand Cayman Island in 1967 to participate in the fishing for sea turtles, took twelve years to produce. He has said that he could have spent another twelve years on it, that he never got sick of it. "I had fun fooling with it, trying to make it work, trying to make the pieces resonate, strung out like beads on a string."[12]

Stylistically, it is a departure from his previous fiction. While *At Play in the Fields of the Lord* is a densely textured work in terms of its themes, characters, and action, *Far Tortuga* is a stark, spare, work stripped of the typical literary contrivances and restrictions. Matthiessen has noted that it was "a purposeful change." He had gotten sick of all the metaphor.

The book is filled with the voices of the characters and the silences in between. It is a book of impressions and sensations without explanation or direction, where the empty spaces are as important and meaningful as the written words. As a novel, it comes close to being a true prose poem.

The experimental nature of the work elicited a wide range of critical reaction. It also makes it a demanding book for the reader. The closeness of the various voices and the lack of identification of the speakers take some getting used to. Matthiessen has said that it is a book that is appreciated more by writers than by critics. At least until the time of his Watson trilogy, Matthiessen believed it to be his best book. However, the book that many critics and readers believe to be his best was his next work of nonfiction, *The Snow Leopard*.

Matthiessen had become interested in Zen as a result of his second wife, Deborah Love, whom he married in 1963. He has told of returning home unexpectedly from a trip in August 1969 to find three "inscrutable small men," Zen masters, in his driveway in "weird costumes." His wife had turned to Zen from the years of drug experimentation that she and Matthiessen had followed. When he was in South America, he had experimented with ayahuasca, a jungle hallucinogen that is at the center of Lewis Moon's drug induced dream sequence in *At Play in the Fields of the Lord*. He and his wife continued to use drugs — mescaline, LSD, and psilocybin — throughout the sixties.

The relationship between Matthiessen and his wife was strained at this time, and she tried to keep her Zen practice separate from him. But despite being put off at first, Matthiessen's innate curiosity led him to begin investigating Zen and asking his wife for information. In December 1970 she took him to a weekend silent retreat, or *sesshin*. He practiced *zazen*, "sitting Zen," for twelve hours each day, an experience he described as dreadfully painful for the inexperienced. Hobbled and wiser, he "swore that this barbaric experience would never be repeated." However, within a few weeks, he was doing *zazen* every day.

As his involvement in Zen increased, his drug use stopped. He had used drugs to discover a "place where you understood something much more clearly."[13] Zen now provided the same experience.

When it was discovered that Deborah had inoperable cancer, their practice of Zen brought them closer together and provided some solace for both of them. She died in January 1972. In October and November of the next year, Matthiessen joined zoologist George Schaller on a trek across the Himalayas in search of two rare species — the snow leopard and the *bharal*, or Himalayan blue sheep. For Matthiessen it was also a search for personal enlightenment. The challenge of the 250-mile journey provided him the opportunity to reconcile himself to the loss of this wife, to the world around him, as well as to his own spiritual identity.

Matthiessen's account of both his outer and inner journeys, *The Snow Leopard*, was published in 1979 to widespread critical and popular acclaim. It received a National Book Award for contemporary thought, and the paperback edition was awarded the American Book Award in 1980. It remains his most famous work of nonfiction and, to his regret, probably the best known of all of his books. It is a book that defines as well as confines him in the minds of many readers and critics. Each successive book, especially the travel accounts, is measured against the lyricism, beauty, and introspection of this one. But more importantly, for Matthiessen, who has persistently insisted that he sees himself as and wishes his legacy to be that of a fiction writer, *The Snow Leopard* "fixes me into a nonfiction pigeonhole. I don't disown the book, but I feel my fiction is the heart of my work." And he has come "to a pretty pass where I kind of resent" it.[14]

While *The Snow Leopard* may be Matthiessen's best known work, *In the Spirit of Crazy Horse* is certainly his most controversial. He first heard of Leonard Peltier, an American Indian activist, when he was doing research for *Indian Country*, a collection of essays chronicling efforts of traditional Native Americans to defend their culture and land from corporate America and the federal government.

Peltier was serving two consecutive life terms for the killing of two F. B. I. agents during a shoot-out at the Pine Ridge reservation in South Dakota on June 26, 1975. Initially, Matthiessen was not interested in Peltier because he was a member of the radical national American Indian Movement (AIM). But as he heard more about him and the circumstances surrounding the murders and Peltier's trial,

Matthiessen became convinced that Peltier, regardless of his guilt or innocence, had been framed and railroaded into an illegal conviction.

Although he thought that a Native American writer should write the story, Matthiessen was unable to interest the few he spoke with. Russell Means, an AIM leader, suggested that Matthiessen's reputation would help bring attention to Peltier's case, and so he agreed to do it. What he originally envisioned as a long essay took three years to write. The book would embroil him in legal turmoil for an additional eight years.

In the Spirit of Crazy Horse is less a literary work than a political one. The book was published in 1983 and was intended by Matthiessen to be the primary organizing tool to rally support for Peltier and to get him a new trial. In trying to make his case and convince the reader of his cause, Matthiessen presents an exhausting and overwhelming construction of documents, testimony, and interviews. He admits that the book is an evidentiary brief for a new trial. "The primary aim was to get Peltier out of prison, not to write a literary book. Once Leonard is out, if I have time and energy, I would love to cut it down by a third."[15]

Almost immediately, David Price, an F.B.I. agent, and William J. Janklow, the South Dakota governor and former state attorney general, filed two libel suits against Matthiessen and his publisher, Viking Press. The suits claimed the book libeled Price and Janklow by printing unsubstantiated charges against them. As a result of the law suits Viking withdrew the book from circulation, thereby denying Leonard Peltier the support and publicity that his supporters and Matthiessen hoped would gain him a new trial.

After seven years of litigation and nearly three million dollars spent defending the book, Matthiessen and Viking Press prevailed, and *In the Spirit of Crazy Horse* was reissued. It was one of the longest libel cases in publishing history and drained a good deal of Matthiessen's attention and resources.

During the seven years of litigation over *In the Spirit of Crazy Horse* Matthiessen continued work on other nonfiction projects to support specific causes and interests. He published *Indian Country* in 1984. With *In the Spirit of Crazy Horse*, it forms a formidable attack upon the federal government's relationship with and mistreatment of Native Americans.

In 1986 he published both *Nine-Headed Dragon River*, an attempt to convey the essence of Zen experience drawn from his journals, and *Men's Lives: The Surfmen and Baymen of the South Fork*, a tribute to and a plea for the East End fishermen he had worked with in the 1950s and among whom he still lives. Like the two books on the Indian problems, these works were written to assist certain groups.

He published *Nine-Headed Dragon River* as a means to raise funds for a Zen center in Riverdale. The profits from the book go to the Zen Community of New York. Still, Matthiessen was hesitant about the book, worried about the appearance of proselytizing: "one is always appalled by the idea of wearing your so-called spirituality on your sleeve."[16]

Matthiessen hoped to use the profits from *Men's Lives* to help the fishermen by establishing alternate fish processing factories and reseeding the shellfish beds.[17] He also hoped to draw public attention to legislation that was affecting the fishermen's ability to support themselves. Although it was a book he says he always intended to write, he was pushed into it sooner than he expected because of the fishermen's increasingly dire economic situation. "These guys were in an emergency. They were pushed off the map by the tourist economy.... We wanted to help them out. It was too late. We should have started ten years ago."[18] Matthiessen acknowledges that the books he undertakes for specific causes are not necessarily good literary books:

> [These books] were all written to help out certain groups. I don't regret it, but I don't have any illusions about the literary quality of those books. Those books are not as good as *The Snow Leopard*, or *The Tree Where Man Was Born*. They're not. And they could have been. I knew how to make them good. But I couldn't make them good from a literary point of view and accomplish my purposes. It's very difficult to do.[19]

Still, the nineties saw three more books of nonfiction on Africa, Nepal, and Lake Baikal as well as a compilation of previously published essays on Africa. *African Silences* (1991) combines accounts of his visits to west Africa in 1978 and to central Africa in 1986, focusing on the destruction of the African wildlife, particularly the elephant, and the simultaneous ruination of the wilderness in the face of the developing African nations' economies. The following year Matthiessen joined the artist Mary Frank in a collaborative effort which drew selections from his previous books on Africa. Part of the proceeds from that book, *Shadows of Africa*, went to benefit Wildlife Conservation International.

At the invitation of the musician and environmentalist Paul Winter, in 1990 Matthiessen joined an expedition to Lake Baikal in Siberia. Baikal is the deepest and oldest freshwater lake in the world, and it is being threatened by increasing industrial development. Winter invited Matthiessen in the hope that the author could help focus attention on the imminent destruction of the region's ecosystem.

In the spring of 1992 Matthiessen returned to Nepal with photographer and ethnographer Thomas Laird. They become the first westerners in thirty years to enter the city of Lo Monthang in the Nepalese Kingdom of Lo. *East of Lo Monthang* is a beautifully realized but little noticed record of their visit to this remote Buddhist culture.

Despite his continued nonfiction work, the decade of the nineties was immensely important in the development of Matthiessen's fiction. By the end of the decade he published three new volumes of fiction that comprise the Watson trilogy, which constitutes one of the most ambitious projects in modern American literature.

In 1990 Matthiessen published *Killing Mister Watson*. With the exception of two new stories included in *On the River Styx and Other Stories*, published the year before, it was the first new fiction he had published since *Far Tortuga* in 1975. The Watson story had a long gestation. Matthiessen first learned about Edgar J. Watson when he was 17 during a trip along the west coast of Florida with his father, who pointed out Chathum River flowing out of the Everglades and commented that three or four miles up that river was a house that had belonged to a man named Watson who had been killed by his neighbors. "The seed was planted: a man killed by his neighbors! Why? The whole thing had a gothic and romantic ring to it."[20] The idea stayed with him. His curiosity eventually led him to search out whatever historical information he could find on the man and to gather oral histories from those who still remembered Watson and his exploits in southwest Florida. But he was not interested in writing a local history or even a historically accurate biography. Instead, he wanted to discover "the underlying truth, the real truth" behind Watson's story and in that truth to reveal the story of American mythologizing and to create a metaphor for the American experience. Matthiessen has said, "I see [Watson] as a great American allegory, he's really Uncle Sam."[21]

Killing Mister Watson introduced the character of Edgar J. Watson and his murder by twenty of his neighbors. Watson's fate is decided in the book's first chapter, and the remainder of the book is an account of the man through the perspective of those who knew him and killed him. It is Faulknerian in its concept and narrative technique.

The second book of the trilogy, *Lost Man's River*, appeared in 1997. Watson's son, Lucius, estranged from his father as a boy, attempts to come to some understanding of his father and to separate the facts from the rumors that surround his name.

Two years later Matthiessen completed the trilogy with *Bone by Bone*, the Watson story as told by the man himself.

The three novels were originally conceived and written as one book, but it evolved and eventually grew to a 2,000-page manuscript. Matthiessen cut the manuscript essentially into thirds and reworked the material to make each section self-sustaining. But in their conception and intent, the three books belong together as a whole, and Matthiessen is reworking and rewriting the material to reassemble it as the one novel it was originally intended to be.

With the completion of his most ambitious work of fiction, the two publications that followed the Watson trilogy highlighted Matthiessen, the nonfiction writer. *The Peter Matthiessen Reader* is a compilation of excerpts from his nonfiction works between 1959 and 1991. In January of 2000, *Tigers in the Snow* appeared. It is a record of the plight of the Siberian tiger and the efforts of the Siberian Tiger Project to study and protect them. Matthiessen had been invited to visit the project in the hopes that his involvement would help focus attention on the perilous state of the tigers.

That Matthiessen is one of the most important nature writers of the last century seems indisputable. Some critics are less sure of his lasting reputation as a novelist. Yet it is a testament to his strength as a fiction writer that there is no critical consensus as to what is his best work. *At Play in the Fields of the Lord, Far Tortuga, Killing Mister Watson,* and *Bone by Bone* all have their advocates.

Certainly there is a strong connection between his fiction and his nonfiction. His best fiction is informed by his nature writing, and this goes beyond the descriptive passages of flora and fauna in the novels. There are the shared themes of the beauty of the natural world, the consequences of human greed, and the loss of traditional cultures to increasing global homogeneity. Repeatedly, eloquently, and presciently he has warned of the dangers to our planet and to ourselves from the realpolitiks of the twentieth-century. His best fiction —*At Play in the Fields of the Lord, Far Tortuga,* and the Watson trilogy — has emerged from his concerns and experiences in real life:

> I have a curiosity about things, a restless mind. I get into things more than I can handle, into overwork and stress. I keep trying to slow it all down, eliminate a few interests, but I'm embattled in the sense of being very concerned about the future of the world my son and grandsons will inherit.[22]

More than once, Matthiessen has spoken of the tendency of American writers to go on writing longer than they should, of producing weak work late in life. He has said that he hopes that he will know "when my work becomes repetitive or stupid or senile or when I'm just coasting, sneaking by on past work."[23] He need not worry. For more than four decades he has consistently produced significant, innovative, and passionate work. There are few American writers, old or young, who can combine Matthiessen's grace, intelligence, empathy and extraordinary observational and notational powers with his willingness to take literary risks. He is one of America's great literary polymaths, and a writer of consistent and profound humanity.

Notes

1. Peter Matthiessen, "New York: Old Hometown," *Architectural Digest,* 46 (November 1989), 56.

2. John Wakeman, ed., *World Authors 1950–1970* (New York: H. W. Wilson Co., 1975), 956.

3. "New York: Old Hometown," 60.

4. Shawn Adamson, "Interviewing Mister Matthiessen," *Proteus* (1994), 73.

5. Kay Bonetti, "An Interview with Peter Matthiessen," *The Missouri Review,* 12 (1989), 113.

6. *Zen and the Writing Life* (San Anselmo, CA: Audio Wisdom, 1994). Cassette.

7. Michael Shnayerson, "Higher Matthiessen," *Vanity Fair*, 54 (December 1991), 128.

8. In actuality, only one article appeared in *Sports Illustrated*: "Slaughter and Salvation," November 16, 1959.

9. William Styron, "Introduction," in D. Nicholas, *Peter Matthiessen: A Bibliography 1951–1979* (Canoga Park, CA: Orirana Press, 1979), xv–xvi.

10. "Peter Matthiessen," *Words from the Land*, ed. Stephen Trimble (Reno: University of Nevada Press, 1995), 243.

11. Wendy Smith, "PW Interviews Peter Matthiessen," *Publishers Weekly*, 229 (9 May 1986), 241.

12. Smith, 241.

13. Shayerson, 128.

14. Jerry Carroll, "Writer's Restless Mind Keeps Him Working," *San Francisco Chroncile*, 22 November 1997, D1.

15. Tom Shone, "A War of Attrition Against Their Own," *The Independent*, 1753 (30 May 1992), 31.

16. Smith, 241.

17. Smith, 240.

18. *Authors & Artists for Young People*, vol. 6, ed. Agnes Garrett and Helga P. McCue (Detroit: Gale Research, Inc., 1991), 137.

19. Bonetti, 122.

20. Michael Sims, "A Series of Tiny Astonishments," *BookPage* (2000), http://www.bookpage.com/0002bp/peter_matthiessen.html.

21. Andrew Clements, "Wild at Heart," *The Guardian*, 26 October 1999, 14.

22. Carroll, D1.

23. Lawrence Shainberg, "Emptying the Bell," *Tricycle*, 3 (Fall 1993), 47.

PART I

WORKS BY PETER MATTHIESSEN

A. Books and Broadsides

FICTION

A1. *Race Rock*, 1954

[in black:] RACE ROCK / *A novel by* / Peter Matthiessen / [colophon] / *Harper & Brothers, Publishers* / *New York*

Collation: pp. [i–x] 1–306 [307–308]. 5½" × 8⅜6".

Pagination: p.[i] half-title; p. [ii] blank; p. [iii] title page; p. [iv] "RACE ROCK / *Copyright, 1954, by Peter Matthiessen* / *printed in the United States of America* / *All rights in this book are reserved.* / *No part of the book may be used or reproduced* / *in any manner whatsoever without written per-* / *mission except in the case of brief quotations* / *embodied in critical articles and reviews. For* / *information address Harper & Brothers* / *49 East 33rd Street, New York 16, N. Y.* / FIRST EDITION / B D / *Library of Congress catalog card number: 54-6020*"; p. [v] [dedication:] "*To* / *My Wife*"; p. [vi] blank; p. [vii] [eight line epigraph] / "RAINER MARIA RILKE, *Duino Elegies*"; p.[viii] blank; p. [ix] second half-title; p. [x] blank; pp. 1–306 text; p. [307] "*Set in Linotype Electra* / *Format by Katharine Sitterly* / *Manufactured by the Haddon Craftsmen, Inc.* / Published by HARPER & BROTHERS, *New York*"; p. [308] blank.

Binding: Blue cloth covered boards. Spine, reading across: [in yellow:] RACE / ROCK / [rule] / MATTHIESSEN / [rule] / HARPER. Endpapers front and back of stiff white paper. Issued in a dust jacket.

Price: $3.50.

_____. London: Secker and Warburg, 1955.
_____. New York: Bantam Books, 1957. Published as *The Year of the Tempest*.
_____. London: Heinemann, 1966.
_____. London: Panther, 1969.
_____. New York: Vintage Books, 1988.

A2. *Partisans*, 1955

[within a decorative frame:] [in black:] PARTISANS / a novel by / PETER MAT-

THIESSEN / 1955 / THE VIKING PRESS NEW YORK

Collation: pp. [i–viii] [1–2] 3–178 [179–184]. 5¼" × 8".

Pagination: pp. [i–ii] blank; p. [iii] half-title; p. [iv] "ALSO BY PETER MATTHIESSEN / RACE ROCK"; p. [v] title page; p. [vi] "COPYRIGHT ©1955 BY PETER MATTHIESSEN / FIRST PUBLISHED BY THE VIKING PRESS IN SEPTEMBER 1955 / PUBLISHED ON THE SAME DAY IN THE DOMINION OF CANADA / BY THE MACMILLAN COMPANY OF CANADA LIMITED / Library of Congress catalog card number: 55-9639 / [colophon] / PRINTED IN U.S.A. BY THE VAIL-BALLOU PRESS, INC."; p. [vii] [an epigraph from Feodor Dostoevski's *Diaries* followed by an epigraph from A. Rossi's *Physiologie du P.C.F.*]; p. [viii] blank; p. [1] second half-title; p. [2] blank; pp. 3–178 text; pp. [179–184] blank.

Binding: Blue paper covered boards with a gray paper shelf-back. Spine, reading downward: [in brown:] PETER / MATTHIESSEN [within a decorative frame:] PARTISANS [reading across:] VIKING. On front of the shelf-back, reading downward: [in brown:] PETER / MATTHIESSEN [in a decorative frame:] PARTISANS. Endpapers front and back of stiff white paper. Issued in a dust jacket.

Price: $3.00.

_____. Toronto: Macmillan, 1955.
_____. London: Secker and Warburg, 1956.
_____. Milano: Coriere della Sera, 1956. Tr. Vittoria Comucci. [*Fantasmi a Parigi*].
_____. New York: Avon, 1957. Published as *The Passionate Seekers*.
_____. London: Heinemann, Ltd., 1966.
_____. New York: Vintage Books, 1987.
_____. London: Collins-Harvill, 1990.

A3. *Raditzer*, 1961

[in black:] RADITZER / [upside down anchor] / PETER MATTHIESSEN /

[ornamental rule] / *New York* / : *Viking Press* : / *1961*

Collation: pp. [i–vi] [1–2] 3–65 [66] 67–103 [104] 105–152 [153–154]. 5⅜″ × 8″.

Pagination: p. [i] half-title; p. [ii] "*Also by Peter Matthiessen* / *Fiction* / RACE ROCK / PARTISANS / *Nonfiction* / WILDLIFE IN AMERICA"; p. [iii] title page; p. [iv] "*Copyright © by Peter Matthiessen* / *All rights reserved* / *First published in 1961 by Viking Press, Inc.* / *625 Madison Avenue, New York 22, N.Y.* / *Published simultaneously in Canada by* / *The Macmillan Company of Canada Limited* / *Library of Congress catalog card number: 61-6034* / *Printed in the U.S.A. by H. Wolff, New York* / *All the characters* / *in this novel are fictitious*"; p. [v] [dedication:] "*To* / S & D / *with love*"; p. [vi] blank; p. [1] second half-title; p. [2] blank; pp. 3–152 text; pp. [153–154] blank.

Binding: Dark blue paper covered boards with a white cloth shelf-back. Spine, reading downward: [in blue:] MATTHIESSEN [across:] [two inverted anchors] [reading downward:] RADITZER [reading across:] *Viking*. Endpapers front and back of stiff white paper. Issued in a dust jacket designed by H. Lawrence Hoffman with an author photograph by Mary Gimbel.

Price: $3.00.

_____. Toronto: Macmillan, 1961.
_____. London: Heinemann, 1962.
_____. Paris: Stock, 1962. Tr. Michel Deutsch.
_____. New York: Dell, 1965.
_____. New York: Viking, 1965.
_____. New York: Vintage Books, 1987.

A4. *At Play in the Fields of the Lord*, 1965

[on left of double-spread title page:] [in black:] AT PLAY IN THE / [ornamental device] [on right of double-spread title page:] [in black:] Peter Matthiessen / FIELDS OF THE LORD / RANDOM HOUSE / *New York* / [colophon]

Collation: pp. [i–x] 1–373 [374]. 5½″ × 8⅜″.

Pagination: p. [i] "BOOKS BY PETER MATTHIESSEN / NONFICTION" / [lists three titles] / "FICTION" / [lists four titles]; p. [ii] blank; p. [iii] half-title; pp. [iv–v] title

page; p. [vi] "First Printing / © Copyright, 1965, by Peter Matthiessen / All rights reserved under International and Pan-American Copyright Con- / ventions. Published in New York by Random House, Inc., and simultane- / ously in Toronto, Canada, by Random House of Canada Limited. / Library of Congress Catalog Card Number: 65-21230 / Manufactured in the United States of America / By The Haddon Craftsmen, Scranton, Pennsylvania"; p. [vii] [dedication:] "For / Luke and Carey / Rue and Alex"; p. [viii] blank; p. [ix] "*At Play in the Fields of the Lord* / The way to innocence, to the uncreated and to God leads / on, not back, not back to the wolf or to the child, but ever further / into sin, ever deeper into human life. / — Hermann Hesse"; p. [x]; pp. 1–373 text; p. [374] "ABOUT THE AUTHOR" / [ten-line statement] / [colophon].

Binding: Light beige cloth covered boards with a black cloth shelf-back. Spine, reading across: [in gold:] AT / PLAY / IN THE / FIELDS / OF THE / LORD / [rule] / Peter / Matthiessen / [colophon] / RANDOM / HOUSE. Front, in center: [in gold:] [decorative design]. Endpapers front and back of stiff white paper. Issued in a dust jacket.

Price: $5.95.

_____. London: Heinemann, 1966.
_____. Leiden: Sijthoff, 1966. Tr. J. F. Kliphaus and R. W. M. Kliphaus Vlaskamp. [*Spelend in de Velden des Herden*].
_____. München: Droemer Knaur; Zurich: Droemer, 1966. Tr. Paul Baudisch. [*Ein Pfeil in den Himmel*].
_____. New York: New American Library, 1967. A Signet Book.
_____. Paris: Gallimard, 1967. Tr. M. Rambaud. [*En Liberté dans les Champs du Seigneur*].
_____. Barcelona: Plaza & Janés, 1968. Tr. Rosalía Vazquez. [*Jugando en Los Campos del Señor*].
_____. Copenhagen: Fremad, 1968. Tr. Peter Jerndorff Jessen. [*Syndig Leg Med Rene Sjaele*].
_____. London: Panther, 1968.
_____. Stockholm: Forum, 1968. Tr. Kjell Ekstrom. [*Lek Pa Guds Grona Angar*].
_____. New York: Bantam Books, 1976.
_____. New York: Random House, 1978. With *Far Tortuga*.

_____. London: Granada, 1980. A Panther book.

_____. Toronto and New York: Bantam Windstone edition.

_____. Praha: Odeon, 1983. Tr. Šimon Pellar. [*Hráči na vinici Páně*].

_____. New York: Vintage Books, 1987.

_____. London: Collins Harvill, 1988.

_____. Oslo: Aventura, 1988. Tr. Finn B. Larsen. [*Junelens Evangeluim*].

_____. Amsterdam: Contact, 1991. Second ed. Tr. J. F. Kliphaus and R W. M. Kliphaus Vlaskamp. [*Oerwoud*].

_____. New York: Vintage Books, 1991.

_____. New York: Flamingo [HarperCollins], 1991.

_____. Milano: Frassinelli, 1992. Tr. Eileen Romano. [*Giocando nei Campi del Signore*].

_____. Tokyo: Hayakawashobo, 1992. Tr. Kazue Saito. [*Kami no Niwa Ni Asobite*].

_____. Madrid: Siruela, 1992. Tr. Jose Luis Lopez Munos. [*Jugando en los Campos del Senor*].

_____. Amsterdam: Pandora, 1996. Third ed. Tr. J. F. Kliphaus and R. W. M. Kliphaus Vlaskamp. [*Oerwoud*].

_____. New York: Crown Books, 1996.

A5. *Seal Pool*, 1972

[on right of double-spread title page with a colored illustration across both sides:] [in black:] SEAL POOL / By PETER MATTHIESSEN / Illustrated by / WILLIAM PÈNE DU BOIS / Doubleday & Company, Inc., / Garden City, New York

Collation: pp. [1–6], 7–10 [11] 12–13 [14] 15–17 [18] 19–22 [23] 24–25 [26] 27–30 [31] 32–37 [38] 39–42 [43] 44–45 [46] 47–50 [51] 52–54 [55] 56–57 [58] 59–62 [63] 64–66 [67] 68–69 [70] 71–74 [75] 76–78 [79–80]. 5⅜" × 8⅛".

Pagination: pp. [1] blank; pp. [2–3] title page; p. [4] "LIBRARY OF CONGRESS CATALOG CARD NUMBER: 73-104984 / TEXT COPYRIGHT ©1972 BY PETER MATTHIESSEN / ILLUSTRATIONS COPYRIGHT ©1972 BY WILLIAM PÈNE DU BOIS / ALL RIGHTS RESERVED / PRINTED IN THE UNITED STATES OF AMERICA / FIRST EDITION"; p. [5] [dedication:] "*For the young of all species*"; pp. [6]–[79] text and illustrations; p. [80] [statements about the author and illustrator].

Binding: White paper covered boards printed in yellow, brown, red, blue, green, pink, and black. Front: [in black:] Peter Matthiessen / [in white:] SEAL / POOL / [in black:] Illustrated by William Pène du Bois. Back, centered: [colored illustration]. Spine, reading downward: [in black against multicolored pastel stripes:] SEAL POOL Matthiessen/Pène du Bois Doubleday. Endpapers front and back of white paper. Issued in a dust jacket.

Price: $4.95.

_____. London: Angus and Robertson, 1974. Published as *The Great Auk Escape*.

A6. *Far Tortuga*, 1975

[in black:] PETER MATTHIESSEN / FAR TORTUGA / Random House [colophon] NEW YORK

Collation: pp. [i–viii] [1–2] 3–7 [8–9] 10 [11] 12–24 [25] 26–32 [33] 34–42 [43] 44–50 [51–53] 54–88 [89] 90–95 [96] 97–102 [103] 104–116 [117] 118–121 [122] 123–127 [128–129] 130–134 [135] 136–137 [138] 139–163 [164] 165 [166] 167–174 [175] 176–180 [181–182] 183–201 [202] 203–216 [217] 218–252 [253] 254–258 [259] 260 [261] 262–268 [269] 270–281 [282] 283–324 [325–326] 327 [328] 329–360 [361] 362–365 [366–372] 373 [374] 375–378 [379] 380–387 [388] 389–390 [391] 392–395 [396] 397–403 [404–405] 406–408. 6¼" × 9¼".

Pagination: p. [i] half-title; p. [ii] "BOOKS BY PETER MATTHIESSEN / NONFICTION" / [lists seven titles] / "FICTION" / [lists five titles]; p. [iii] title page; p. [iv] "Copyright ©1975 by Peter Matthiessen / All rights reserved under International and Pan-American Copy- / right Conventions. Published in the United States by Random / House, Inc., New York, and simultaneously in Canada by Random / House of Canada Limited, Toronto. / *Library of Congress Cataloging in Publication Data*" / [four lines] / "Manufactured in the United States of America / 4 6 8 9 7 5 3"; p. [v] [dedication:] "FOR MARIA"; p. [vi] "ACKNOWLEDGMENTS" / [nine line statement]; p. [vii] "Death, Thou comest / When I had Thee least in mind. / —*Every-*

man"; p. [viii] blank; p. [1] second half-title; p. [2] blank; pp. 3–408 text.

Binding: Light blue paper covered boards with a darker blue cloth shelf-back. Spine, reading downward: [in dark blue:] FAR TORTUGA / Peter Matthiessen [in light blue:] RANDOM HOUSE [across:] [colophon]. Front, center in upper half: [in dark blue:] P º M. Endpapers front and back of stiff blue paper are printed in blue and show maps of the Caribbean and the Cayman Islands. Issued in a dust jacket designed by Kenneth Miyamoto and illustrated by Walter Rane, with a photograph of Matthiessen by Nancy Crampton.

Price: $10.95.

_____. New York: Bantam, 1976.

_____. New York: Random House, 1978. With *At Play in the Fields of the Lord.*

_____. Stockhom: Forum, 1978. Tr. Hans Dahlberg.

_____. Budapest: Európa, 1981. Tr. Bartos Tibor. [*Titkos Tortuga*].

_____. New York: Vintage Books, 1984.

_____. New York: Vintage Books, 1988.

_____. London: Collins Harvill, 1989.

_____. Paris: Éd. de l'Olivier, 1993. Tr. Brice Matthieussent.

_____. Paris: Seuil, 1995. Tr. Brice Matthieussent.

A7. *Midnight Turning Gray,* 1984

[in black:] MIDNIGHT TURNING GRAY / SHORT STORIES By / PETER MATTHIESSEN / & / Ampersand Press / Roger Williams College / Bristol, RI 02809

Collation: pp. [1–8] 9–94 [95–96]. 6" × 9".

Pagination: p. [1] half-title; p. [2] blank; p. [3] title page; p. [4] "Acknowledgment is made to the following publications in which / these stories first appeared: / *The Atlantic Monthly:* "Sadie" and "The Fifth Day" / *Harper's Bazaar:* "The Wolves of Aquila" / *Harper's Magazine:* "Travelin Man" / *New World Writing:* "Late in the Season" / *The Paris Review:* "A Replacement" / "Midnight Turning Gray" is reprinted from *The Saturday Evening / Post* ©1963 The Curtis Publishing Company. / Library of Congress Catalogue Card Number: 83-82381 / ISBN 0-96047-5-6 / *Midnight Turning Gray* Copyright ©1984 by Peter Matthiessen /

Composition by Coastal Composition / Box 2600, Ocean Bluff, MA 02065 / Layout and design by Coastal Composition and Ampersand Press / Printed in U.S.A. / Published by Ampersand Press, Creative Writing Program, / Roger Williams College, Bristol, RI 02809"; p. [5] [dedication:] "*for Sherry* / My friend for nearly fifty years — Good Lord!— who / pestered me to return to fiction before the smoke clears."; p. [6] blank; p. [7] "CONTENTS"; p. [8] blank; pp. 9–94 text, pp. [95–96] blank.

Binding: Gray colored paper wrappers. Spine, reading downward: [in black:] MIDNIGHT TURNING GRAY PETER MATTHIESSEN & AMPERSAND. Front cover: [in black:] MIDNIGHT / TURNING / GRAY / SHORT STORIES By / PETER MATTHIESSEN. Back cover, in upper left quadrant: [in black:] $5.50. Opposite, in upper right quadrant: [in black:] ISBN: 0-9604740-5-6. Centered in middle, in black, is a thirteen line statement about the author. At bottom: [in black:] & / Ampersand Press / Roger Williams College / Bristol, RI 02809.

Contents: Sadie / The Fifth Day / Midnight Turning Gray / Late in the Season / Travelin Man / A Replacement / The Wolves of Aquila

Price: $5.50.

A8. *On the River Styx and Other Stories,* 1989

[in gray:] ON / THE /RIVER /STYX AND / OTHER / STORIES / [in black:] PETER / MATTHIESSEN

Collation: pp. [i–ix] x [xi–xii] [1–3] 4–13 [14] 15–23 [24] 25–32 [33] 34–46 [47] 48–70 [71] 72–91 [92] 93–105 [106] 107–137 [138] 139–167 [168] 169–208 [209–212]. 5¾" × 8¼".

Pagination: p. [i] blank; p. [ii] "ALSO BY / PETER MATTHIESSEN / *Fiction*" / [lists five titles] / "*Nonfiction*" / [lists thirteen titles]; p. [iii] half-title; p. [iv] [colophon] / "RANDOM / HOUSE / NEW / YORK"; p. [v] title page; p. [vi] "Copyright 1951, 1953, ©1957, 1958, / 1963, 1978, 1985, 1988, 1989 / by Peter Matthiessen / All rights reserved under International / and

Pan-American Copyright Conventions. / Published in the United States by / Random House, Inc., New York, and / simultaneously / in Canada by Random House of / Canada Limited, Toronto. / 'Sadie' and 'The Fifth Day' were first / published in *The Atlantic*. 'Late in the Season' / was first published in *New World Writing* / (NAL). 'Travelin Man' was first published in / *Harper's Magazine*. 'The Wolves of Aguila' / was first published in *Harper's Bazaar*. 'Horse / Latitudes' was published by *Antaeus* (originally / published in *Venture* as 'Horace and Hassid'). / 'Midnight Turning Gray' was first published in / *The Saturday Evening Post*. 'On the River / Styx' was first published in *Esquire*. 'Lumumba / Lives' was first published in *Wigwag*. / Most of the stories in this collection were / originally published in book form in *Midnight / Turning Gray*, published by Ampersand Press in / 1984." / [four lines of Library of Congress Cataloging-in-Publication Data] / "ISBN 0-394-55399-3 / Manufactured in the United States of America / 24689753 / First Edition / Book design by Charlotte Staub"; p. [vii] [dedication:] "FOR SHERRY / *My friend* / *for fifty years,* / *who pestered me to* / *return to fiction* / *before the smoke* / *clears*"; p. [viii] blank; p. [ix]–x "AUTHOR'S / NOTE"; p. [xi] "CONTENTS"; p. [xii] blank; p. [1] second half-title; p. [2] blank; pp. [3]–208 text; p. [209] "ABOUT THE AUTHOR" / [seventeen-line statement]; pp. [210–212] blank.

Binding: Cream paper covered boards with a red cloth shelf-back. Spine, reading downward: [in gold:] ON THE RIVER STYX / AND OTHER STORIES PETER / MATTHIESSEN [colophon] RANDOM / HOUSE. On front in upper left quadrant of shelf-back: [in gold:] P. M. Endpapers front and back of stiff white paper. Issued in a dust jacket designed by Paul Bacon with a photograph of Matthiessen by Rue Matthiessen.

Contents: Sadie / The Fifth Day / The Centrepiece / Late in the Season / Travelin Man / The Wolves of Aguila / Horse Latitudes / Midnight Turning Gray / On the River Styx / Lumumba Lives

Price: $17.95

_____. London: Collins Harvill, 1989.
_____. New York: Vintage Books, 1990.
_____. Paris: Gallimard, 1992. Tr. Suzanne Mayoux. [*Les Loups d'Aguila et Autres Nouvelles*].
_____. Madrid: Siruela, 1993. [*En la Laguna Estigia y otros relatos*].

A9. *Killing Mister Watson*, 1990

[within a gray single-rule frame with a curved bottom joining the colophon:] [in black:] KILLING / MISTER / WATSON / [decorative rule] / PETER MATTHIESSEN / [colophon] / [in gray:] [rule] / [in black:] RANDOM HOUSE NEW YORK

Collation: pp. [i–viii] [1–3] 4–10 [11] 12–20 [21] 22–23 [24] 25–42 [43] 44–46 [47] 48–57 [59–59] 60–65 [66] 67–73 [74] 75–94 [95] 96 [97] 98–104 [105] 106–109 [110] 111–113 [114] 115–127 [128] 129–144 [145] 146–147 [148] 149–150 [151] 152–172 [173] 174–175 [176] 177–178 [179] 180–181 [182] 183–187 [188] 189–193 [194] 195–201 [202] 203–204 [205] 206–218 [219] 220 [221] 222–224 [225] 226 [227] 228–231 [232] 233–235 [236] 237–243 [244] 245–249 [250] 251–252 [253] 254 [255] 256–261 [262] 263–274 [275–276] 277 [278] 279–280 [281] 282–283 [284] 285–286 [287] 288–289 [290] 291–292 [293] 294–308 [309] 310–312 [313] 314 [315] 316–323 [324] 325–326 [327] 328–337 [338] 339 [340] 341 [342–343] 344 [345] 346–361 [362] 363–372 [373–376]. 6¼" × 9¼".

Pagination: p. [i] half-title; p. [ii] "ALSO BY / PETER MATTHIESSEN / *Fiction*" / [lists six titles] / "*Nonfiction*" / [lists thirteen titles]; p. [iii] title page; p. [iv] "Copyright ©1990 by Peter Matthiessen / Maps copyright ©1990 by Anita Karl and Jim Kemp / All rights reserved under International and Pan-American Copyright / Conventions. Published in the United States by Random House, Inc., New / York, and simultaneously in Canada by Random House of Canada Limited, / Toronto. / Library of Congress Cataloging-in-Publication Data" / [seven lines] / "Manufactured in the United States of America / 24689753 / First Edition / Book design by Lilly Langotsky"; p. [v] "TO THE PIONEER FAMILIES OF SOUTHWEST FLORIDA" /

[twenty line statement]; p. [vi] blank; p.
[vii] "AUTHOR'S NOTE" / [decorative
rule] / [fourteen line statement]; p. [viii]
blank; p. [1] title page; p. [2] blank; pp.
[3]–372 text; p. [373] "ABOUT THE
AUTHOR" / [sixteen line statement]; pp.
[374–376] blank.

Binding: Blue paper covered boards
with a dark blue cloth shelf-back. Spine,
reading across: [in gold:] KILLING / MIS-
TER / WATSON / [decorative rule] /
PETER / MATTHIESSEN / [colophon] /
RANDOM / HOUSE. Front, in upper left
quadrant, on the shelf-back: [in gold:] PM
/ [rule]. Endpapers front and back are
printed in a mottled blue and gray and show
a map of the Ten Thousand Islands area of
the Everglades. Issued in a dust jacket
designed and illustrated by Paul Bacon with
a photograph of Matthiessen by Jonathan
Becker.

Price: $21.95.

_____. London: Collins Harvill, 1990.
_____. Milano: Frassinelli, 1991. [*Uccidere Mis-
ter Watson*].
_____. New York: Flamingo (HarperCollins),
1991.
_____. New York: Vintage Books, 1991.
_____. Thorndike, ME: Thorndike Press, 1991.
Large print edition.
_____. Paris: Éd. de l'Olivier, 1992. Tr. Brice
Matthieussent. [*Monsieur Watson Doit
Mourir*].

A10. *Lost Man's River*, 1997

[against a field of thirty-eight vertical
gray bars:] [in black:] LOST / [rule] /
MAN'S / [rule] / RIVER / [rule] / PETER
MATTHIESSEN / [on white:] [colophon]
/ Random House / New York

Collation: pp. [i–xiv] [1–3] 4–6 [7]
8–47 [48] 49–57 [58] 59–98 [99] 100–153
[154] 155–242 [243] 244–302 [303]
304–333 [334] 335–390 [391] 392–458
[459] 460–506 [507] 508–539 [540–546].
6¼" × 9¼".

Pagination: p. [i] blank; p. [ii] "Also by
Peter Matthiessen / Fiction" / [lists seven
titles] / "Nonfiction" / [lists fifteen titles];
p. [iii] half-title; p. [iv] blank; p. [v] title
page; p. [vi] "Copyright ©1997 by Peter
Matthiessen / All rights reserved under

International and Pan-American Copyright
/ Conventions. Published in the United
States by Random / House, Inc., New York,
and simultaneously in Canada by / Random
House of Canada Limited, Toronto. /
Library of Congress Cataloging-in-Publication Data" / [seven lines] / "Random House
website address: http://www.randomhouse
.com / Printed in the United States of America on acid-free paper / 2 4 6 8 9 7 5 3 /
First Edition / *Book design by J. K. Lambert*";
p. [vii] ""Author's Note / and Acknowledgments" / [twelve line statement reprinted
from *Killing Mister Watson*] / [twelve line
statement of acknowledgment]; p. [viii]
blank; p. [ix] [dedication:] "*For dear Maria
with much love and gratitude / for her generous forbearance and great good sense / throughout the long course of this work*"; p. [x] blank;
p. [xi] [epigraph:] " 'The dread of something after death, the undiscovered country, from whose, / bourn no traveller returns
… makes us rather bear those ills we have
than / fly to others that we know not of.'
/ —*Hamlet*, Act II"; p. [xii] blank; pp. [xiii–
xiv] "E. J. WATSON" / [family members];
p. [1] second half-title; p. [2] blank; pp. [3]–
539 text; p. [540] blank; p. [541] "About
the Author" / [thirteen line statement]; p.
[542] blank; p. [543] "About the Type" /
[three line statement]; pp. [544–546] blank.

Binding: Dark green paper covered
boards with a black paper shelf-back. Spine,
reading across: [in gold:] LOST / [rule] /
MAN'S / [rule] / RIVER / [rule] Peter /
Matthiessen / [rule] / [colophon] / Random
House. Front, centered on the dark green
paper near the top: [blind stamping:] P M
/ [rule]. Endpapers front and back printed
in green and ivory show a map of the Ten
Thousand Islands area of the Everglades.
Issued in a dust jacket designed by Andy
Carpenter with an author photograph by
Nancy Crampton.

Price: $26.95.

_____. London: Harvill Press, 1998.
_____. New York: Vintage Books, 1998. First
Vintage International edition.
_____. London: Harvill Press, 1999.

A11. *Bone by Bone*, 1999

[against a field of thirty-eight vertical

gray bars:] [in black:] BONE / [rule] / BY / [rule] / BONE / [rule] / Peter Matthiessen / [on white beneath the field of vertical bars:] A Novel / [colophon] / Random House / New York

Collation: pp. [i–xiii] xiv [1–3] 4–62 [63] 64–104 [105] 106–149 [150] 151–204 [205] 206–235 [236] 237–275 [276] 277–293 [294] 295–321 [322] 323–362 [363] 364–410 [411–418]. 6¼" × 9⅛".

Pagination: p. [i] blank; p. [ii] "Also by Peter Matthiessen / Fiction" / [lists eight titles] / "Nonfiction" / [lists fifteen titles]; p. [iii] half-title; p. [iv] blank; p. [v] title page; p. [vi]"Copyright ©1999 by Peter Matthiessen / All rights reserved under International and Pan-American Copyright / Conventions. Published in the United States by Random / House, Inc., New York, and simultaneously in Canada by / Random House of Canada Limited, Toronto. / Library of Congress Cataloging-in-Publication Data" / [eight lines] / "Random House website address: www.atrandom.com / Printed in the United States of America on acid-free paper / 2 4 6 8 9 7 5 3 / First Edition / *Book Design by J. K. Lambert*"; p. [vii] [dedication:] "*To my old friends (and agents) Candida Donadio and Neil Olson / and my new friend (and editor) Deb Futter (and Becky and Lee, and Beth / and Benjamin, and many other friends at Random House) / with sincere gratitude for their great patience and support in the long throes / of what can only be called a twenty-year obsession*"; p. [viii] blank; p. [ix] [five line epigraph from Emily Dickinson] / [two line epigraph from John Milton's *Paradise Lost*] / [two line epigraph from John Keats] / [two line epigraph from Governor John Hammond of South Carolina]; p. [x] blank; p. [xi] "Author's Note / and Acknowledgments" / [twelve line statement reprinted from *Killing Mister Watson*] / [eleven line statement of acknowledgment]; p. [xii] blank; pp. [xiii]–xiv "E. J. WATSON" / [family members]; p. [1] second half-title; p. [2] blank; pp. [3]–410 text; pp. [411–412] blank; p. [413] "About the Author" / [fifteen line statement]; p. [414] blank; p. [415] "About the Type" / [three line statement]; pp. [416–418] blank.

Binding: Ocher colored paper covered boards with a black paper shelf-back. Spine, reading across: [in gold:] BONE / [rule] / BY / [rule] / BONE / [rule] / Peter / Matthiessen / [rule] / [colophon] / Random House. Front, centered on the ocher paper near the top: [blind stamping:] P M / [rule]. Endpapers front and back printed in tan and ivory show a map of the Ten Thousand Islands area of the Everglades. Issued in a dust jacket designed by Andy Carpenter with an author photograph by Linda Girvin.

Price: $26.95.

———. New York: Vintage International, 2000.

NONFICTION

A12. *Wildlife in America*, 1959

[on left of double-spread title page:] [in black:] [drawings of animals along left hand side and bottom:] WILDLIFE / *Introduction by* / RICHARD H. POUGH / *Drawings by* / BOB HINES [on right of double-spread title page:] [in black:] IN AMERICA / *by Peter Matthiessen* / NEW YORK : *Viking Press* : MCMLIX / [continuation of drawing along the bottom of the page]

Collation: pp. [1–10] 11–15 [16] [sixteen unnumbered pages of colored plates] [17–18] 19–228 [sixteen unnumbered pages of monochrome plates] 229–266 [267–268] 269–304. 6¾" × 9¾".

Pagination: p. [1] "WILDLIFE / IN AMERICA / ALSO BY PETER MATTHIESSEN" / [lists two titles]; pp. [2–3] title page; p. [4] "*For E.C.M and E.A.M. / with love and many thanks* / [rule] / "COPYRIGHT ©1959 BY PETER MATTHIESSEN / LINE ILLUSTRATIONS IN THE TEXT COPYRIGHT ©1959 BY BOB HINES / PUBLISHED IN 1959 BY THE VIKING PRESS, INC. / 625 MADISON AVENUE, NEW YORK 22, N.Y. / PUBLISHED IN CANADA BY / THE MACMILLAN COMPANY OF CANADA LIMITED / PORTIONS OF THE TEXT APPEARED IN *Sports Illustrated* / LIBRARY OF CONGRESS CATALOG

CARD NUMBER: 59-11635 / PRINTED IN U.S.A."; p. [5] "*Contents*"; pp. [6–7] "*Illustrations*"; pp. [8–9] "*The North American Continent*" [map]; p. [10] blank; pp. 11–12 "ACKNOWLEDGMENTS"; pp. 13–15 "*Introduction*"; p. [16] blank; pp. [17]–266 text and drawings; pp. [267] "*Appendices / Reference Notes / Bibliography / Index*"; p. [268] blank; pp. 269–280 "*Appendix I*"; pp. 281–284 "*Appendix II*"; pp. 285–288 "*Reference Notes*"; pp. 289–294 "*Bibliography*"; pp. 295–304 "*Index*".

Binding: Green cloth covered boards with a white cloth shelf-back. Spine, reading downward: [in green:] *Peter Matthiessen* / [on a green field surrounded by a single rule frame:] [in gold:] WILDLIFE IN AMERICA / [beneath the frame:] [in green:] *Viking Press*. Front, on the green cloth: [four rows of animal silhouettes]. Endpapers front and back printed in green decorated by "Symbols, or Totems, of the Plains Indians by George Catlin" with a note about the designs. Issued in a dust jacket.

Contents: Acknowledgments / Introduction by Richard H. Pough / The Outlying Rocks / The Tropical Border / The Eastern Slope / Fur Countries and Forest Lakes / Ocean Coasts and the High Seas / Hidden Worlds / Plains, Prairies, and the Shining Mountains / The High Air of a Continent / The End of the Wilderness Road / Old Fields / Land of the North Wind / Another Heaven and Another Earth / Appendix I: The Rare, Declining, and Extinct Vertebrate Animal Species of North America North of the Mexican Boundary / Appendix II: A Chronology of Representative Legislation Affecting North American Wildlife / Reference Notes / Bibliography / Index

Price: $10.00.

_____. London: Deutsch, 1960.
_____. New York: Penguin Books, 1964.
_____. New York: Viking Press, 1964. Viking Compass book.
_____. New York: Viking Press, 1966. Viking Compass book.
_____. New York: Viking Press, 1969.
_____. New York: Penguin Books, 1977.
_____. New York: Viking Press, 1987. Re-

vised and updated edition. Elizabeth Sifton books.
_____. New York: Penguin Books, 1995. Penguin nature classics.
See **C5**.

A13. *The Cloud Forest*, 1961

THE / CLOUD / FOREST / [single rule] / *A Chronicle of the South American Wilderness* / [single rule] / PETER MATTHIESSEN / [colophon] / *Viking Press* • *New York* / *1961*

Collation: pp. [i–v] vi [vii–viii] 1–88 [twelve unnumbered pages of photographs] 89–184 [twelve unnumbered pages of photographs] 185–280. 5½" × 8⅜".

Pagination: p. [i] half-title; p. [ii] "Also by / Peter Matthiessen / FICTION" / [lists three titles] / "NONFICTION" / [lists one title]; p. [iii] title page; p. [iv] [dedication:] "FOR / *Andrés Porras Cáceres* / my excellent friend and mentor on the Urubamba, whose wiser / head prevailed / AND FOR / *Lucha and Alfredo Porras Cáceres* / whose kind welcome in Lima and at La Honda, in January, / March, and May, made so much difference / Copyright ©1961 by Peter Matthiessen / All rights reserved / First published in 1961 by Viking Press, Inc. / 625 Madison Avenue, New York 22, N.Y. / Published simultaneously in Canada by / The Macmillan Company of Canada Limited / Portions of this book originally appeared in *The New Yorker* / Library of Congress catalog card number: 61-10989 / Printed in the U.S.A. by Vail-Ballou Press"; pp. [v]–vi "ACKNOWLEDGMENTS"; p. [vii] "CONTENTS"; p. [vii] "ILLUSTRATIONS"; pp. 1–269 text; pp. 270–280 "INDEX".

Binding: Black cloth covered boards. Spine, reading downward: [in gold:] THE CLOUD FOREST [reading across:] *Viking Press* [reading down:] MATTHIESSEN. Front, centered in the upper half: [blind stamping of the colophon]. Front endpapers of stiff white paper printed in black, gray, and green showing a map of South America and Matthiessen's route. Back endpapers of stiff white paper printed in black, gray, and green showing a map of central Peru and Matthiessen's route. Issued in a dust jacket designed by Jean Zallinger.

Contents: Part I: 1. Sargasso Sea and Southward / 2. Amazonas / 3. Sierra / 4. Tierra del Fuego / Notes on the Cities / 5. Mato Grosso / Part II: 6. Beyond Black Drunken River / Epilogue / Index
Price: $6.50

_____. London: Andre Deutsch, 1962.
_____. New York: Ballantine Books, 1963.
_____. New York: Pyramid Books, 1966.
_____. New York: Ballantine Books, 1973.
_____. New York: Penguin Books, 1987. Elisabeth Sifton books. Penguin travel library.
_____. London: Collins Harvill, 1988.
_____. Paris: Payot, 1992. Tr. Jacques Chabert. [*Urubamba*].
_____. New York: Penguin Books, 1996. Penguin nature classics.

See **C7–C9**.

A14. *Under the Mountain Wall,* 1962

[on the left and on the left-half of the right of a double-spread title page:] [photograph] [on a green right-half of the right of a double-spread title page:] [in black:] Under / the / Mountain / Wall / [in white:] a chronicle of / two seasons / in the / stone age / [in black:] Peter / Matthiessen / Viking Press / *New York*

Collation: pp. [i–viii] ix [x] xi–xvi [sixteen unnumbered pages of photographs] [1–2] 3–256 [sixteen unnumbered pages of photographs] xvii–xx [xxi] xxii–xxxii. 6" × 9¼".

Pagination: p. [i] half-title; p. [ii] blank; p. [iii] "*Also by Peter Matthiessen* / FICTION" / [lists three titles] / "NON-FICTION" / [lists two titles]; pp. [iv–v] title page; p. [vi] "*Copyright ©1962 by Peter Matthiessen / All rights reserved / First published in 1962 by Viking Press, Inc. / 625 Madison Avenue, New York 22, New York / Published simultaneously in Canada by / The Macmillan Company of Canada Limited / All photographs copyright 1962 by the Film Study Center, / Peabody Museum, Harvard University, Cambridge 38, Massachusetts. / They may not be reproduced in any form, except for the use of / not more than four photographs as illustrations for a review of the book, / without written permission of the Film Study Center. / A portion of the text has appeared in*

somewhat different / form in Harper's. / *Library of Congress catalog card number 62-16796 / Printed in the U.S.A. by The Vail-Ballou Press*"; p. [vii] [dedication:] "*For Deborah, with love* / [single rule] / *In warm memory of / MICHAEL ROCKEFELLER / whose interest and generosity were a major / contribution to the Harvard-Peabody Expedition of 1961. / Though he did not live to see the achievement of the Expedition, / his participation was crucial to its success.*"; p. [viii] blank; p. ix "Contents"; p. [x] blank; pp. xi–xiv "Preface"; pp. xv–xvi "Photographic Section I: THE KURELU"; pp. [1]–256 text; pp. xvii–xix "Photographic Section II: THE PEOPLE OF THE BOOK"; p. xx "Acknowledgments"; p. [xxi] [diagram of the village of Wuperainma]; pp. xxii–xxv "Glossary of Personal Names"; p. xxvi "Dani Words Used Commonly in Text"; pp. xxvii–xxxii "Index".

Binding: Black cloth covered boards. Spine, reading across: [in gold:] Under / the / Mountain / Wall / [in green:] Peter /Matthiessen / Viking. Front, in the upper half to the right of center: [blind stamping of ornamental device]. Front endpaper of stiff white paper printed in green and black showing a map of the Southern Kurelu. Back endpaper of stiff white paper printed in green showing an unfinished drawing by Michael Rockefeller. Issued in a dust jacket designed by Chermayeff & Geismar Associates with an author photograph by Luisa Gilardenghi.

Contents: Preface / List of Illustrations, Section I / Photographic Section I: The Kurelu / Under the Mountain Wall / Photographic Section II: The People of the Book / List of Illustrations, Section II / Acknowledgments / Diagram: Village of Wuperainma / Glossary of Personal Names / Dani Words Used Commonly in Text / Index
Price: $7.50.

_____. London: Heinemann, 1963.
_____. Paris: Gallimard, 1963.
_____. Meppel [Netherlands]: Boom & Zoon, 1964. Tr. Bep Vuyk. [*De Zonen Van Nopoe*].
_____. Munich: Droemer Knauer; Zurich: Droemer, 1964. Tr. Annemarie Bierbrauer.

[*Das Verborgene Tal: Chronik einer Reise in die Stenzeit*].
_____. Tokyo: Bungeishunjushinsha, 1964. Tr. Okado Kazuo. [*Nijusseiki No Sekkijin: Nyuginia Danizoku no Kiroku*].
_____. Copenhagen: Fremad, 1965. Tr. Hagmund Hansen. [*Stenalderfolket På Ny Guinea*].
_____. Paris: Gallimard, 1967. Tr. Guy Durand. [*Deux Saisons à L'Âge de Pierre*].
_____. Stuttgart: Europäischen Buchklub, 1967. Tr. Annemarie Bierbrauer. [*Das Verborgene Tal: Chronik einer Reise in die Stenzeit*].
_____. New York: Ballantine, 1969.
_____. New York: Ballantine, 1972.
_____. New York: Penguin Books, 1987. As *Under the Mountain Wall: A Chronicle of Two Seasons in Stone Age New Guinea*. [This will remain the title for subsequent editions].
_____. London: Collins Harvill, 1989.
_____. Amsterdam: Contact, 1990. Tr. Beb Vuyk. [*Een Vallei in de Steentijd*].
_____. Paris: Payot, 1990. Tr. Guy Durand. [*Deux Saisons à L'Âge de Pierre*].
_____. Paris: Payot, 1993. Tr. Guy Durand. [*Deux Saisons à L'Âge de Pierre*].
_____. London: Harvill Press, 1995.
_____. New York: Penguin Books, 1996. Penguin nature classics.
_____. Barcelona: Liberduplex, 2000. Tr. José Manuel Álvarez Flofez. [*Al Pie de la Mohta(a)*].

A15. *Oomingmak*, 1967

[in black:] OOMINGMAK / The Expedition to / the Musk Ox Island / in the Bering Sea / *by Peter Matthiessen* / Illustrated with photographs / HASTINGS HOUSE • Publishers / NEW YORK
Collation: pp. [i–ii] [1–6] 7–15 [16] 17–18 [19] 20 [21–22] 23–31 [32] 33–38 [39] 40–42 [43] 44–48 [49] 50–62 [63] 64–67 [68] 69–74 [75–76] 77–80 [81–82] 83–85 [86–87]. 5¼" × 8¼".
Pagination: p. [i] half-title; p. [ii] "BOOKS BY PETER MATTHIESSEN" / [lists eight titles]; p. [1] title page; p. [2] "The photographs were taken by the author except where the / photographer's name is given. Permission for the / reproduction (page 1) of 'Musk Ox' by Kiawak was / granted by Eskimo Fine Arts, Ottawa 4, Ontario, Canada. / This book first appeared

in a shorter version in / the *New Yorker* magazine. / Copyright ©1967 by Peter Matthiessen / All rights reserved. No part of this book / may be reproduced without / written permission of the publisher. / Published simultaneously in Canada / by Saunders, of Toronto, Ltd., Toronto 28. / Library of Congress Catalog Card Number: 67-16253 / *Printed in the United States of America*"; p. [3] [dedication:] "For John Teal, / friend of the musk ox," / [photograph of Teal] / "and for / Penny, Pammie, Ptarmie and Demi-John Teal / who made life at Nash Harbor so much finer"; p. [4] blank; p. [5] second half-title; p. [6] [map of Nunivak Island]; pp. 7–80 text and photographs; p. [81] "INDEX"; p. [82] blank; pp. 83–85 index; p. [86] blank.
Binding: Reddish brown cloth covered boards. Spine, reading downward: [in silver:] MATTHIESSEN OOMINGMAK [in black:] HASTINGS HOUSE. Front, centered on upper half: [in silver:] [musk ox design]. Centered on lower half: [in black:] OOMINGMAK / The Expedition to / the Musk Ox Island / in the Bering Sea. Endpapers front and back contain doublespread photographs. Issued in a dust jacket.
Price: $3.95.
See **C16.**

A16. *The Shorebirds of North America*, 1967

[in black:] [within a double rule frame:] The / Shorebirds / of / North America / *Editor and Sponsor* / GARDNER D. STOUT / *Text by* / PETER MATTHIESSEN / *Paintings by* / ROBERT VERITY CLEM / *Species Accounts by* / RALPH S. PALMER / THE VIKING PRESS NEW YORK
Collation: pp. [1–6] 7 [8–10] 11–13 [14–18] 19–23 [24–26] 27–29 [30–32] 33–37 [38] 39 [40–42] 43–45 [46–48] 49–55 [56–58] 59–61 [62–64] 65–71 [72–74] 75–77 [78–80] 81–87 [88–90] 91–93 [94–96] 97–103 [104–106] 107–109 [110–112] 113–119 [120–122] 123–125 [126–128] 129 [130] 131–135 [136–138] 139–140 [141–142] 143 [144–146] 147–153 [154–156] 157–159 [160–162] 163–169 [170–172] 173–175 [176–178] 179–185 [186–188] 189–191 [192–

194] 195–201 [202–204] 205–207 [208–
210] 211–217 [218–220] 221–223 [224–226]
227–233 [234–236] 237–239 [240–242]
243–249 [250–252] 253–259 [260–262]
263–270. 9¾" × 13¾".
Pagination: p. [1] half-title; p. [2] blank;
p. [3] title page; p. [4] *"Peter Matthiessen's
text ©1967 by Peter Matthiessen / All other
text and captions © by Gardner D.
Stout / All
rights reserved / First published in 1967 by
Viking Press, Inc. / 625 Madison Avenue,
New York, N. Y. 10022 / Published simultaneously in Canada by / The Macmillan Company of Canada Limited / Library of Congress
catalog card number: 67-19920 / Text printed
in the U.S.A. / Color plates printed in
Switzerland by Offset & Buchdruck A.G. /
under the supervision of Chanticleer Press, Inc.
/* Grateful acknowledgment is made to the
following for permission to quote copy- /
righted material:" / [ten-line statement] /
"Most of the text by Peter Matthiessen,
written especially for this book, has also /
appeared in *The New Yorker* in somewhat
different form under the title "The / Wind
Birds."; p. [5] "CONTENTS"; p. [6] blank;
pp. 7, 11–13 *"Introduction,"*; p. [8–9] "Plate
1"; p. [10] blank; p. 13 "ACKNOWLEDG-
MENTS"; pp. [14–15] "Plate 2"; p. [16]
blank; p. [17] second half-title; p. [18]
blank; pp. 19–129 text and plates; p. [130]
blank; pp. 131–132 "ACKNOWLEDG-
MENTS"; pp. 133–135 "SELECTED BIB-
LIOGRAPHY"; pp. [136–137] "Plate 17";
p. [138] blank; pp. 139–[141] "APPENDIX
BY RALPH S. PALMER / PLUMAGE
DESCRIPTIONS"; p. [142] blank; pp.
143–267 "SPECIES ACCOUNTS" and
plates; pp. 268–270 "INDEX".
Binding: Off-white cloth covered
boards. Spine, reading across: [in gold on a
brown field:] [thick rule] / [two thin rules]
/ *The* / *Shorebirds* / *of* / *North* / *America* / •
/ *Stout* / • / *Matthiessen* / • / *Clem* / • /
Palmer / [two thin rules] / [thick rule] / [in
gold on a separate brown field toward the
bottom of the spine:] [thick rule] / [two
thin rules] / VIKING / [two thin rules] /
[thick rule]. Endpapers front and back of
stiff brown paper. Issued in a dust jacket
with a painting on the front cover by Robert
Verity Clem.

Contents: Introduction by Gardner D.
Stout / Text by Peter Matthiessen / Selected
Bibliography / Appendix by Ralph S.
Palmer: Plumage Descriptions and Species
Accounts / Index.
Price: $22.50.
See A21 and C19–C20.

A17. *Profile: Cesar Chavez*, 1969
[in black:] [within a single rule frame:]
[left side: drawing of Chavez] [right side:]
PROFILE: / CESAR / CHAVEZ / By /
PETER MATTHIESSEN / [beneath
frame:] Reprinted from the June 21 and
June 28, 1969 issues of The New Yorker /
El Taller Grafico, United Farm Workers,
Box 62, Keene, CA. 93531
Collation: p. [1] 2–24. 7¾" × 10¾".
Pagination: p. [1] title page and cover;
pp. 2–24 text.
Binding: Plain white paper covers. Title
page serves as front cover.
———. Los Angeles, CA: UAW Western
Region Six, 1969.

A18. *Sal Si Puedes*, 1969
[in black:] *Peter Matthiessen* / [single
rule] / Sal Si Puedes / [thin single rule] /
[thick single rule] / [thin single rule] /
CESAR CHAVEZ / and the New American
Revolution
Collation: pp. [i–x] [1–2] 3–336
[337–338] 339–359 [360–362] 363–372
[373–374]. 5½" × 8¼".
Pagination: p. [1] blank; p. [2] "Books
by Peter Matthiessen / NONFICTION" /
[lists four titles] / "FICTION" / [lists four
titles]; p. [3] half-title; p. [4] "Random
House [colophon] *New York*"; p. [5] title
page; p. [6] "Copyright ©1969 by Peter
Matthiessen / All rights reserved under
International and Pan-American Copyright
Con- / ventions. Published in the United
States by Random House, Inc., New / York,
and simultaneously in Canada by Random
House of Canada Limited, / Toronto. / A
portion of the contents of this book
appeared originally in *The New / Yorker*, in
somewhat different form." / [fourteen lines
of permissions] / "Library of Congress Catalog Card Number: 70-85581 / Manufac-

tured in the United States of America by The Book Press, / Brattleboro, Vermont / Typography and binding design by Pauline Weiner / FIRST PRINTING 9 8 7 6 5 4 3 2"; p. [7] [dedication:] "To the farm workers and the American future"; p. [8] blank; p. [9] [excerpt from the 1967 Report of the President's National Advisory Commission on Rural Poverty]; p. [10] blank; p. [1] second half-title; p. [2] blank; pp. 3–336 text; pp. [337]–359 *"Epilogue"*; p. [360] blank; pp. [361]–372 *"Appendix"*; p. [373] *"About the Author"* / [five line statement]; p. [374] blank.

Binding: Black cloth covered boards. Spine, reading downward: [in red:] *Peter Matthiessen* / [single rule] Sal Si Puedes [reading across:] [colophon] / RANDOM HOUSE. Front, in upper right quadrant: [in purple:] P / M. Endpapers front and back of stiff white paper. Issued in a dust jacket designed by Jay J. Smith with a photograph of Chavez by Bob Fitch.

Price: $6.95.

_____. New York: Dell Publishing Company, 1969. A Delta book.

_____. New York: Dell Publishing Company, 1971. A Delta book.

_____. New York: Random House, 1972. First revised edition.

_____. New York: Dell Publishing Company, 1973. A Laurel edition.

_____. New York: Random House, 1973. Revised edition.

See **C22–C23**.

A19. *Blue Meridian*, 1971

[in black:] Blue / Meridian / THE SEARCH / FOR THE / GREAT WHITE / SHARK [with a gray silhouette of a shark to the right] / Peter Matthiessen / RANDOM HOUSE / *New York* / [colophon]

Collation: pp. [i–xiv] [1–2] 3–18 [xv–xxii] 19–20 [21] 22–31 [32] 33–89 [90] 91–92 [93] 94–121 [122] 123–146 [xxiii–xxx] 147–204 [205–210]. 6½" × 9¼".

Pagination: pp. [i–ii] blank; p. [iii] half-title; p. [iv] blank; p. [v] "BOOKS BY PETER MATTHIESSEN / *Nonfiction*" / [lists five titles] / *"Fiction"* / [lists four titles]; p. [vi] blank; p. [vii] title page; p. [viii] "Copyright ©1971 by Peter Matthiessen /

All rights reserved under International / and Pan-American Copyright Conventions. / Published in the United States / by Random House, Inc., New York, / and simultaneously in Canada / by Random House of Canada Limited, Toronto. / *Photographs taken on the expedition are / reproduced by permission of Cinema Center Films. / Copyright ©1970 by Cinema Center Films.* / Portions of this book first appeared in / *Esquire, Audubon* and *Playboy*. / ISBN: 0-394-46216-5 / Library of Congress Catalog Card Number: 76-139241 / Manufactured in the United States of America / by The Book Press, Brattleboro, Vt. / 2 3 4 5 6 7 8 9 / First Edition"; p. [ix] *"Acknowledgments"* / [twenty-seven line statement] / "P. M."; p. [x] blank; p. [xi] [dedication:] "For my brother / *George Carey Matthiessen*"; p. [xii] blank; p. [xiii] [four line epigraph] / — JONATHAN COUCH, / *Fishes of the British Islands* (1862); p. [xiv] blank; p. [1] second half-title; p. [2] blank; pp. 3–18 text; pp. [xv–xxii] photographs; pp. 19–146 text; pp. [xxiii–xxx] photographs; pp. 147–204 text; p. [205–206] blank; p. [207] *"About the Author"* / [eleven-line statement]; pp. [208–210] blank.

Binding: Off-white cloth covered boards with a blue cloth shelf-back. Spine, reading downward: [in gold:] Peter Matthiessen Blue Meridian [colophon] RANDOM HOUSE. Front, in upper right quadrant: [in silver:] [silhouettes of five sharks]. Endpapers front and back are printed in orange and blue and show a map of the Voyage of the Blue Water Films Expedition.

Price: $8.95.

_____. New York: New American Library, 1971. A Signet Book. Paperback.

_____. London: Harvill Press, 1995.

_____. New York: Penguin Books, 1997. Penguin Nature Classics. Paperback.

See **C27–C30**.

A20. *The Tree Where Man Was Born*, 1972

[in black:] PETER MATTHIESSEN / [thin rule] / THE TREE / WHERE MAN / WAS BORN / ELIOT PORTER / [thin rule] / THE AFRICAN / EXPERIENCE /

E. P. DUTTON & CO., INC. / NEW YORK / 1972
Collation: pp. [1–11] 12–14 [15] 16 [17–21] 22–29 [30–31] 32–41 [42] 43–48 [49] 50–75 [76] 77–83 [84–85] 86–90 [91–93] 94–110 [111] 112–122 [123] 124–139 [140–141] 142–152 [153–154] 155–157 [158–160] 161–165 [166–167] 168–176 [177–178] 179–188 [189–190] 191 [192] 193–197 [198–199] 200–209 [210–211] 212–247 [248]. 9½" × 11".
Pagination: p. [1] half-title; p. [2] blank; p. [3] "Also by Peter Matthiessen" / [lists nine titles] / "Also by Eliot Porter" / [lists eight titles]; p. [4] blank; p. [5] title page; p. [6] "Published 1972, in the United States by E. P. Dutton & Co., Inc., New York, / and simultaneously in Canada by Clarke, Irwin & Co., Ltd., Toronto and Vancouver / First Edition / All rights reserved under International and Pan-American Copyright Conventions / Library of Congress Catalog Card Number: 75-158598 / SBN: 0-525-22265-0 / Conceived, edited, and designed by E. P. Dutton & Co., Inc. / Printed in association with Chanticleer Press, Inc., New York, / and Amilcare Pizzi (S.P.A. Milan, Italy. / Portions of the text originally appeared, in somewhat different form, / in *The New Yorker* magazine. Copyright ©1972, *The New Yorker*."; p. [7] [dedication:] "*In Memoriam* / DEBORAH / LOVE / MATTHIESSEN / in love / and / gratitude"; p. [8] "Author's Note"; pp. [9–11] photographs; pp. 12–14 photographs; p. [15] photograph; p. 16 photograph; p. [17] "Contents"; pp. [18–20] maps of East Africa; pp. [21]–234 text and photographs; pp. 235–236 "Acknowledgments"; p. 237 "Glossary"; pp. 238–240 "Notes"; pp. 241–242 "Selected Bibliography"; pp. 243–247 "Index"; p. [248] blank.
Binding: Brown cloth covered boards. Spine, reading downward: [in gold:] PETER MATTHIESSEN THE TREE WHERE MAN WAS BORN / ELIOT PORTER THE AFRICAN EXPERIENCE [reading across:] [colophon] / DUTTON. Endpapers front and back of stiff white paper. Issued in a dust jacket.
Contents: Photographs / Maps / I. The Tree Where Man Was Born / II. White Highlands / Photographs / III. Northwest Frontier / Photographs / IV. Siringet / Photographs / V. In Maasai Land / VI. Rites of Passage / Photographs / VII. Elephant Kingdoms / Photographs / VIII. Great Caldron Mountains / Photographs / IX. Red God / X. At Gidabembe / Acknowledgments / Glossary / Notes / Selected Bibliography / Index.
Price: $17.50

_____. London: Collins, 1972.
_____. New York: Crescent Books, 1972.
_____. New York: MJF Books, 1972.
_____. [New York]: Avon, 1974. Paperback.
_____. Örebro: I. P. C., 1974. Tr. Mikael Mörling. [*Trädet där människan föddes: Afrikansk erfarenhet*].
_____. Tokyo: Kôdan-sha, 1980. Tr. Kuroda Akiko. [*Hito no Umareta ki*].
_____. New York: E. P. Dutton & Co., Inc., 1983. Paperback.
_____. London: Picador in association with Collins, 1984.
_____. London: Havill, 1994. Paperback.
_____. New York: Penguin Books, 1995. Penguin Nature Classics. Paperback.
_____. Palma de Mallorca: José J. de Olañeta, 1998. Tr. Ángela Pérez. [*El Árbol en que Nació el Hombre*].
_____. 1999. Second edition.
See **C11, C33–C35.**

A21. *The Wind Birds,* 1973

THE WIND BIRDS / by / PETER MATTHIESSEN / Drawings by / Robert Gillmor / A Studio Book / THE VIKING PRESS / NEW YORK
Collation: pp. [1–10] 11 [12] 13–20 [21–22] 23–36 [37–38] 39–46 [47–48] 49–56 [57–58] 59–68 [69–70] 71–80 [81–82] 83–100 [101–102] 103–112 [113–114] 115–126 [127–128] 129–136 [137–138] 139–149 [150] 151–153 [154] 155–159 [160]. 8" × 9⅞".
Pagination: p. [1] half-title; p. [2] "Also by Peter Matthiessen" / [lists ten titles]; p. [3] title page; p. [4] "Text Copyright ©1967, 1973 by Peter Matthiessen / Illustrations Copyright ©1973 by Robert Gillmor / All rights reserved / The text by Peter Matthiessen was originally published in 1967, in / different form, in *The Shorebirds of North America*, Gardner D. / Stout ed. /

This edition published in 1973 by Viking Press, Inc. / 625 Madison Avenue, New York, N.Y. 10022 / Published simultaneously in Canada by / The Macmillan Company of Canada Limited / SBN 670-77096-5 / Library of Congress catalog card number: 72-11906 / Printed in U.S.A. / Most of the text originally appeared in *The New Yorker*. / Grateful acknowledgment is made to the following for permission to / quote copyrighted material: / Doubleday & Company, Inc.: From *An Introduction to Haiku* by Harold / G. Henderson. Copyright ©1958 by Harold G. Henderson. Reprinted by / permission. / The Macmillan Company (New York), Macmillan & Co. Ltd. (London), and / Mr. M. B. Yeats for 'Paudeen' (page 11) from *Collected Poems* by W. B. / Yeats. Copyright 1916 by The Macmillan Company, renewed 1944 by Bertha / Georgie Yeats. / New Directions Publishing Corporation, J. M. Dent & Sons Ltd., and the / Trustees for the Copyrights of the late Dylan Thomas for 'In the White / Giant's Thigh' (page 139) from *The Collected Poems of Dylan Thomas*. / Copyright 1953 by Dylan Thomas. / Viking Press, Inc., for lines from *The Fables of La Fontaine* (page 59), / translated by Marianne Moore. Copyright 1954 by Marianne Moore."; p. [5] [dedication:] "*For Mary Matthiessen Wheelwright*"; p. [6] [drawing]; p. [7] "PREFACE AND ACKNOWLEDGMENTS"; p. [8] [drawing]; p. [9] [fourteen-line epigraph] / "*—J. Henri Fabre*"; pp. [10]–[150] text and drawings; pp. 151–[154] "SELECTED BIBLIOGRAPHY"; pp. 155–[160] "*Index*".

Binding: Slate blue paper covered boards with a blue cloth shelf-back. Spine, reading downward: [in gold:] MATTHIESSEN *The Wind Birds* VIKING. Endpapers front and back of white paper. Issued in a dust jacket designed by Nicolas Ducrot.

Price: $9.95.

_____. Shelburne, VT: Chapters Publishing Ltd., 1994. The Curious Naturalist series.
_____. Magnolia, MA: Peter Smith Publisher, Inc., 1999.

See **A16** and **C19–C20**.

A22. *The Snow Leopard*, 1978

[in black:] the snow leopard / peter matthiessen / THE VIKING PRESS NEW YORK

Collation: pp. [i–xii] [1–3] 4–6 [7–11] 12–21 [22] 23–25 [26] 27–30 [31] 32 [33] 34–35 [36] 37–38 [39] 40 [41] 42–47 [48] 49–51 [52] 53–57 [58] 59–60 [61] 62–67 [68–73] 74 [75] 76–80 [81] 82–83 [84] 85–88 [89] 90–96 [97] 98–100 [101] 102–109 [110] 111–114 [115] 116–121 [122] 123–128 [129] 130–134 [135] 136 [137] 138–143 [144] 145–146 [147] 148 [149] 150–153 [154] 155–158 [159] 160–163 [164] 165–168 [169] 170–172 [173] 174–176 [177] 178–179 [180–185] 186–189 [190] 191–196 [197] 198–201 [202] 203–206 [207] 208–209 [210] 211–213 [214] 215–217 [218] 219–220 [221] 222–223 [224] 225–229 [230] 231–233 [234] 235–238 [239] 240–242 [243] 244–246 [247] 248–249 [250] 251–252 [253] 254–257 [258–263] 264–270 [271] 272–274 [275] 276–279 [280] 281–284 [285] 286–290 [291] 292–295 [296] 297–298 [299] 300–302 [303] 304–305 [306] 307–309 [310] 311 [312] 313 [314] 315–317 [318] 319 [320] 321 [322–323] 324 [325] 326–330 [331] 332–338 [339–340]. 6'' × 9⅛''.

Pagination: p. [i] half-title; p. [ii] blank; p. [iii] "ALSO BY PETER MATTHIESSEN / NONFICTION" / [lists seven titles] / "FICTION" / [lists five titles]; p. [iv] [photograph]; p. [v] title page; p. [vi] "Copyright ©Peter Matthiessen, 1978 / All rights reserved / Published in 1978 by Viking Press / 625 Madison Avenue, New York, N.Y. 10022 / Published simultaneously in Canada by / Penguin Books Canada Limited / A portion of this book / originally appeared in *The New Yorker* / A limited edition of this book / has been privately printed / LIBRARY OF CONGRESS CATALOGING IN PUBLICATION DATA" / [nine lines] / "Printed in the United States of America / Set in Linotype Janson / *Frontispiece photograph by George B. Schaller / Maps by Paul J. Pugliese*"; p. [vii] [dedication:] "*For / Nakagawa Soen Roshi / Shimano Eido Roshi / Taizan Maezumi Roshi / GASSHO / in gratitude, affection, / and respect*"; p. [viii] blank; p. [ix] "contents"; p. [x] blank; p. [xi] [epigraph] / RAINER

MARIA RILKE"; p. [xii] blank; pp. [1]–321 text; p. [322] blank; pp. [323]–324 "acknowledgments"; pp. [325]–330 "notes"; pp. [331]–338 "index"; pp. [339–340] blank.

Binding: Dark blue cloth covered boards. Spine, reading downward: [in silver:] peter matthiessen [in light blue:] [medallion] [in silver:] the snow leopard [reading across:] VIKING. Endpapers front and back of stiff blue paper printed in black. The front endpaper shows a map of the Tibetan Plateau of Nepal. The back endpaper shows a map of Inner Dolpo. Issued in a dust jacket with a jacket photograph by George B. Schaller and a photograph of Matthiessen by Nancy Crampton.

Contents: Prologue / I. Westward / II. Northward / III. At Crystal Mountain / IV. The Way Home / Acknowledgments / Notes / Index

Price: $12.95.

_____. Franklin Center, PA: Franklin Library, 1978. Limited first edition.

_____. New York: Viking Press, 1978. Limited edition of 199 copies.

_____. New York: Viking Press, 1978. Book Club edition.

_____. London: Chatto & Windus, 1979.

_____. New York: Bantam, 1979.

_____. London: Pan, 1980.

_____. Milano: A. Mondadori, 1980. Tr. Francesco Franconeri. [*Il Leopardo delle Nevi*].

_____. München and Bern: Scherz, 1980. Tr. Maria Csollány and Stephan Schuhmacher. [*Auf der Spur des Schneeleoparden*].

_____. Amsterdam: Karnak, 1981. Tr. Victor Verduin. [*De Sneeuwluipaard*].

_____. Buenos Aires: Sudamericana, 1981. Tr. Moreno de Sáenz. [*El Leopardo de las Nieves*].

_____. Stockhom: Alba, 1981. Tr. Maj Frisch. [*Snöleoparden*].

_____. Toronto and New York: Bantam Windstone edition, 1981.

_____. München and Bern: Scherz, 1982. Second edition.

_____. Paris: Gallimard, 1983. Tr. Suzanne Nétillard. [*Le Léopard des Neiges*].

_____. München: Droemersche Verlagsanstalt Knaur, 1985. [*Auf der Spur des Schneeleoparden*].

_____. New York: Penguin Books, 1987. "Elisabeth Sifton books."

_____. Warsaw: Czytelnik, 1988. Tr. Blanka Kuczborska. [*Eniena Pantera*].

_____. London: Collins Harvill, 1989.

_____. Paris: Gallimard, 1991. Tr. Suzanne Nétillard. [*Le Léopard des Neiges*].

_____. Milano: Frassinelli, 1993. Tr. Francesco Franconeri. [*Il Lepardo delle Nevi*].

_____. New York: Penguin Books, 1996. "Penguin nature classics."

_____. Praha: Volvox Gloator, 1997. Tr. Jirí Hrubý. [*Snezný Levhart*].

_____. T'ai-pei Shih: Chi Chieh Feng, 1997. Tr. Pi-yün Sung. [*Hsüeh Pao*].

_____. London: Vintage, 1998.

See **C47–C48**.

A23. *Sand Rivers*, 1981

[in black:] Peter Matthiessen / SAND / RIVERS / photographs by / Hugo van Lawick / THE VIKING PRESS NEW YORK

Collation: pp. [i–viii] [1–2] 3–24 [25–32] 33–48 [49–56] 57–69 [70] 71–72 [156] 157–168 [169–176] 177–183 [184] 185–192 [193–200] 201–210 [211–212] 213 [214–216]. 6¾" × 9¾".

Pagination: p. [i] half-title; p. [ii] blank; p. [iii] title page; p. [iv] "Text Copyright ©1981 by Peter Matthiessen / Photographs Copyright © by Hugo van Lawick / All rights reserved / First published in 1981 by Viking Press / 625 Madison Avenue, New York, N.Y. 10022 / Published simultaneously in Canada by / Penguin Books Canada Limited / Library of Congress Cataloging in Publication Data" / [six lines] / "ISBN 0-670-61696-6 / Printed in the United States of America / Designed and produced by Aurum Press Ltd., London / Set in Linotron Trump Medieval" / [colophon]; p. [v] [dedication:] "For Eck and Donnie Eckhart / and / For John Owen"; p. [vi] blank; p. [vii] "ACKNOWLEDG-MENTS" / [twelve line statement]; p. [viii] blank; p. [1] second half-title; p. [2] [photograph of Matthiessen and van Lawick]; pp. 3–210 text and photographs; p. [211] "NOTES"; p. [212] blank; p. 213 [notes]; pp. [214–216] blank.

Binding: Off white cloth covered boards. Spine, reading downward: [stamped in blue:] SAND RIVERS [stamped in maroon:] Peter Matthiessen / Hugo van Lawick [reading across:] [in blue:]

VIKING. Endpapers front and back are printed in brown and show a map of the Selous Game Reserve. Issued in a dust jacket.

Price: $19.95.

_____. London: Aurum Press, 1981.

_____. New York: Bantam Books, 1982. Paperback.

See **C64–C67**.

A24. *In the Spirit of Crazy Horse,* 1983

[on left of a double-spread title page:] [in black:] [single rule with decorative devices at either end] / PETER MATTHIESSEN / IN THE [on right of double-spread title page:] [in black:] [single rule with decorative devices at either end:] / SPIRIT OF / CRAZY HORSE / THE VIKING PRESS [decorative device] NEW YORK / [on left of double-spread title page:] [single rule with a decorative device at either end] [on right hand side of double-spread title page:] [single rule with a decorative device at either end]

Collation: pp. [i–xi] xii [xiii] xiv [xv–xx] xxi–xli [1–4] 5–32 [33–34] 35–58 [59–60] 61–83 [84–85] 86–103 [104–105] 106–127 [128–129] 130–151 [152–156] 157–171 [172–173] 174–192 [193–194] 195–221 [222–223] 224–251 [252–253] 254–283 [284–285] 286–321 [322–323] 324–375 [376–380] 381–411 [412–413] 414–451 [452–453] 454–476 [477–478] 479–498 [499–500] 501–524 [525–526] 527–546 [547–548] 549–575 [576–577] 578–611 [612–613] 614–628 [629–630]. 6" × 9¼".

Pagination: p. [i] half-title; p. [ii] blank; p. [iii] "*ALSO BY PETER MATTHIESSEN* / NONFICTION" / [lists nine titles] / "FICTION" / [lists five titles]; p. [iv–v] title page; p. [vi] "Copyright ©1980, 1983 by Peter Matthiessen / All rights reserved / First published in 1983 by Viking Press / 40 West 23rd Street, New York, N.Y. 10010 / Published simultaneously in Canada by / Penguin Books Canada Limited / An excerpt from this book originally appeared / in *The New York Times* in different form. / LIBRARY OF CONGRESS CATALOGING IN PUBLICATION DATA" /

[nine lines] / "Maps by David Lindroth / Printed in the United States of America / Set in CRT Garamond"; p. [vii] [dedication:] "For all who honor and defend those people / who still seek to live in the wisdom of Indian way"; p. [viii] blank; p. [ix]–xii "*ACKNOWLEDGMENTS*"; p. [xiii]–xiv "*CONTENTS*"; p. [xv] [map of the Lakota Territory]; p. [xvi] [map of the Pine Ridge Reservation]; p. [xvii] [map of the Jumping Bull Property]; p. [xviii] blank; pp. [xix]–xli "*INTRODUCTION*"; p. [xlii] blank; pp. [1]–575 text; p. [576] blank; pp. [577]–611 "*NOTES*"; p. [612] blank; pp. [613]–628 "*INDEX*"; pp. [629–630] blank.

Binding: Light orange colored paper-covered boards with a brown cloth shelf-back. Spine, reading downward: [in gold:] IN THE SPIRIT OF / CRAZY HORSE [two rules across spine] PETER / MATTHIESSEN. Front, in upper right quadrant: [in gold:] [within a single rule frame:] PM. Issued in a dust jacket designed by R. Adelson with a photograph by Josef Muench.

Price: $20.95

_____. New York: Penguin Books, 1991. With an epilogue by Matthiessen and an afterword by Martin Garbus.

_____. London: Harvill, 1992.

_____. London: Collins-Harvill, 1992. Paperback.

A25. *Indian Country,* 1984

[within a single rule frame:] [in black:] INDIAN / COUNTRY / [single rule] / PETER MATTHIESSEN / [ornamental device] / THE VIKING PRESS • NEW YORK

Collation: pp. [i–xi] xii [xiii–xiv] [1–3] 4–13 [14–17] 18–63 [64–67] 68–102 [103–105] 106–126 [127–129] 130–163 [164–167] 168–199 [200–203] 204–220 [221–223] 224–237 [238–241] 242–257 [258–261] 262–289 [290–293] 294–312 [313–315] 316–330 [331] 332–338. 6⅛" × 9¼".

Pagination: p. [i] half-title; p. [ii] "ALSO BY PETER MATTHIESSEN / [single rule] / NONFICTION" / [lists ten titles] / "FICTION" / [lists five titles]; p. [iii] title page; p. [iv] "Copyright ©1979,

1980, 1981, 1984 by Peter Matthiessen / All rights reserved / First published in 1984 by Viking Press / 40 West 23rd Street, New York, N.Y. 10010 / Published simultaneously in Canada by / Penguin Books Canada Limited / Portions of this book appeared originally in slightly different / form, in *Audubon*; *Geo*; "Tropic Magic," Sunday Supplement, / *Miami Herald*; *The Nation*; *The New York Review of Books*; *The / New York Times*; *Newsweek*; *Parabola*; *Rocky Mountain* magazine; / and *The Washington Post*. / LIBRARY OF CONGRESS CATALOGING IN PUBLICATION DATA" / [eight lines] / "Grateful acknowledgment is made to Professor Simon J. Ortiz / for permission to reprint a selection from "Fight Back: For the / Sake of the People, for the Sake of the Land," by Simon J. Ortiz, / INAD-UNM, 1980. / Printed in the United States of America / Set in Garamond / Designed by Mary A. Wirth / Endpaper map by David Lindroth"; p. [v] [dedication:] "[single rule] / To Craig Carpenter, my teacher and guide on my first / journeys into Indian Country, whose fierce encourage- / ment of the last traditionals among his people is one / good reason why they still exist."; p. [vi] blank; p. [vii] "ACKNOWLEDGMENTS"; p. [viii] blank; p. [ix] [epigraph from Sealth, a Duwamish chief]; p. [x] blank; pp. [xi]–xii "FOREWORD"; p. [xiii] "CONTENTS"; p. [xiv] blank; pp. [1]–330 text; pp. [331]–338 "INDEX".
Binding: Light gray paper covered boards with a maroon cloth shelf-back. Spine, reading downward: [in gold:] PETER MATTHIESSEN / [single rule] / INDIAN COUNTRY [reading across:] VIKING. Endpapers front and back of stiff white paper are printed in gray and black and show a map of Indian country in the western United States. Issued in a dust jacket designed by R. Adelson with a photograph by Harold Davis and an author photograph by Barbara Hall.
Contents: Foreword / Native Earth / The Long River / Mesas / Lost Eloheh Land / Akwesasne / The High Country / Black Hills / At the Western Gate / East of Mount Shasta / Great Basin / Four Corners / To Big Mountain / Index

Price: $17.95
____. London: Collins Harvill, 1985.
____. London: Flamingo, 1986.
____. New York: Penguin Books, 1992.
See **C52**, **C55–C56**, **C59–C60**, **C62**, and **C63**.

A26. *Nine-Headed Dragon River*, 1986

[in black:] [within a single rule frame with ornamental borders top and bottom:] NINE-HEADED / DRAGON / RIVER / ZEN JOURNALS 1969–1985 [below the frame:] Peter Matthiessen / [colophon] / SHAMBHALA • BOSTON / 1986
Collation: pp. [i–ix] x [xi] xii [xiii–xvi] [1–3] 4–19 [20] 21–29 [30] 31–37 [38] 39–44 [45] 46–59 [60] 61–67 [68–71] 72–89 [90] 91–113 [114–117] 118–132 [133] 134–140 [141] 142–147 [148] 149–157 [158] 159–169 [170] 171–183 [184] 185–196 [197] 198–208 [209] 210–222 [223] 224–234 [235] 236–246 [247] 248–259 [260–263] 264 [265] 266–275 [276–277] 278–279 [280–281] 282–288. 6" × 9".
Pagination: p. [i] half-title; p. [ii] blank; p. [iii] title page; p. [iv] "SHAMBHALA PUBLICATIONS, INC. / 314 Dartmouth Street / Boston, Massachusetts 02116 / ©1985 Zen Community of New York / All rights reserved / 9 8 7 6 5 4 3 2 1 / FIRST EDITION / Printed in the United States of America / Distributed in the United States by Random House / and in Canada by Random House of Canada Ltd. / Material that appears in Chapters 7 and 8 is from *The / Snow Leopard*, by Peter Matthiessen, ©Peter Matthies- / sen, 1978. Reprinted by permission of Viking Penguin, / Inc. / *Library of Congress Cataloging-in-Publication Data*" / [nine lines] / "ISBN 0-87773-325-2 / 0-394-55251-2"; p. [v] [dedication:] "*To my excellent teacher and kind friend Bernard / Tetsugen Glassman-sensei, with admiration, / gratitude, and deep affection.*" / [ornamental device] / [eight line epigraph] / "*Shobogenzo /* — EIHEI DOGEN"; p. [vi] blank; p. [vii] "CONTENTS"; p. [viii] [twelve line poem] / "from *Treasury of the True Dharma Eye /* — NYOJO ZENJI"; pp. [ix]–x "FOREWORD"; pp. [xi]–xii "PREFACE";

pp. [xiii] "AUTHOR'S NOTE"; p. [xiv] blank; p. [xv] "ACKNOWLEDGMENTS"; p. [xvi] blank; pp. [1]–259 text; p. [260] blank; p. [261] [map]; p. [262] [genealogical tree of Shakyamuni Buddha]; pp. [263]–264 "CHAPTER EPIGRAPH SOURCES"; pp. [265]–275 "NOTES"; p. [276] blank; pp. [277]–279 "GLOSSARY"; p. [280] blank; pp. [281]–288 "INDEX".

Binding: Dark blue cloth covered boards. Spine, reading downward: [in gold]: MATTHIESSEN NINE-HEADED DRAGON RIVER [colophon] SHAMBHALA. Front, centered in upper half: [in gold:] [ornamental device]. Endpapers front and back of stiff gray paper. Issued in a dust jacket designed by Paul Bacon with photographs by Peter Cunningham.

Contents: Foreword / Preface / Author's Note / Acknowledgments / America: Rinzai Journals 1969–1976 / Nepal: Himalayan Journals 1973 / Japan: Soto Journals 1976–1982 / Appendixes / Notes / Glossary / Index

Price: $16.95

_____. London: Collins Harvill, 1986.

_____. Amsterdam: Contact, 1987. Tr. Aleid C. Swierenga. [*De Rivier van de Negenkoppige Draak*].

_____. Boston: Shambhala, 1987. Shambhala Dragon editions. Paperback.

_____. New York: Flamingo [HarperCollins], 1987.

_____. Amsterdam: Contact, 1995. Second edition. Tr. Aleid C. Swierenga. [*Zen-Dagboeken*].

_____. Boston: Shambhala, 1998.

_____. Palma de Mallorca: José J. de Olañeta, 1999. Tr. Ángela Pérez. [*El Río del Dragón de Nueve Cabezas*].

A27. *Men's Lives*, 1986

[in black:] MEN'S LIVES / PETER MATTHIESSEN / THE SURFMEN AND BAYMEN OF THE SOUTH FORK / [in gray:] RANDOM HOUSE [colophon] NEW YORK

Collation: pp. [i–viii] ix [x] xi [xii] [1] 2–8 [9–10] 11–27 [28] 29–53 [54] 55–58 [59] 60–71 [72] 73–113 [114] 115–117 [118] 119–124 [125] 126–133 [134] 135–182 [183] 184–218 [219] 220–249 [250] 251 [252] 253–256 [257] 258–259 [260] 261–263 [264] 265–266 [267–268] 269–277 [278–279] 280–283 [284–285] 286 [287–288] 289–292 [293] 294–301 [302] 303–305 [306] 307–310 [311–312] 313–339 [340]. 8" × 9½".

Pagination: p. [i] half-title; p. [ii] [photograph]; p. [iii] title page; p. [iv] "MEN'S LIVES / Text copyright ©1986 by Peter Matthiessen / Original pencil drawings ©1986 by Ralph Carpenter / All photographs are protected by the photographers' / individual copyrights as listed on pages 334–338. / All rights reserved under International / and Pan-American copyright conventions. / Published in the United Sates by Random House, Inc., / New York and simultaneously in Canada by / Random House of Canada Limited, Toronto / Library of Congress Cataloging-in-Publication Data" / [seven lines] / "Manufactured in the United States of America / 9 8 7 6 5 4 3 2 / FIRST EDITION"; p. [v] [photograph]; p. [vi] blank; p. [vii] [epigraph:] *"It's not fish ye're buyin, it's men's lives.* / Sir Walter Scott"; p. [viii] blank; p. ix "Contents"; p. [x] blank; p. xi *"Acknowledgments"*; p. [xii] blank; pp. [1]–249 text; p. [250] blank; pp. 251–316 *"Plates"*; pp. 317–324 *"Notes"*; pp. 325–333 drawings and engravings; pp. 334–338 *"List of Illustrations"*; p. 339 [acknowledgment by Adelaide de Menil]; p. [340] "[photo of a ray] / Set in Bembo and Carlson by Waldman Graphics, Inc., Pennsauken, N.J. / Plates printed by Rembrandt Press, Milford, Connecticut. / Text printed by Kingsport Press, Kingsport, Tennessee. / Design by Helen Buttfield / Editorial Assistant: Charles Allcroft Production Assistants: Eric Darton, Anthony Feyer, April Johnson, Kate Kehrig."

Binding: Dark blue cloth covered boards. Spine, reading downward: [in gold:] MEN'S LIVES PETER MATTHIESSEN [reading across:] [colophon] / RANDOM / HOUSE. Endpapers front and back of stiff white paper printed in black, blue, and tan with a map of the South Fork of Long Island and Block Island Sound. Issued in a dust jacket with a front cover photograph by Dan Budnik and a back cover photograph by Lynn Johnson.

Contents: Acknowledgments / Preface /

The Old Days / The Fifties / Modern Times / Epilogue / Plates / Notes / Drawings and Engravings / List of Illustrations / List of Plates
Price: $29.95

_____. [New York:] Rock Foundation, 1986. 2 vols. Vol. 2 has subtitle: Photographs. Issued in a slipcase.

_____. London: Collins Harvill, 1988.

_____. New York: Vintage Books, 1988.

Note: There was also a presentation copy given to attendees of a $500.00-a-plate benefit dinner. Each copy was numbered by a tipped in page and contained an original print of one of the photographs for the book. Each photograph was signed by the photographer. The copies were presented in a folding clamshell box.

A28. *African Silences*, 1991

[in black:] [decorative rule] / [white outline within black letters:] AFRICAN / SILENCES / [decorative rule] / [decorative frieze] / [decorative rule] / PETER MATTHIESSEN / [decorative rule] / [colophon] /RANDOM HOUSE / NEW YORK

Collation: pp. [i–xii] [1–3] 4 [5] 6–53 [54–55] 56–95 [96–97] 98–218 [219] 220–225 [226–228]. 5½" × 8¼".

Pagination: p. [i] "ALSO BY / PETER MATTHIESSEN" / [lists twenty titles]; p. [ii] blank; p. [iii] half-title; p. [iv] blank; p. [v] title page; p. [vi] "Copyright ©1991 by Peter Matthiessen / All rights reserved under / International and Pan-American Copyright Conventions. Published in the / United States by Random House, Inc., New York / and simultaneously in Canada by Random House / of Canada Limited, Toronto. / Portions of this work were originally published in / *Audubon* and *Outside* magazines. / 'Pygmies and Pygmy Elephants: The Congo Basin' was originally published in *Antaeus* as / 'Congo Basin: The Search for the Forest Elephants,' / parts I and II. / Library of Congress Cataloging-in-Publication Data" / [ten lines] / "Manufactured in the United States of America / 24689753 / First Edition / *Book design by Oksana Kushnir*"; p. [vii] [dedication:] "*For George Schaller, Jonah Western, / Iain Douglas-Hamilton, Alec Forbes-Watson, / Peter

Enderlein, Brian Nicholson, and / other mentors and companions of immemorial / long days on foot in Africa."; p. [viii] blank; p. [ix] "ACKNOWLEDGMENTS" / [ten line statement]; p. [x] blank; p. [xi] "CONTENTS"; p. [xii] blank; p. [1] second half-title; p. [2] blank; pp. [3]–4 "PROLOGUE"; pp. [5]–218 text; pp. [219]–225 "EPILOGUE"; p. [226] blank; p. [227] "ABOUT THE AUTHOR" / [twenty-one line statement]; p. [228] blank.

Binding: Mottled gray and white paper-covered boards with an olive-green cloth shelf-back. Spine, reading downward: [in gold:] PETER / MATTHIESSEN [decorative rule] AFRICAN SILENCES [decorative rule] [reading across:] [colophon] / RANDOM / HOUSE. Front, in lower right quadrant: [in gold:] [decorative device]. Endpapers front and back are printed in green and mottled gray and white and show maps of the West Africa Wildlife Survey — 1978 and the Congo Basin Forest Elephant Survey — 1986. Issued in a dust jacket designed by R. D. Scudellari with a monoprint by Mary Frank on the cover and a photograph of Matthiessen by Nancy Crampton on the back.

Contents: Prologue / African Silences: Senegal, Gambia, Ivory Coast (1978) / Of Peacocks and Gorillas: Zaire (1978) / Pygmies and Pygmy Elephants: The Congo Basin (1986) / Epilogue.

Price: $21.00.

_____. London: Harvill, 1991.

_____. New York: Vintage Books, 1992.

_____. London: Harvill, 1992. Paperback.

_____. Paris: Payot, 1994. Tr. Jean-Pierre Ricard. [*Silences Africains*].

_____. Barcelona: Península, 1999. Tr. Ángela Pérez. [*Los Silencios de África*].

See **C87** and **C92**.

A29. *Baikal*, 1992

[in black:] BAIKAL / SACRED SEA OF SIBERIA / ESSAY BY PETER MATTHIESSEN / PHOTOGRAPHS BY BOYD NORTON / FOREWORD BY YEVGENY YEVTUSHENKO / AFTERWORD BY DAVID BROWER / Edited by Chez Liley / SIERRA CLUB BOOKS / San Francisco

Collation: pp. [i–viii] ix [x] xi–xiv

[xv–xvi] [1–2] 3–4 [5–6] 7–8 [9–10] 11–12 [13–14] 15–16 [17–20] 21–22 [23–24] 25–26 [27–28] 29–30 [31–34] 35–36 [37] 38 [39] 40–44 [45] 46–47 [48–50] 51–52 [53] 54 [55–56] 57–58 [59] 60–63 [64–66] 67–68 [69–70] 71 [72] 73 [74] 75–76 [77–80] 81–82 [83–84] 85 [86] 87–89 [90–92]. 9½" × 8⅜".

Pagination: p. [1] blank [blue-gray]; p. [2] [color photograph]; p. [3] title page; p. [4] [text is divided into two columns:] [left hand column:] [twelve line statement about The Sierra Club] / [five line statement concerning a share of the book's proceeds going to Baikal Watch]. [Right hand column:] "This essay by Peter Matthiessen appeared in altered form in the / February 14, 1991 issue of the *New York Review of Books*. Copyright / 1991 NYREV, Inc. / Compilation copyright ©1992 by Baikal Watch / Essay copyright ©1992 by Peter Matthiessen / Foreword copyright ©1992 by Yevgeny Yevtushenko / Afterword copyright ©1992 by Baikal Watch / Photographs copyright ©1992 by Boyd Norton / unless otherwise noted / Other photographs copyright © by / the photographer credited / All other text copyrights appear on pages 87–89, which constitute an / extension of this copyright page. / Photographs: page ii, by Ben Simmons; pages xvi and 2, by / Boris Dmitriev. / All rights reserved under International and Pan-American Copyright / Conventions. No part of this book may be reproduced in any form / or by any electronic or mechanical means, including information / storage and retrieval systems, without permission in writing from / the publisher. / Library of Congress Cataloging-in-Publication Data" / [ten lines] / "PRODUCTION Susan Ristow / COMPOSITION Wilsted & Taylor / Printed by Dai Nippon Printing Co. (Hong Kong) Ltd. / 10 9 8 7 6 5 4 3 2 1"; p. [v] [color photograph] / [dedication:] "For Paul Winter and Chez Liley / and all our excellent friends / on board the *Baikal*"; p. [vi] [color photograph]; p. [vii] "CONTENTS"; p. [viii] [color photograph]; p. [ix] [twenty-nine line excerpt] / "VALENTIN RASPUTIN from 'Baikal'"; p. [x] [color photograph]; pp. xi–xiv "FOREWORD"; p. [xv] [maps of Siberia and Lake Baikal]; p. [xvi] [color photograph]; pp. [1]–[79] text and photographs; p. [80] blank; pp. 81–82 "AFTERWORD"; P. [84] [color photograph]; p. [85] blank; p. 85 "ACKNOWLEDGMENTS"; p. [86] [color photograph]; pp. 87–89 "NOTES" [and] "SOURCES AND PERMISSIONS"; p. [90] blank; p. [91] [color photograph]; p. [92] blank [blue gray].

Binding: Dark blue cloth covered boards. Spine, reading downward: [in silver:] BAIKAL MATTHIESSEN/NORTON SIERRA CLUB BOOKS. Front, across top third, a blind stamping of BAIKAL. Endpapers front and back of silver paper. Issued in a dust jacket with photograph of Matthiessen by Nancy Crampton and of Norton by Barbara Norton.

Contents: Foreword by Yevgeny Yevtushenko / Part One / Part Two / Part Three / Part Four / Part Five / Afterword by David Brower / Acknowledgments / Notes / Sources and Permissions

Price: $25.00

_____. London: Thames & Hudson, 1992.

_____. Vancouver: Douglas & McIntyre, 1992.

See **C98**.

A30. *The Poorest of the Poor — By Far — Are the Indian People*, 1992

Berkeley, CA: Black Oak Books. Broadside. 17" × 8¼". Tan paper printed in black, reddish brown, and green. The passage is from *In the Spirit of Crazy Horse*. Produced by Black Oak Books to benefit the Leonard Peltier Defense Committee. Designed and printed in an edition of 150 copies at Okeanos Press.

A31. *Shadows of Africa*, 1992

[on the left hand side of a double-spread title page:] [in black:] SHADOWS / Peter Matthiessen / [drawing] / HARRY N. ABRAMS, INC., PUBLISHERS, NEW YORK [on the right hand side of a double-spread title page:] [in white:] OF AFRICA / Mary Frank

Collation: pp. [1–7] 8–13 [14] 15–20 [21] 22–33 [34] 35–40 [41] 42–44 [45]

46–57 [58–59] 60 [61] 62–64 [65–66] 67–76 [77] 78–80 [81–82] 83–88 [89] 90 [91] 92–93 [94] 95–97 [98–99] 100–117 [118] 119–120. 10¼" × 9¾".

Pagination: p. [1] half-title; pp. [2–3] title page; p. [4] "Project Director: Robert Morton / Editor: Harriet Whelchel Designer: Samuel N. Antupit / *Library of Congress Cataloging-in-Publication Data*" / [eight lines] / "Illustrations copyright ©1992 Mary Frank. Mary Frank / is represented by Zabriskie Gallery, New York / Text copyright ©1972, 1981, 1991, 1992 Peter Matthiessen / The African journals in this book were excerpted from the / sources given below and are reprinted with the generous / cooperation of the publishers: *The Tree Where Man Was Born* / (Dutton, 1972), *Sand Rivers* (Viking, 1981), and *African Silences* / (Random House, 1991). Additional sources are "Botswana," / in *Audubon Magazine* (January 1981), and "Tanzania," in / *Audubon Magazine* (May 1981). Portions of *The Tree Where Man / Was Born* and *Sand Rivers* appeared earlier in *The New Yorker*. / Published in 1992 by Harry N. Abrams, Incorporated, / New York. A Times Mirror Company. All rights reserved. / No part of the contents of this book may be reproduced / without the written permission of the publisher / Printed and bound in Japan"; p. [5] "CONTENTS"; p. [6] [dedication:] "*To the courage and dedication of the rangers and wardens of the African national parks*" / [small drawing] / "With appreciation to my son, Pablo, / for his endless curiosity and interest in the / world of animals; and for Leo — M.F. / In fervent hope that my small grandsons, / Christopher, Joseph, and Andrew, together / with all of the world's children, may still / find remnants of the splendor of the world / when they grow up — P.M."; pp. [1]–119 text and drawings; p. 120 "ACKNOWLEDGMENTS" / [eight line statement] / "PHOTOGRAPH CREDITS" / [eight line statement].

Binding: Dark green cloth covered boards. Spine, reading downward: [in gold:] Matthiessen Frank SHADOWS OF AFRICA [reading across:] Abrams. Front, centered at top: [in gold:] SHADOWS / OF AFRICA. Endpapers front and back are of stiff white paper with drawings in black. Issued in a dust jacket with paintings by Mary Frank on the front and back, and photograph of Matthiessen and Frank by Barbara Bordnick.

Contents: Part 1: 1961, 1969–1970 / Part 2: 1976–1978 / Part 3: 1979, 1986 / Epilogue / Acknowledgments / Photograph Credits.

Price: $34.95.

A32. *East of Lo Monthang: In the Land of Mustang*, 1995

[across a double-spread title page with a white border at the top and bottom: a color photograph of a Tange village] [on the right side of the double-spread title page above the photograph:] [in black:] EAST OF [decorative flourish] / LO MONTHANG / IN THE LAND OF MUSTANG [small ornamental devices are between the letters of Mustang] [on the right side of the double-sided spread title page below the photograph:] [in black:] [colophon] / SHAMBHALA / *Boston* / 1995

Collation: pp. [1–13] 14–16 [17]18–19 [20–21] 22 [23] 24 [25] 26 [27–28] 29–31 [32] 33–48 [49–50] 51–52 [53] 54 [55–56] 57–58 [59] 60–63 [64–65] 66–76 [77] 78–80 [81] 82 [83] 84–87 [88–89] 90–105 [106–107] 108 [109–110] 111–118 [119–120] 121–122 [123] 124–127 [128] 129–132 [133] 134 [135] 136–138 [139] 140 [141] 142 [143] 144–160 [161–162] 163–164 [165] 166–167 [168] 169 [170] 171–175 [176–177] 178–180 [181–183] 184–185 [186–187] 188–192. 9⅛" × 12".

Pagination: p. [1] half-title; pp. [2–3] title page; pp. [4–11] photographs; p. [12] "EAST OF LO MONTHANG: IN THE LAND OF MUSTANG / Shambhala Publications, Inc. / Horticultural Hall / 300 Massachusetts Avenue / Boston, Massachusetts 02115 / TEXT ©1995 PETER MAT-THIESSEN / PHOTOS & CAPTIONS ©1995 THOMAS LAIRD / All rights reserved. No part of this book may be reproduced in any form or by any means, / electronic or mechanical, including photocopying, recording, or by any information storage / and retrieval system, without permission in writing from the publisher. /

9 8 7 6 5 4 3 2 1 / First Edition / Printed in Hong Kong / Distributed in the United States by Random House, Inc., / and in Canada by Random House of Canada Ltd. / Library of Congress Cataloging-in-Publication Data" / [ten lines] / "Edited by Elizabeth Rudy / Copyedited by Mary Orr / Designed by David Hurst" / [single rule] / [seven lines of credits for the preceding photographs]; p. [13] "CONTENTS"; p. 14 map of Mustang District, Nepal; pp. 15–190 text and photographs; p. 191 "ACKNOWLEDGMENTS"; p. 192 [photograph].

Binding: Dark red cloth covered boards. Spine, reading downward: [in gold:] MATTHIESSEN / LAIRD EAST OF LO MONTHANG IN THE LAND / OF MUSTANG [reading across:] [colophon] [reading downward:] SHAMBHALA. Endpapers front and back of stiff paper with a black and white photograph. Issued in a dust jacket designed by David Hurst with photographs by Thomas Laird.

Contents: Wings of Daybreak / Ghost-Eaters and Border Towns / Himalayan Rain Shadow / Saligrams / The Three Treasures / Track of Jackal, Print of Snowcock / The Precariousness of Life / Silent Mountains / Sao Gompa / *Mehti* and Snow Leopard / Lo Monthang / "Like A Hidden Valley" / Raja Jigme / The Tiji Ceremony / Champa Temple / The Temples of Lo Monthang / The Demon's Red Remnants / Epilogue

Price: $35.00

_____. Boston: Shambhala Publications, 1996.
_____. Collingdale, PA: DIANE Publishing Co., 1998.

A33. The Peter Matthiessen Reader, 2000

[in gray:] THE / [in black:] PETER / MATTHIESSEN / [in gray:] READER / [in black:] NONFICTION 1959–1991 / [in gray:] Edited with an Introduction by [in black:] McKay Jenkins / [colophon] / VINTAGE BOOKS / [in gray:] A Division of Random House, Inc. / New York

Collation: pp. [a–d] [i–ix] x [xi] xii–xxix [xxx] [1–3] 4–17 [18] 19–67 [68–69] 70–85 [86] 87–102 [103] 104–125 [126] 127–136 [137] 138–200 [201] 202–242

[243] 244–266 [267] 268–289 [290] 291–314 [315] 316–336 [337] 338–359 [360–366]. 5" × 8".

Pagination: p. [a] "Praise for PETER MATTHIESSEN" / [five brief testimonials]; p. [b] blank; p. [c] "THE PETER MATTHIESSEN READER / NONFICTION 1959–1991" / [eleven line statement about Matthiessen] / [seven line statement about Jenkins]"; p. [d] blank; p. [i] "Books by Peter Matthiessen / Nonfiction" / [lists fifteen titles] / "Fiction" / [lists nine titles]; p. [ii] blank; p. [iii] half-title; p. [iv] blank; p. [v] title page; p. [vi] [dedication:] "For Brian and Denny / — M. J. / A VINTAGE ORIGINAL, JANUARY 2000 / *Copyright ©1999 by McKay Jenkins and Peter Matthiessen* / All rights reserved under International and Pan-American Copyright Conventions. / Published in the United States by Vintage Books, a division of Random House, / Inc., New York, and simultaneously in Canada by Random House of Canada / Limited, Toronto / Page 361 constitutes an extension of this copyright page. / Vintage and colophon are registered trademarks of Random House, Inc. / Library of Congress Cataloging-in-Publication Data" / [nine lines] / "www.vintagebooks.com / Printed in the United States of America / 10 9 8 7 6 5 4 3 2 1"; p. [vii] "Editor's Acknowledgments" / [five line statement]; p. [viii] blank; pp. [ix]–x "Contents"; pp. [xi]–xxix "Introduction; p.[xxx] blank; p. [1] second half-title; p. [2] blank; pp. [3]–359 text; p. [360] blank; p. [361] "Permissions Acknowledgments"; p. [362] blank; pp. [363–364] "ALSO BY PETER MATTHIESSEN"; pp. [365–366] blank.

Binding: Stiff white paper covers. Front: [a black and white photograph of Matthiessen holding and petting a tiger cub:] [upper right quadrant:] [in black:] "Our greatest modern nature writer / in the lyrical tradition." / (*The New York Times Book Review.*" / [centered:] [in white:] THE / [in green:] PETER / MATTHIESSEN / [in white:] READER / A SELECTION OF NONFICTION / EDITED AND WITH AN INTRODUCTION BY McKAY JENKINS. Spine: [photograph continued:] [reading downward:] [in black:] Edited by

McKay Jenkins [in white:] THE [in green:] PETER MATTHIESSEN [in white:] READER [reading across:] [colophon] / Vintage. Back cover: [against a black background:] [upper left quadrant:] [in white:] NATURE WRITING/ANTHOLOGY / [centered:] [in green:] "Matthiessen is a great travel companion.... His knowledge of / plants, animals and people is breathtaking." — *The Boston Globe* / [in white:] [two paragraph statement regarding Matthiessen and the book] / left lower quadrant:] [in green:] U. S. $14.00 / Can. $21.00 / COVER DESIGN BY CHIN-YEE LAI / COVER PHOTOGRAPH BY ZENBOY PRODUCTIONS, INC./ / JESSIE CLOSE / A VINTAGE ORIGINAL [right lower quadrant:] [in black on a white field:] ISBN 0-375-70272-5 / [bar code] / [beneath white field:] [in green:] www.vintagebooks .com.

Contents: Introduction / from *Wildlife in America* (1959) — The Outlying Rocks / from *The Cloud Forest* (1961) — Beyond Black Drunken River / from *Under the Mountain Wall* (1962) — The Death of Weake / from *The Shorebirds of North America* (1967) / from *Sal Si Puedes: Cesar Chavez and the New American Revolution* (1969) / from *Blue Meridian* (1971) / from *The Tree Where Man Was Born* (1972) — Rites of Passage, — Elephant Kingdoms, — At Gidabembe / from *The Snow Leopard* (1978) (At Crystal Mountain / from *Indian Country* (1984) — Lost Eloheh Land / from *Men's Lives* (1986) / from *African Silences* (1991) — Of Peacocks and Gorillas: Zaire, — Pygmies and Pygmy Elephants: The Congo Basin / from *In the Spirit of Crazy Horse* / Permissions Acknowledgments

Price: $14.00.

A34. *Tigers in the Snow*, 2000

[in black:] TIGERS IN THE SNOW / [in orange:] *Introduction and photographs by* / MAURICE HORNOCKER / [in black:] PETER MATTHIESSEN / [in orange:] NORTH POINT PRESS / *A division of Farrar, Straus and Giroux* / New York

Collation: pp. [a–b] [i–viii] ix–xviii [1–2] 3–14 [15] 16–25 [26] 27–28 [29] 30–36 [37–38] 39–45 [46] 47–48 [49]

50–102 [103] 104–105 [106] 107–112 [113] 114–119 [120] 121–131 [132] 133–134 [135] 136–146 [147] 148–172 [173] 174 [175–176] 177–185 [186]. 6¾" × 9¼".

Pagination: p. [a] "*Also by Peter Matthiessen*" / [lists two columns of titles beneath the headings of "FICTION" and "NONFICTION"; p. [b] blank; p. [i] half-title; p. [ii] title page; p. [iii] [photograph]; p. [iv] "North Point Press / A division of Farrar, Straus and Giroux / 19 Union Square West, New York 10003 / Copyright ©2000 by Peter Matthiessen / Introduction and photographs copyright ©2000 by Maurice Hornocker / All rights reserved / Distributed in Canada by Douglas & McIntyre Ltd. / Printed in the United States of America / Designed by Jonathan D. Lippincott / Map designed by Jeffrey L. Ward / First edition, 2000 / Grateful acknowledgment is made to *The New Yorker* and *Audubon* magazine, in which / some of the material in this book first appeared, in an altered form. / Library of Congress Cataloging-in-Publication Data" / [ten lines] / "All tiger photographs are by Maurice Hornocker except for those on pp.125 and 142, which / are by Marc Moritsch, and p. 162, which is by Howard Quigley. / *Art credits:*" [ten lines of credits]; p. [v] [dedication:] [twenty-two line dedication to "the tiger biologists cited in this / book"; p. [vi] blank; p. [vii] [five epigraphs]; p. [viii] blank; pp. ix–xviii "*INTRODUCTION*"; pp. [1]–174 text and photographs; pp. [175]–185 "*NOTES*"; p. [186] blank.

Binding: Burnt orange paper covered boards with a black cloth covered shelfback. Spine, reading downward: [in gold:] *TIGERS IN THE SNOW* / *PETER MATTHIESSEN* / [colophon]. Front, centered in upper half of paper covered board: [in black:] *P M*. Endpapers front and back of stiff white paper are printed in blue, yellow, black, and orange and show maps of Asia and the range of the tiger. Issued in a dust jacket designed by Paul Buckley with photographs by Maurice Hornocker, with an author photograph by Linda Girvin and a photograph of Hornocker by Leslie Hornocker.

Price: $27.00.

EDITED WORKS

A35. *North American Indians*, 1989
[in black:] [within a double rule frame:]
North American / Indians / [single rule with
arrows on either end] / GEORGE CATLIN
/ EDITED AND WITH / AN INTRO-
DUCTION BY / *Peter Matthiessen* / [colo-
phon] / VIKING
    Collation: pp. [i–vii] viii–xix [xx–xxiii]
xxiv–xxxiii [xxxiv–xxxviii] [1] 2–8 [9] 10–11
[12–13] 14–17 [18] 19–21 [22] 23 [24–25]
26–29 [30–31] 32 [33] 34–38 [39] 40 [41]
42–44 [45] 46–48 [49] 50–52 [53–54] 55
[56–57] 58–59 [60] 61–62 [63] 64–69
[70–71] 72 [73] 74–79 [80–81] 82–84 [85]
86 [87–88] 89–91 [92] 93–97 [98] 99–100
[101] 102 [103] 104–108 [109–110] 111–120
[121] 122–127 [128] 129–133 [134] 135–140
[141] 142–144 [145] 146–147 [148] 149 [150]
151–172 [173] 174–184 [185] 186–187 [188]
189–192 [193] 194–197 [198] 199–201 [202]
203 [204] 205–206 [207] 208–212 [213]
214–218 [219] 220–225 [226] 227–228
[229] 230–234 [235] 236–247 [248] 249–
254 [255] 256–266 [267] 268–269 [270]
271–275 [276] 277–279 [280] 281–283
[284] 285 [286] 287–290 [291] 292–293
[294–295] 296 [297] 298–300 [301] 302–
303 [304–305] 306 [307] 308–311 [312]
313–314 [315] 316–318 [319] 320–326 [327]
328 [329] 330 [331] 332 [333] 334 [335–
336] 337–341 [342–344] 345–346 [347]
348–354 [355] 356–359 [360] 361 [362–
363] 364–365 [366] 367–370 [371] 372
[373] 374–375 [376] 377 [378] 379 [380–
381] 382 [383] 384–386 [387] 388–389
[390] 391–399 [400] 401 [402] 403–405
[406] 407 [408–409] 410–411 [412] 413–416
[417] 418–419 [420] 421–439 [440–441]
442–448 [449] 450 [451] 452 [453] 454–
455 [456] 457–485 [486–487] 488–497
[498] 499–522. 5'' × 7¾''.
    Pagination: p. [i] half-title; p. [ii]
"PENGUIN NATURE LIBRARY" / [list of
sixteen titles]; p. [iii] title-page; p. [iv]
"VIKING / Published by the penguin
Group / Viking Penguin, a division of Penguin Books USA Inc., / 40 West 23rd
Street, New York, New York 10010, U. S. A.
/ Penguin Books Ltd, 27 Wrights Lane, /

London W8 5TZ, England / Penguin
Books Australia Ltd, Ringwood, / Victoria,
Australia / Penguin Books Canada Ltd, 2801
John Street, / Markham, Ontario, Canada
L3R 1B4 / Penguin Books N. Z.) ltd,
182–190 Wairau Road, / Aukland 10, New
Zealand / Penguin Books Ltd, Registered
Offices: / Harmondsworth, Middlesex,
England / This edition first published in
simultaneous hardcover and paperback /
editions by Viking Penguin, a division of
Penguin Books USA Inc. 1989 / 1 3 5 7 9
10 8 6 4 2 / Introduction copyright © Peter
Matthiessen, 1989 / All rights reserved / Art-
work courtesy of the National Museum of
American Art, Smithsonian / Institution,
Gift of Mrs. Joseph Harrison, Jr. /
LIBRARY OF CONGRESS CATA-
LOGING IN PUBLICATION DATA" /
[nine lines] / "Printed in the United States
of America / Set in Bulmer / Designed by
Ann Gold" / [eight line copyright notice];
pp. [v] [double rule] / "*PENGUIN
NATURE LIBRARY* (/ [statement on the
series] / "— Edward Hoagland"; p. [vi]
blank; pp. [vii]–xix *"INTRODUCTION"*;
p. [xx] blank; p. [xxi] *"EDITOR'S NOTE"*;
p. [xxii] blank; pp. [xxiii]–xxxiii *"CON-
TENTS"*; pp. [xxxiv–xxxv] [two-page map
spread showing "A BRIEF CHRONOL-
OGY OF CATLIN'S TRAVELS"; p. [xxxvi]
[map] / "*U. States Indian Frontier in 1840*";
p. [xxxvii] second half-title; p. [xxxviii]
blank; pp. [1]–485 text; p. [486] [map] /
"*The moves of the Mandans and the place of
their extinction.*"; pp. [487]–497 *"APPEN-
DIX"*; p. [498] blank; pp. 499–522
"INDEX".
    Binding: Tan paper covered cloths with
a tan cloth shelf-back. Spine, reading
downward: [in gold:] GEORGE / CATLIN
NORTH AMERICAN / INDIANS [read-
ing across:] VIKING. Endpapers front and
back of stiff white paper. Issued in a dust
jacket.
    Price: $24.95.
_____. New York: Penguin Books, 1989.
_____. Paris: A. Michel, 1992. Tr. Danièle and
Pierre Bondil. [*Les Indiens d'Amérique du
Nord*].
_____. New York: Penguin Books, 1996.

B. Short Fiction

1951

B1. "Sadie." *Atlantic Monthly*, 187 (January), 55–58.

Tension between Dewey Floyd, a former poacher and dog handler, and his brother-in-law, Joe Pentland, leads to the killing of a favorite dog and murder.
Reprinted in **A7–A8**.

B2. "The Fifth Day." *Atlantic Monthly*, 188 (September), 60–63.

Differences surface between two men, Dave Winton, a young college student, and Joe Robitelli, an older, working-class "tough," while they help drag the bay for the body of a drowned man.
Reprinted in **A7–A8**.

1952

B3. "The Centrepiece." In *The Observer Prize Stories*. With an introduction by Elizabeth Bowen. London: William Heinemann, Ltd., pp. 104–113.

A boy remembers December 1941 when his grandmother gathered the family together to celebrate a traditional German Christmas complete with the family's five foot long holiday centerpiece of Saint Nicholas and his reindeer. Young cousin Millicent (Silly Milly) refuses to participate in anything German and remains in the car. During the dinner a fallen candle sets the centerpiece on fire, destroying the family's symbol of tradition and the past, but restoring something more important.
Reprinted in **A8**.

B4. "Martin's Beach." *Botteghe Oscure Reader*, 10, pp. 310–318.

Because of his health, nine year old Martin Stark is confined to playing on the beach outside of his home. One day he and his brother, Joey, discover a Snowy Owl wintering in the bog at the far end of the beach. Martin develops a special attachment to the owl but an accident causes him to lose both his brother and the owl.

B5. "The Tower of the Four Winds." *Cornhill*, 166 (Summer), 143–149.

Misunderstanding Spanish manners and the question of a man's pride, a man tries to recapture the week of friendship and merriment he experienced with another at the festival of San Fermin.

1953

B6. "Late in the Season." *New World Writing*, no. 3, pp. 320–328.

The fate of a large snapping turtle is the catalyst of and subject for a dispute between Cici and Frank Avery and a revelation about their one year marriage.
Reprinted in **A7–A8**.

B7. "A Replacement." *Paris Review*, no. 1 (February), [47]–56.

At the close of World War II a disillusioned German lieutenant finds the possibility of hope in the appearance and survival of a young, wounded American pilot.
Reprinted in **A7**.

1956

B8. "Lina." *Cornhill*, 169 (Fall), 53–58.

After the deaths of her parents, Lina goes to live with Count Erardi and his wife in their villa on the Tuscan hillside. A sheltered and timid woman, her life of seclusion precipitates a sense of estrangement from her home, her time, and her self.

1957

B9. "The Traveling Man." *Harper's Magazine*, 214 (February), 57–65.

A black convict, Traver, escapes from a chain gang to an uninhabited barrier island off the Carolina coast. There he plays a game of wit and survival with a white poacher who is hunting him.

Reprinted as "Travelin' Man" in **A7–A8**, and **B10**.

1958

B10. "Travelin' Man." In *Prize Stories 1958: The O. Henry Awards*. Ed. Paul Engle. Garden City, NY: Doubleday, pp. 293–309.

See **B9**.

B11. "The Wolves of Aguila." *Harper's Bazaar*, 87 (August), 76–77, 148–150.

Will Miller is a contract wolf hunter for ranchers and government agencies in the Southwest. He has become uneasy with his growing recognition that he is contributing to the end of a wild place and to his own way of life. He swears never to kill a wolf again but is drawn back to the Gran Desierto in search of two wolves. He finds, instead, two mysterious young boys and his final destiny.

Reprinted in **A7–A8** and **B25**.

1963

B12. "Midnight Turning Gray." *Saturday Evening Post*, 236 (28 September), 56–58, 60, 62, 64–67.

Ann Pryor is a young, naïve, and idealistic volunteer worker at a mental hospital. She tries to help Ernest Hamlin, a patient she believes does not belong there, raising his hopes and assuring his confinement.

Reprinted in **A7–A8**.

1964

B13. "Horace and Hassid." *Venture: The Traveller's World*, 1 (October), 17–18, 21–22, 25.

A humorous account of the relationship and misadventures of two passengers,

Horace and Hassid, aboard a freighter sailing from Brooklyn to Belém. These two "natural enemies" and enforced cabin mates provide the only company for each other during their 40 day voyage.

Reprinted as "Horse Latitudes" in **B15**.

1974

B14. "An Excerpt from *Far Tortuga*." *Paris Review*, no. 60 (Winter), [39]–[77].

See **A6**.

1978

B15. "Horse Latitudes." *Antaeus*, 29 (Spring), 7–14.

Originally published as "Horace and Hassid" in **B13**. Reprinted in **A7–A8**.

1985

B16. "On the River Styx." *Esquire*, 104 (August), 79–81, 84–85, 87.

Burkett, an environmental lawyer, and his wife, Alice, take a fishing trip to a small town in the Ten Thousand Islands of Florida. Burkett hopes to catch robalo or "snook" but finds himself embroiled in the racial hatred, social relations, and criminal dealings of the area.

Reprinted in **A8**.

1988

B17. "Lumumba Lives." *Wigwag*, "Preview Issue," (Summer), 43–[56].

Henry Harkness returns from foreign service in Africa and involvement with the C. I. A. Disowned by his father, an Assistant Secretary of State, for being morally dead, Henry tries to escape his sense of alienation in his own life and in a changing and changed America.

Reprinted in **A8** and **B22**.

1990

B18. "From *Killing Mr. Watson.*" *Paris Review*, no. 114 (Spring), [89]–97.
See **A9**.

1993

B19. "Speck in the Glades." *Esquire*, 120 (July), 80–83.
Excerpt from *Lost Man's River*.
See **A10**.

1995

B20. From *At Play in the Fields of the Lord*. In *Tales From the Jungle: A Rainforest Reader*. Ed. Daniel R. Katz and Miles Chapin. Foreword by George Plimpton. New York: Crown Trade Paperbacks, pp. 302–313.
Chapter 10 from the novel.
See **A4**.

1997

B21. "From *Lost Man's River.*" *Paris Review*, no. 144 (Fall), 20–25.
See **A10**.

B22. "Lumumba Lives." In *The Peregrine Reader*. Ed. Mikel Vause and Carl Porter. Salt Lake City, UT: Gibbs Smith Publisher, pp. 257–258.
Reprint of **B17**.

1998

B23. "The Killing of the Warden." *Audubon*, 100 (November/December), 36–38, 40, 42, 44. With photographs by Clyde Butcher.
An excerpt from *Bone by Bone*.
See **A11**.

1999

B24. "Bone by Bone." *Paris Review*, no. 150 (Spring), [216]–221.
An excerpt from the novel.
See **A11**.

2000

B25. "The Wolves of Aguila." In *The Campfire Collection: Spine-Tingling Tales to Tell in the Dark*. Ed. Eric B. Martin. San Francisco: Chronicle Books, pp. 128–146.
Reprint of **B11**.

C. Articles and Essays

1953

C1. "Six Drawings for Faulkner's *These Thirteen*." *Paris Review*, no. 2 (Summer), [72]. Text and drawings, pp. [72–78].

This brief note prefaces the drawings by Epinouze. The artist is compared to Faulkner in his interest in the "primordial elements in man and nature."

1954

C2. With George Plimpton. "The Art of Fiction V: William Styron." *Paris Review*, no. 5 (Spring), [42]–57.

An interview with Styron. Reprinted in **C4**, **C6** and **C77**.

1958

C3. "Annals of Crime: Peut-Être un Peu Excessif." *New Yorker*, 34 (1 November), 119–120, 122–126, 129–145.

A review of the events surrounding the murder of Dr. Pierre Chevallier, a former Resistance hero, mayor of Orleans, member of the National Assembly, and newly named member of the French Cabinet. His wife, Yvonne, is tried for the murder and subsequently acquitted. Chevallier was killed during an argument about his mistress. Matthiessen presents this as a classic case of a crime of passion; it exhibits all the elements of pure theatre.

C4. With George Plimpton. "The Art of Fiction: William Styron." In *Writers at Work: The Paris Review Interview*. Edited, and with an introduction, by Malcolm Cowley. New York: Viking Press, pp. 268–282.

Reprint of **C2**.

1959

C5. "Slaughter and Salvation." *Sports Illustrated*, 11 (16 November), 82–84, 87–90, 93–94, 96.

Excerpt from *Wildlife in America*. See **A12**.

1961

C6. "CODA: 'I'm not trying to be rosy about things like the atom bomb and war and the failure of the Presbyterian Church. These things are awful.'" In *The Idea of an American Novel*. Ed. Louis D. Rubin, Jr. and John Rees Moore. New York: Thomas Y. Crowell, Company, pp. 368–370.

A brief excerpt from **C2**.

C7. "A Reporter at Large: The Last Wilderness: Amazonas." *New Yorker*, 37 (8 July), 30–32, 34, 39–40, 42–46, 48–57.

An account of Matthiessen's voyage in the Amazonas, the basin of the Amazon River system and one of the last stretches of wilderness in the world. From the coast, he travels to Iquitos, Peru aboard a small British freighter.

Incorporated into **A13**. See also **C8** and **C9**.

C8. "A Reporter at Large: The Last Wilderness: Brazilian Chronicle." *New Yorker*, 37 (12 August), 35–36, 38, 41, 43–45, 48, 50, 52, 55–56, 58–60, 62–67.

Observations from his travels within the interior of Brazil include the frontier life and law of the provincial villages and settlements, the native peoples, and the wildlife.

Incorporated into **A13**. See also **C7** and **C9**.

C9. "A Reporter at Large: The Last Wilderness: Peruvian Journal." *New Yorker*, 37 (September), 51–52, 54, 56, 59, 61–62, 64, 66, 69–70, 72, 74–76, 81–82, 84, 86, 88, 91–92, 94, 96–98, 101–102, 104, 106–111.

Entries from Matthiessen's journal during a trip into the jungles of Río Mapuya in Peru in search of a large fossilized jawbone.

Incorporated into **A13**. *See also* **C7** and **C8**.

1962

C10. "Death of Weake." *Harper's Magazine*, 225 (October), 53–60.

An excerpt from *Under the Mountain Wall* about the death of a young Kurelu boy wounded in tribal warfare.

See **A14**.

C11. "The Tree Where Man Was Born." *The Reporter*, 26 (June 21), 35–38.

A report of his travel to and in Equatoria, the southernmost province of the Sudan, and the Nilotic tribesmen of the area, particularly the Nuer.

Incorporated into **A20**.

1963

C12. "The Atlantic Coast." In *The American Heritage Book of Natural Wonders*. Editor in Charge, Alvin M. Josephy, Jr. [New York]: American Heritage Publishing Co.; book trade distribution by Simon & Schuster. Text, pp. 9–17; photographs with captions, pp. 18–47.

A loving and appreciative description of the Atlantic coast of the United States from St. Croix River, Maine to the Florida Keys. This seaboard "is more striking and varied than any coast of any single country in the world." When it is not beautiful, it is because of the defilement of man. Too much of the coast has succumbed to exploitation and pollution.

1964

C13. "Tierra del Fuego." *Americas*, 16 (February), 35–42.

Excerpts from *The Cloud Forest*. *See* **A13**.

1965

C14. "A Reporter at Large: Sand and Wind and Waves." *New Yorker*, 41 (3 April), 116, 121–122, 124–126, 128, 131–132, 134, 137–138, 140, 142, 144.

With representatives of the National Park Service, Matthiessen visits Assateague Island prior to its designation as a National Seashore. A natural history of the island is given, as is an account of the conflict between nature and the attempted commercial development of the island.

1966

C15. "The Cloud Forest." In *Worlds of Discovery*. Vol. 4. Pyramid Publications.

Not verified. Cited in **H37**.

C16. "A Reporter at Large: Ovibos Moschatus." *New Yorker*, 41 (5 February), 94, 96, 98, 100, 102, 106, 108, 110, 112, 114, 116, 119–123.

Matthiessen participates in an expedition to Nunivak Island, the second largest island in the Bering Sea and the home of the only musk ox (*ovibus moschatus*) in Alaska. Twenty calves are to be captured to start a domestic herd to provide breeding stock to establish herds in the North.

Expanded as *Oomingmak*, **A15**.

1967

C17. "The Last Great Strand." *Audubon*, 69 (March), 64–71. Photography by Frederick Kent Truslow. Painting by Don Richard Eckelberry.

An account of a visit to Corkscrew Swamp Sanctuary in Big Cypress, Florida, home of the largest forest of bald cypress left in America. This three mile remnant of bald cypress is shelter to a colony of large black-and-white wood storks (wood ibis). The Swamp is threatened by Gulf American Corporation and Sun Coast Realty's land reclamation and development, and the diversion of the natural water flow for private profit.

C18. "A Reporter at Large: To the Miskito Bank." *New Yorker*, 43 (28 October), 120, 122, 124, 127–128, 130, 133–134, 136, 138, 140, 143–146, 149–150, 152–164.

An excellent account of Matthiessen's trips to the Cayman Islands and his relationship with Captain Cadian Ebanks. Matthiessen participates in the hunt for green turtles in tortugas aboard Ebanks's boat, *Wilson*. He discusses the changes taking place in the Caymans and in the turtle fishing industry as they both become more modernized and commercialized. Matthiessen provides a wonderful portrait of Captain Ebanks; this is one of his most successful essays. His experiences provide the basis for *Far Tortuga*.

C19. "A Reporter at Large: The Wind Birds — I." *New Yorker*, 43 (27 May), 40–44, 46, 49–50, 52, 55–56, 58, 61–62, 64, 66, 68, 73–74, 76, 78, 80, 85–86, 88, 90, 92, 95–96, 98, 101–102.

A survey of the natural history of shore birds as well as Matthiessen's personal observations of the birds near his Sagaponack, Long Island home.
See **A21** and **C20.**

C20. "A Reporter at Large: The Wind Birds – II." *New Yorker*, 43 (3 June), 42–44, 46, 48, 51–52, 54, 56, 58, 61–62, 64, 66, 68, 70–72, 77–80, 82, 84–86, 88, 91–92, 94, 96–98, 101–105.

A continuation of **C19.** *See also* **A21.**

1969

C21. "The Decent Society: The Physical Environment." *Playboy*, 16 (January), 90, 275–277.

Matthiessen contributes one of eleven essays to a symposium on presenting a "practical course" to achieve "a more humane America." The key to the preservation of the environment is to control population. While technology may be able to address material needs, oblique behavioral problems will still exist from overpopulation. Any meaningful environmental renaissance must start with the whole concept of cities, yet America and the federal government maintain a rural mentality. The American city must be redesigned and rebuilt. The restoration of the environment requires a greater corporate conscience and sense of responsibility. There is too much corporate influence in the federal government. The nation must move away from the idea that any growth is good growth. The American public must become involved to reclaim and maintain the environment.

C22. "Profiles: Organizer — I." *New Yorker*, 45 (21 June), 42–44, 46, 48, 50, 55–56, 58–60, 62–64, 66–85.

This is a compelling, albeit biased, portrait of Cesar Chavez and La Causa — the organization of the first effective farm workers' union in America, the United Farm Workers (UFW). Matthiessen weaves a report of his time spent with Chavez with biographical elements, an account of the beginning of Chavez's social activism, and the underlying century-old effort of California farmers to pit groups of poor people against each other and depress wages. The story of Chavez and his efforts to organize the UFW includes his hunger strikes, the boycott of California grapes, and the overall battle against race prejudice.
Continued in **C23.** Incorporated in slightly different form in *Sal Si Puedes*, **A18.**

C23. "Profiles: Organizer — II." *New Yorker*, 45 (28 June), 43–44, 46, 51–52, 54, 56, 58–71.

The second of the two part portrait of Cesar Chavez and the organization of the United Farm Workers.
See **C22.** Incorporated in slightly different form in *Sal Si Puedes*, **A18.**

1970

C24. *Everglades.* Patricia Caulfield. Selections from the writings of Peter Matthiessen. Essay by John G. Mitchell. Edited, with an introduction, by Paul Brooks. San Francisco: Sierra Club.

Selections from various Matthiessen works are used to accompany photographs. Excerpts from the following works appear on the cited pages: *Raditzer*, p. 91; *The Shorebirds of North America*, pp. 79, 87, 110; *Wildlife in America*, pp. 19, 74, 82, 84, 85, 88, 95, 98, 100, 120, 126, 128, 130, 132, 134; "The Last Great Strand," half-title, pp. 18, 21, 22, 27, 70, 77, 80, 81, 112, 125; *At Play in the Fields of the Lord*, pp. 15, 16, 24, 30, 72, 115, 117, 122; *Sal Si Puedes*, p. 135; and "Travelin' Man," pp. 67, 109.

C25. "Kipahulu: From Cinders to the Sea." *Audubon*, 72 (May), 10–23. With photographs by Robert Wenkam.

An account of a four day trip with naturalist Jack Kind and his son in the Haleakala National Park on Maui. Beginning at the rim of Haleakala Volcano, Matthiessen walks through one of the last great strongholds of Hawaii's surviving native birds until he reaches the ocean.

Reprinted in **C108**.

C26. "The River-Eater." *Audubon*, 72 (March), 52–53.

A brief essay on the destruction of the wild Kissimmee River in south Florida by the U. S. Army Corps of Engineers' straightening and regulating of it. This is seen as symbolic of the "idiot's progress" which is strangling the region.

1971

C27. "… And God Created Great Whales." *Reader's Digest*, 98 (April), 117–121.

Excerpt from *Blue Meridian*.
See **A19**.

C28. "In the Blue Mist." *Audubon*, 73 (January), 4–12.

Adapted from *Blue Meridian*, this essay recounts Matthiessen's experience with Peter Gimbel and his shark filming expedition. He relates his first dives in a shark cage and his encounter with a large nurse shark in a cave in the wall of Blue Hole on the Yellow Banks between New Providence and the Exumas.

See **A19**.

C29. "Shark!" *Playboy*, 18 (March), 98–100, 152, 181, 183–187.

Excerpt from the conclusion of *Blue Meridian*.
See **A19**.

C30. "Waiting for the Last Whales." *Esquire*, 75 (February), 64–65, 124, 126.

This excerpt from *Blue Meridian* is an account of a day aboard a Norwegian whale-catcher off the coast of Natal is given.

See **A19**.

1972

C31. "Great Caldron Mountains." *Audubon*, 74 (November), [4]–21. Photography by Eliot Porter.

Excerpt from *The Tree Where Man Was Born*.
See **A20**.

C32. "Lignumvitae—the Last Key." *Audubon*, 74 (January), 20–31. Photographs by Patricia Caulfield.

Matthiessen gives his "impressions" of the only high island in the northern Keys that the Oversea Highway does not touch. As a result of its isolation, Lignumvitae is relatively unspoiled and has not suffered the same fate as the other Keys. It contains the last of the virgin hammocks — West Indian tropic hardwoods surrounded by another type of vegetation — in the Keys.

C33. "A Reporter at Large: The Tree Where Man Was Born — I." *New Yorker*, 48 (16 September), 39–42, 44, 47–48, 50, 55–56, 58–60, 62, 67–68, 70–74.

A report on Matthiessen's stay in East

Africa in early 1969. This provides the basis for the "Siringet" and "In Maasai Land" chapters of *The Tree Where Man Was Born*.
See **A20** and **C34–C35**.

C34. "A Reporter at Large: The Tree Where Man Was Born — II." *New Yorker*, 48 (23 September), 39–46, 48, 51–52, 54, 59–60, 62.

A continuation of his account of his visit to East Africa in 1969. This essay is expanded and revised as the chapters "Rites of Passage" and "Elephant Kingdoms" in *The Tree Where Man Was Born*.
See **A20**, **C33** and **C35**.

C35. "A Reporter at Large: The Tree Where Man Was Born — III." *New Yorker*, 48 (30 September), 47–48, 50, 52, 54, 59–60, 67–75.

The final part of his account of his travels in East Africa, this is revised as chapters "White Highlands" and "At Gidabembe" in *The Tree Where Man Was Born*.
See **A20** and **C33–C34**.

C36. "Search for the White Death." In *Men of Courage: True Stories of Present-Day Adventures in Danger and Death*. Ed. William Parker. Chicago: Playboy Press, pp. [163]–176.

An excerpt from *Blue Meridian*.
See **A19**.

1973

C37. "In the Dragon Islands." *Audubon*, 75 (September), 4–49. Photography by Les Line.

"Field notes" from a two-week cruise aboard a gaff-rigged schooner in the Galápagos archipelago exploring the islands' flora and fauna.
Reprinted in **C42**.

C38. "Under the Silent Sky." *Reader's Digest*, 102 (January), 197–203.

Excerpts from *The Tree Where Man Was Born* are used for captions to accompany the photographs of Eliot Porter.
See **A20**.

C39. "Wind Birds." *Audubon*, 75 (May), [38–43]. Drawings by Robert Gillmor.

Brief excerpts from *The Wind Birds* on shorebird migration, the sanderling or white sandpiper, and curlews.
See **A21**.

1975

C40. "Happy Days." *Audubon*, 77 (November), 64–68, 70, 74, 76, 78, 80, 84–88, 90–95. Paintings by James McMullan.

Matthiessen returns with his father, a former member, to the Santee Gun Club in South Carolina where they used to go each year to hunt. The land has been deeded to the Nature Conservancy and transferred to the South Carolina Wildlife & Marine Resources Department. This account of "a sentimental journey" merges personal reminiscence with a natural history of the region.

C41. "The Wind Birds." In *Bridge Hampton Works and Days*. Ed. Anne Freedgood, Kelsey Marechal, and Barbara Wright. New York: Vintage Books, pp. 102–107.

Excerpts from the book.
See **A21**.

1976

C42. "In the Dragon Islands." In *The Audubon Wildlife Treasury*. Ed. Les Line. Philadelphia: J. B. Lippincott Co., pp. 25–44.

Reprint of **C37**.

1977

C43. "Foreword." In *To Forget the Self: An Illustrated Guide to Zen Meditation*. John Daishin Buksbazen. Photography by John Daido Loori. Los Angeles: Zen Center of Los Angeles, Inc., pp. xiv–xv.

This book is "a wonderful introduction to Zen Buddhism, and also an invitation to new life." The universality and benefits of Zen, particularly *zazen*, sitting meditation, are briefly discussed. Through *zazen* "comes an intuitive understanding that what we seek lies nowhere else but in this present moment."

C44. "Return to Bladensfield." In *Quest/ 77*, 1 (September/October), 5–12.

An excerpt from "Homegoing" in *The Children of Bladensfield*.
See **C46.**

C45. "A Track on the Beach." *Audubon*, 79 (March), 68–69, 72, 74, 76, 78, 80, 97–98, 100, 102, 104–106. Drawing by Peter Parnall.

An account of Matthiessen's two year attempt to verify the identity of a bird he sighted on Tuckernuck Island off the west end of Nantucket. He believes he may have seen the eastern race of the pinneated grouse or prairie chicken. Also known as the heath hen, this bird was declared extinct over thirty years before he first sights a track on a Tuckernuck beach in 1966.

1978

C46. "Homegoing." In *The Children of Bladensfield*. Evelyn D. Ward. New York: Viking Press [A Sand Dune Press book], pp. 114–141.

Matthiessen made his first trip to his mother's [Elizabeth Bleeker Carey] family ancestral home in Virginia in 1956. He recalls his trip and meeting with his uncle, William Randolph Ward. An account of his maternal family history and the fate of the Wards and Careys and their home since the Civil War is given as he remembers his subsequent visits to Bladensfield.
See **C44.**

C47. "A Reporter at Large: The Snow Leopard — I." *New Yorker*, 54 (27 March), 39–46, 49–50, 52, 57–58, 60, 63–64, 66, 70–72, 74, 77–78, 80, 85–86, 88–92, 94.

With some variation and omissions of journal entries for certain dates, this coincides with the Prologue, "Westward," and "Northward" sections of *The Snow Leopard*.
See **A22** and **C48.**

C48. "A Reporter at Large: The Snow Leopard — II." *New Yorker*, 54 (3 April), 41–42, 45–46, 48, 50, 55–56, 58, 60–63, 66, 68–72, 74, 79–80, 82, 84, 87–92.

This is the majority of the entries that comprise the section, "At Crystal Mountain," in *The Snow Leopard*.
See **A22** and **C47.**

C49. "The Snow Leopard." *Book Digest*, 5 (November), 68–94.

An extended excerpt from the book.
See **A22.**

C50. "A Whale in Spring." *Westigan Review of Poetry*, 3, pp. 38–39.

Two brief notes of natural observation from near Matthiessen's home in Sagaponack, Long Island. The sighting of two humpback whales, the first he has seen off Long Island in a decade, recalls another time in the summer of 1959 when he saw the great whales —fin backs and orcas, as well as distant humpbacks. The second note concerns the discovery of a solitary Atlantic salmon, now a remnant of the past, caught in a haul seine.

Parts of these notes are incorporated in the preface to *Men's Lives*.
See **A27.**

C51. "Common Miracles." In *Search*. Ed. Jean Sulzberger. San Francisco: Harper & Row, pp. 25–30.

A series of "outdoor notes" from *sesshins* at Beecher Lake, the site of the International Dai Bosatu Zendo, in 1974, and also where the ashes of Matthiessen's second wife, Deborah, are buried. In a series of four *sesshins* noted as March, June, August, and September, he offers his observations on the generous natural world around him.

C52. "Journeys to Hopi: National Sacrifice Area." *Rocky Mountain Magazine*, 1 (July/ August), 49–64.

Matthiessen visits the land of the Hopi Nation and examines their efforts to preserve their traditional and sacred ways. A brief history of the Hopi and their relationship with the federal government and the Navaho is given. The government and corporate interests are exploiting the Hopi land in order to mine the mineral rich area. There is complicity by the Hopi and Navaho Tribal Councils in the Bureau of Indian Affairs' corporate influenced decisions and policies.

Included in a revised version in **A25**.

C53. "The Price of Tellico." *Newsweek*, 94 (17 December), 21.

It is argued that the closing of the Tennessee Valley Authority's (TVA) Tellico Dam has stopped the last stretch of free-flowing river in northeast Tennessee, destroyed the last natural spawning beds of the snail darter, and submerged the homes of thousands of displaced families. The creation of still another artificial lake has also destroyed a serious part of the heritage of the Cherokee nation, including the last great sacred center and an unprecedented number of physical records of American prehistory. The TVA's action is a transgression against all of us. The river should be allowed to flow and the valley restored.

See also **C57**.

C54. "Stop the GO Road." *Audubon*, 81 (January), 48–65. Photography by Philip L. Fradkin.

The Sisiyou wilderness area in California's Klamath region is threatened by the U. S. Forest Service's paving of an old track road — the Gasquet-Orleans Road. The GO Road raises both environmental and enthographic concerns in the area while benefiting only the lumber corporations.

See **H32** and **H39–H40**.

C55. "Tolakwe, Portal of Souls: Last Stand at The Western Gate." *The Nation*, 229 (2 August–1 September), 135–138.

Point Concepcion, the "Western Gate" of the indigenous peoples of south-central California, is threatened by the proposed construction of a liquefied natural gas (LNG) terminal. Matthiessen recounts the efforts of the Chumash, "the Keepers of the Western Gate," to protect this ancient sacred site from the Western LNG power consortium which has cavalierly disregarded environmental and spiritual concerns.

Included in a revised version in **A25**.

1980

C56. "High Noon in the Black Hills." *New York Times Magazine*, 13 July, pp. 30–32, 34, 38–40.

The first invasion of the Lakota Sioux's sacred Black Hills of South Dakota occurred when gold was discovered in the early 1800s. Today's invasion is because of uranium. The Union Carbide Corporation and the Tennessee Valley Authority are close to beginning uranium mining and milling operations near Edgemont, the site of the state's first uranium discovery. The people, both white and Indian, are protesting the uranium mining's threat to their health and to the environment. The Black Hills Alliance, a grass roots environmental group of Indians and whites, is working to educate and protect the public. They are taking the corporations to court concerning alleged violations of existing environmental laws, even though the state shows no interest in doing so. They are working to protect themselves, their families, and the sacred Black Hills.

Included in a revised version in **A25**.

C57. "How to Kill a Valley." *New York Review of Books*, 27 (February 7), 31–36.

An examination of the sordid politics behind the Tennessee Valley Authority's Tellico Dam project. It is "one of the oldest and most evil-smelling public works projects in the country." Matthiessen visits the Little Tennessee River before the valley is flooded and discusses the historical and archaeological significance of the valley as well as its importance to the Cherokee Nation. The proponents of the dam, including Senator Howard Baker, have circumvented legality and fair hearings and have done a great injustice to the American people.

See also **C53**.

C58. "Introduction." In *Galapagos: Islands Lost in Time*. Tui De Roy Moore. New

York: Viking Press (A Studio Book), p. 12.

On assignment with Les Line in the Galapagos Islands for *Audubon* magazine, Matthiessen was unable to take the desired crucial photograph of a giant tortoise. It was suggested that they look at some photographs taken by a nineteen year old girl on the island, Tui De Roy. He and Line were "stunned with pleasure and surprise" at the quality of the photographs and her remarkable talent. She is a well informed and affectionate observer of the natural world.

C59. "A Land Sacred to Indians Is Despoiled by the White Man: Battle for Big Mountain." *Geo*, 2 (March), 8–23, 26–30.

Big Mountain in Black Mesa, Arizona is the ancestral homeland and sacred site of the Hopi and Navajo. It is threatened by proposed uranium mining and power plants. The effects of such ventures at Shiprock, New Mexico and the consequences for the land and the people are examined. This proposal is part of an "ignoble pattern" of governmental and corporate dealing with Native Americans which results in the environmental, as well as economic, destruction of their lands.

Included in a revised version in **A25**.

C60. "The Siege of the Mohawks." *Washington Post*, 14 September, "Outlook," pp. C1, C4–C5.

A dispute between two armed Mohawk factions on the St. Regis Reservation along the St. Lawrence River in New York is investigated. One group represents the Tribal Council, the other, the traditionals. While state police are supposedly protecting each faction from the other, it has been suggested that state authorities are siding with the tribal faction in order to prevent the Mohawks from achieving a united, sovereign Mohawk nation. Matthiessen visits with the traditionals and state authorities to discuss the factors that have incited the conflict between the two factions and the state's ambiguous role in both initiating and perpetuating it.

Included in a revised version in **A25**.

1981

C61. "Introduction." *Taproot*, (Summer), 1.

In a brief introduction to a collection of workshop writings by older adults, Matthiessen remarks on two aspects of the work which he finds "particularly striking." The insistence on memory (as opposed to nostalgia) echoes the great universal oral tradition. The works' direct, spare expression, free of literary concerns, allows for a true beauty to emerge from the work.

C62. "Native Earth." *Parabola*, 6 (Fall), 6–17.

The Native Americans' ability to live at one with nature with no interest in modifying it was in sharp contrast to the European colonists and early American frontiersmen who viewed nature as a "wilderness" to tame. The Indians understood the *rightness* of nature. They recognized the interconnectedness of all things, and this holistic approach to their daily existence is evidence of their not separating themselves from nature. For them there is no distinction between mind and body. Similarities exist between their beliefs and Zen teachings. The "awareness" of the traditional peoples can be regained by all people to achieve a harmonious existence with their habitat. The first step is to regain respect for the earth and to live and work in service with nature, not battle against it.

Slightly different versions appear in **A25** and **C70**.

C63. "No Man's Land." *Miami Herald*, 8 November, "Tropic Magazine," pp. 8–12, 14–16, 26, 28–29.

In the face of intrusions and the development of the Everglades and the Big Cypress National Preserve, the isolated and fiercely independent Miccosukee Indians struggle to maintain their autonomy. Matthiessen discusses the politics within the Seminole Tribes of Florida and Oklahoma, as well as the destruction of the ecosystem that has long been their home. He proposes that the Miccosukees be given free run of the Everglades to act as its wardens to help save and preserve it.

Included in a revised version in **A25**.

C64. "Peter Matthiessen's Africa. Book One: Botswana." *Audubon*, 83 (January), 68–81.

Matthiessen joins Victor Emanuel and John Rowlett on an ornithological safari with the hope of observing the fish owl. An account of the political and racial turmoil of the region as well as a natural history of the area and its indigenous peoples, particularly the Bushmen, are given.

See also **C65–C66**. Reprinted in **A23**.

C65. "Peter Matthiessen's Africa. Book Two: Tanzania." *Audubon*, 83 (May), 67–83.

A description of the country, peoples, and wildlife of Tanzania during a 1600 mile safari in the summer of 1976.

See also **C64** and **C66**. Reprinted in **A23**.

C66. "Peter Matthiessen's Africa. Book Three: Zaire." *Audubon*, 83 (September), 82–95.

Matthiessen crosses paths in Zaire with George Plimpton and gorillas, among others, in search for the Congo peacock.

See also **C64–C65**. Reprinted in **A23**.

C67. "A Reporter at Large: Sand Rivers." *New Yorker*, 56 (12 January), 43–44, 46, 48, 50, 52, 54, 56, 58, 60–80.

Matthiessen participates in a safari to Selous Game Reserve in Tanzania with Brian Nicholson, the former warden of the Reserve. He provides an account of the formation and development of the Reserve as well as the people he meets and the animals he encounters. An interesting portrait of Nicholson is presented as well; he is a man who doesn't always share Matthiessen's views concerning man's relationship with the natural world.

Reprinted as part of **A23**.

C68. "Sand Rivers." *Book Digest*, 8 (May), 88–96, 98–113.

Extended excerpts from the book.
See **A23**.

C69. "The Sighting of Ross' Gull." *Quest/81*, 5 (September), 36–38, 90.

A June 1980 trip to Churchill, Manitoba, a tundra town and legendary place for bird watchers since it is the terminus for the great bird migrations of the central flyway in the spring and fall, coincides with the unexpected arrival of six Ross' Gulls, a rare arctic bird of eastern Siberia. It is a year of unusual gulls at Churchill. During a later trip, three Ivory Gulls, a species of the circumpolar region, are also observed.

1982

C70. "Native Earth: Man's Harmony with His Surroundings." *American West*, 19 (May/June), 44–49.

An abbreviated version of **C62**.

1983

C71. "American Indians." *New York Times Book Review*, 20 March, p. 38.

A letter in response to Alan M. Dershowitz's review of *In the Spirit of Crazy Horse*. Matthiessen fears that Dershowitz's apparent bias against the American Indian Movement (AIM) and Leonard Peltier may hamper the chances of Peltier appealing his conviction. Dershowitz dutifully accepts the F.B.I.'s unsubstantiated version of events and their claim of considerable circumstantial evidence against Peltier. He ignores the evidence available under the Freedom of Information Act and becomes adversarial in the review. AIM was instrumental in restoring a lost identity and reviving the "dying spirit of the traditional people." It asks for nothing more radical than that the federal government honor its own laws and Constitution.

Dershowitz replies at the letter's conclusion that he has no predisposition either for or against the prosecutors or AIM. He does not doubt that the F. B. I. manipulated evi-

dence, but the information derived from the Freedom of Information Act does not raise serious doubt about Peltier's guilt. Matthiessen is trying to blame his failure as an advocate on a reviewer he didn't persuade. His book fails to provide a proper "sense of perspective."
See I387.

C72. "The Making of an Adventurer." *Travel & Leisure*, 13 (April), 104–105, 148.

A humorous, self-deprecating account of a six week trip to Bonaventure immediately following his engagement party in June of 1950. Bonaventure is a small island off the Gaspé Peninsula in Quebec, home to a colony of pelagic birds. Matthiessen acquires a 19-foot codfish smack for an ill conceived "adventure" back to Long Island before being tied down by marriage. However, his fiancée subsequently informs him of his "unengagement" because of his "churlish behavior" at the party and lack of communication since his departure. He sets sail aboard the *Maudite* (Cursed One) anyway. The proposed journey is mercifully and embarrassingly ended in Port Daniel, Quebec, sixty miles from Bonaventure, when the boat is demasted by a lower than realized bridge. The *Maudite* and its captain continue their trip on the bed of a timber truck and set sail for home from a boatyard in Manchester, Massachusetts. A few months later the engagement is renewed.
See **C96.**

C73. "The Real Indians." *New Age*, 9 (August), 33.

A brief excerpt from *In the Spirit of Crazy Horse* accompanies **H59.**
See **A24.**

C74. "Return of the Big Man: Travels Through Indian America." *The Nation*, 236 (12 February), 167–170, 172–177.

An excerpt from *In the Spirit of Crazy Horse.*
See **A24.**

C75. "A Tribal Conflict." In *1000 Adventures.* Ed. Christian Kallen. New York: Harmony Books, p. [55].

A very brief excerpt from *Under the Mountain Wall.*
See **A14.**

1984

C76. "The Desert Sea." *Geo*, 6 (September), 116–125, 128–131. Photos by Dan Budnik.

A trip aboard the *El Dorado*, an old cabin cruiser, with his son Luke and three photographers to explore the Midriff Islands off Baja California is recounted. Their particular destination is San Pedro Mátir, the most remote of the islands, and the home of a colony of nesting seabirds, especially brown and blue-footed boobies.

1985

C77. "The Art of Fiction V: William Styron." With George Plimpton. In *Conversations with William Styron.* Ed. James L. W. West III. Jackson: University Press of Mississippi, pp. 8–19.

Reprint of **C2.**

1986

C78. "In Memory: This Was the Bay." *Newsday*, 8 July, p. 4.

An excerpt from *Men's Lives.*
See **A27.**

C79. "Peter Matthiessen On the Showdown at Big Mountain." *The Amicus Journal*, 8 (Summer), 24–25.

An extended comment concerning the partition of the Navajo-Hopi Joint Use Area derived from an interview with Trebbe Johnson. The federal government has an opportunity to create a "wave of good feeling" among the Indian peoples if it takes measures to counter the Navajo-Hopi Land Settlement Act. The country has yet to confront its hypocritical mistreatment of the Native Americans. The Big Mountain people should be allowed to continue to live in the Indian Way.
See also **C84.**

1987

C80. "The Farber Case." With Nora Ephron, Bruce Jay Friedman, Nicholas Pileggi, George Plimpton, Jack Richardson, William Styron, Gay Talese, and Joy Williams. *New York Review of Books*, 34 (July 16, 1987), 53.

A letter protesting the "extremely harsh sentence" given Bernard Farber, convicted on three counts of conspiracy to import, actual importation, and conspiracy to distribute hashish. It is believed that Farber received this sentence, despite being a first time offender, because he wouldn't "cooperate" with the government and implicate Norman Mailer in the smuggling of the hashish. Since it is clear that Farber can not or will not involve Mailer, he should be given a shorter, fairer sentence and be allowed to perform community service.

C81. "Treasured Places." *Life*, 10 (July), 44 [35–44].

Matthiessen is one of eight writers who present brief statements on favorite "wild" places. He offers a eulogy for the South Shore of eastern Long Island, Sagaponack Pond, and for the land that "can no longer cleanse itself of our human progress."

1988

C82. "At Crystal Mountain." In *Words From the Land: Encounters with Natural History Writing*. Edited and with an introduction by Stephen Trimble. Salt Lake City, UT: Gibbs M. Smith, Inc., pp. 244–263.

Excerpts from *The Snow Leopard*. *See* **A22** and **C122**.

C83. "Foreword." In *The Way of the White Clouds: A Buddhist Pilgrim in Tibet*. Anagarika Brahacari Govinda. Boston: Shambhala, pp. xi–xiii.

A brief account of the importance of white clouds in Buddhist symbology precedes a thumbnail sketch of Lama Govinda and his disagreement with Matthiessen

concerning the choice of *The Snow Leopard* as the title for Matthiessen's book. He preferred the book be called "The Crystal Mountain."

C84. "Navajo Relocation Attacked." *Akwesasne Notes*, 20 (31 March), 9. <http://www.softlineweb.com/bin/KaStasGw.exe?k_a=bojbl17.9.doc.w&tocfrom=1>. (26 July 1999)

Matthiessen argues against the Relocation Act (P. L. 93–531) whose purpose is to resolve the so-called Navajo-Hopi land dispute but which has forced the relocation of traditional Navajos from their sacred homeland. The act is a clear violation of the First Amendment and presents "one of the most appalling cases of discrimination against Indian people in recent history." It threatens one of the last traditional native communities in North America.
See also **C74**.

C85. "Our National Parks: The Case for Burning." *New York Times Magazine*, 11 December, pp. 38–41, 121–123, 128–129.

Visiting Yellowstone National Park in the autumn following a summer of great fires, Matthiessen examines the consequences of the fires for the park's forest and wildlife. He reviews the evolving land and fire management policies at the Park and the debate within the National Park Service about natural burns and prescribed burning in regenerating the forest and keeping it "natural."
See **C89** and **C104**.

1989

C86. "The Captain's Trail." *Condé Nast Traveler*, 24 (January), 106–111, 130–134.

In the autumn of 1987 Matthiessen and his wife visit the Isle of Föhr, a German holding, in the North Frisians off Denmark's North Sea coast, home of the Matthiessen family scion, Peter Matthies or Matthias Petersen. Föhr is the home of noted seafarers, and Matthies was known as the "Fortunate One" for his success in the whale fisheries. Matthiessen traces his family heritage on the island and describes the geography and the people he meets. His own line is traced through Matthies's fourth son, Otto, who left the island in 1700 and established a prosperous liquor trade in Altona. Three of Otto's sons were the first Matthiessens to settle in England and America.

C87. Congo Basin: The Search for the Forest Elephant" [Part I]. *Antaeus*, no. 63 (Autumn), 150–189.

Matthiessen accompanies Dr. David (Jonah) Western, a resource ecologist for the New York Zoological Society, in a survey of the central African rain forest to census the small forest elephant (*Loxodonta africana cyclotis*). It is believed its numbers have been seriously reduced by the ivory trade. Western also hopes to learn about the "pygmy elephant" which is generally perceived as the last large "unknown" animal in Africa. In between and during their bureaucratic plagued bush flights within the wilderness of the Central African Republic, Gabon, and Zaire [the Congo], Matthiessen reports on their encounters with various ecologists, biologists, and primatologists, touching on gorillas, the white rhino project, and a brief but penetrating portrait of Dian Fossey. This essay also contains one of Matthiessen's funniest pieces of writing — his description of his losing battle with his hosts' pet mongoose while trying to shower, and his subsequent rescue.

See also **C92.** Reprinted in **A28** and, in part, in **C124.**

C88. "George Catlin's Troubled Mission." *Condé Nast Traveler*, 24 (March), 126–131, 170–173.

Matthiessen, who first became interested in Catlin while preparing *Wildlife in America*, presents "an homage to the painter and chronicler" whose "noble ambition" was to record the Indians of the West in his paintings and journals before their native state was corrupted and destroyed. Catlin's journals carry a historic resonance matched only by Meriwether Lewis and Francis Parkman. His paintings of and writings about the Indians are unromanticized and never stereotyped; he records them as individual

human beings. His creation of his "Indian Gallery" of pictures and artifacts based on his fieldwork in the West provides great historical and ethnographic value. Our culture has benefited more from his bold work than from the western art of academic painters. His chronicle of the Wild West remains stirring as both an echo and a meditation.

An expanded version of this essay serves as the introduction to Matthiessen's edited volume of Catlin's *North American Indians*. *See* **A35.**

C89. "Introduction: The Case for Burning." In *Yellowstone's Red Summer*. Alan Carey and Sandy Carey. Flagstaff, AZ: Northland Publishing, pp. [1]–25.

An abbreviated version of **C85.**

C90. "New York: Old Hometown." *Architectural Digest*, 46 (November), 52, 56, 60, 66, 70, 74.

This is a revealing reminiscence about growing up in New York and his early impressions of the city — Le Roy Hospital, where he was born; St. Bernard's School; Central Park; and trips with his grandmother, among others — and his gradual discomfit with a life of "unearned privilege." These memories are viewed against his less frequent visits to the once exhilarating city which is now "oppressive in its noise and filth."

1990

C91. "Among the Griz." *Outside*, 15 (September), 50–56, 100, 102, 106.

A report on accompanying "social outlaw" Douglas Peacock on his unsanctioned observations of the grizzly bears in Glacier National Park. An account of the bears as well as Peacock's experience with and advice about encounters with "Ol' Grizzer" is given.

See **H103** and **H105.**

C92. "Congo Basin: The Search for the Forest Elephant" [Part II]. *Antaeus*, no. 64/65 (Spring/Autumn), 404–424.

The continuation of Matthiessen's account of the search for and survey of the forest elephant and pygmy elephant. With Dr. Western, the savanna ecologist, they discover a wide hybridization zone containing both larger bush elephants and the smaller forest elephant. The reports of pygmy elephants are found to be, in fact, sightings of juvenile forest elephants. "Pure" forest elephants were not able to be located. *See also* **C87**. Reprinted in **A28** and, in part, in **A31**.

C93. "From *The Tree Where Man Was Born.*" In *The Norton Book of Nature Writing.* Ed. Robert Finch and John Elder. New York: W. W. Norton & Co., pp. 693–707.

Extended excerpts from "Rites of Passage," "Elephant Kingdoms" and "Red God."
See **A20**. *See also* **C94**.

C94. "From *The Wind Birds.*" In *The Norton Book of Nature Writing.* Ed. Robert Finch and John Elder. New York: W. W. Norton & Co., pp. 707–708.

A very brief except from the book.
See **A21**. *See also* **C93**.

C95. "Into the Ituri." *Outside*, 15 (May), 70–75, 138–[140]. Photography by Elisabeth Sunday.

Matthiessen spends five days with the Mbuti, Africa's largest Pygmy tribe and the most culturally intact, in the Inturi Forest of Zaire [the Congo]. He is introduced to them by John and Terese Hart, biologists studying the okapi, a relative of the giraffe. The Mbuti are one of the last groups of hunter-gatherers, and Matthiessen accompanies them on a hunt.

C96. "The Making of an Adventure." [sic] In *Boats: An Anthology.* Ed. David Seybold. New York: Grove Weidenfeld, pp. 47–52.

Slightly abbreviated version of **C72**.

1991

C97. "Afterword." In *The Circle of Life: Rituals From the Human Family Album.*

Ed. David Cohen. Introduction by Gabriel García Márquez. Commentary by Arthur Davidson. San Francisco: Harper, pp. 228–231.

Making reference to the photographs in the book, Matthiessen discusses the rituals and rites of passage that "lift us from the petty confusions of existence" and force us to pay complete attention to these human transformations that link us to the world around us and force our attention on the wonder and moment of it all.

C98. "The Blue Pearl of Siberia." *New York Review of Books*, 38 (February 14), 37–47.

Matthiessen presents accounts from his diary from an expedition to Lake Baikal with jazz musician Paul Winter in 1990. Lake Baikal is the most ancient lake on earth and the cleanest large lake in the world. Heedless developing industrialization in Siberia is beginning to threaten the ecology of not only Baikal but of Siberia as a whole. For part of the trip Valentin Rasputin, a controversial Russian writer, accompanies them. Matthiessen provides a profile of Rasputin, discussing his literary and environmental work, as well as examining the question of Rasputin's anti–Semitism.
See **A29** and **H128**.

C99. "Introduction." In *Ancient Futures: Learning from Ladakh.* Helena Norberg-Hodge. San Francisco: Sierra Club Books, pp. xi–xviii.

Ladakh, in the remote trans–Himalayan region of India, is the home of a pure Tibetan Buddhist culture. The self-sufficient economic and traditional technologies practiced by its people are at odds with the modern technologies and Western concepts of progress. But these old ways work and are well suited for the population and the limited resources available. The inappropriate "modern" technologies being introduced and forced upon these people inflict debt, dependence, and pollution on a previously self-sufficient culture. This misguided development results in the fragmentation of Ladakhi life and culture.

C100. "Introduction." In *¡Baja!*. Photographs by Terrence Moore. Text by Doug Peacock. Boston: Bullfinch Press, pp. 13–[29].

In 1990 Matthiessen takes his third trip to Baja, California; the first was in 1946 just after leaving the Navy, and the second was in 1984 with his son (see **C76**). Making occasional comparative references to his 1984 trip, Matthiessen recounts his travels through the south-central Baja, commenting on its natural history and mission architecture.

C101. "Life in the Ruins." *Travel Holiday*, 174 (June), 44–51, 111–112.

This is a report of a trip to Central America with Robert Hughes to fish and to visit two Maya ruins: the terraced pyramids at Tikal in Guatemala, and the coastal trading center of Altun Ha in Belize.

C102. "New Light on Peltier's Case: Who Really Killed the F. B. I. Men." *The Nation*. 252 (13 May), 613, 628, 630–631.

This essay is adapted from the epilogue to the republished *In the Spirit of Crazy Horse*. Matthiessen recounts his meeting and conversation with "X," the American Indian Movement member who supposedly shot two F. B. I. agents at the Pine Ridge Reservation. X's version of the events of June 26, 1975 that led to his killing the agents in what he contends was self-defense, exonerates Leonard Peltier of their murders.
See also **C104**.

C103. "Transcendent Quarry." *Parabola*, 16 (May), 67–69.

This is Section VII of "Seven Perspectives on the Hunt," pp. 54–69. It is a brief excerpt from *The Snow Leopard*.
See **A22**.

C104. "Who Really Killed the F.B.I. Men?" *Akwesasne Notes*, 23 (Summer 1991). <http://indy4.fdl.cc.mn.us/~isk/stories/fbikill.html>. (26 July 1999)
Reprint of **C102**.

1992

C105. "Foreword." In *Exiled In the Land of the Free: Democracy, Indian Nations, and the U. S. Constitution*. Ed. Oren R. Lyons and John C. Mohawk. Preface by Daniel K. Inouye. Santa Fe, NM: Clear Light Publishers, pp. [xi]–xiii.

The "New World" discovered by the Europeans was neither new nor in need of discovery. It was home to the Native Americans who utilized its resources in knowing ways. They were not savage and wild. It has become desirable to denigrate the native peoples to justify the usurpation, rape, and betrayal by the white culture. The principle of sovereignty is the central and underlying concern of all Indian issues and claims.

C106. "Fur Countries and Forest Lakes." In *Treasures of the Place: Three Centuries of Nature Writing in Canada*. Ed. Wayne Grady. Vancouver: Douglas & McIntyre, pp., [178]–187.

Excerpt from *Wildlife in America*. Reprinted in **C140**. *See* **A12**.

C107. "Journey to the Edge of the World." *Condé Nast Traveler*, 27 (November), 148–159, 170–182.

Matthiessen and photographer Thomas Laird are the first Westerners in thirty years to visit the valley of Sao Kohla and the fort city of Lo Monthang, in the remote northernmost region of the Himalayas in Nepal. In this land of the blue sheep and the snow leopard, they ride and camp with nomadic herdsmen, examine the Buddhist influenced culture, and track the trail of the legendary mehti or abominable snowman.

Revised and expanded as *East of Lo Monthang: In the Land of Mustang*. *See* **A32**.

C108. "Kīpahulu: From Cinders to the Sea." In *A World Between Waves*. Ed. Frank Stewart. Washington, D. C.: Island Press, pp. 101–114.

Reprint of **C25**.

C109. "Shadows of Africa." *Audubon*, 94 (November/December), 106–109.

Brief "reflections" on the life of the African wilderness accompanied by the illustrations of Mary Frank. From their book *Shadows of Africa*.

See **A31**.

C110. "The Trials of Leonard Peltier." *Esquire*, 117 (January), 55–57.

A review of recent events concerning the case of Peltier, including Matthiessen's interview with "X," Eighth Circuit Court Judge Gerald H. Heaney's letter, and Senator Daniel Inouye's interest, leading to a hearing for a new trial.

1993

C111. "Alighting Upon the Daurian Steppe." *Harper's Magazine*, 286 (June), 47–55.

An account of an expedition to the breeding grounds of the white-naped crane (*Grus vipio*) in the remote marshes of far northeast Mongolia.

C112. "An Excerpt from Red & Blue Days: Writings on the American West." In *A Clark City Press Reader*. Livingston, MT: Clark City Press, pp. [3]–9.

A collection of brief miscellaneous musings on various subjects related to the American West, including Indian peoples, Doug Peacock, Yellowstone National Park, camping on the Pacific shore, and the Indian concept of art.

From a never published book. Most of these observations appear in one form or another in more developed essays.

C113. "Foreword." In *Totch: A Life in the Everglades*. Loren G. "Totch" Brown. Gainesville, FL: University Press of Florida, pp. vii–viii.

Matthiessen provides a brief testimony to Brown. "Totch" Brown's memoir is not only entertaining but is also an invaluable record of the Everglades country and its people. His combination of an occasionally lawless life with law-abiding and civic-minded principles is not only fascinating

but representative of many men of The Thousand Islands.

C114. "The Masked Lama Dances of Lo." *Tricycle*, 2 (Spring), 10–17. With photographs by Thomas Laird.

A nicely realized account of the masked Lama Dances of the Tiji ceremony, a festival of renewal held each spring in the Kingdom of Lo in Nepal. This three-day reenactment of a myth reflects the Kingdom's dependence on scarce water and the Buddhist teachings of impermanence.

Reprinted in different form in **A32**.

C115. "Postscript: Cesar Chavez." *New Yorker*, 69 (17 May), 82.

A sympathetic portrait of Chavez on the occasion of his death. Matthiessen remembers Chavez's struggles on behalf of the United Farm Workers, and his strength, love and humanity. The piece is accompanied by a photograph of Chavez by Richard Avedon, p. [83].

C116. "A Reporter at Large: The Last Cranes of Siberia." *New Yorker*, 69 (3 May), 76–86.

The development of the Amur Basin by Russia, China, and multinational corporations threatens the ecology of the entire region, including the breeding grounds of the rare white-naped and red-crowned cranes (*Grus japonensis* and *Grus vipio*). An international environmental conference was held to try to initiate a cooperative crane program between Russia and China to help prevent the extinction of the cranes.

Reprinted in **C145**.

1994

C117. "At the End of Tibet." *Audubon*, 96 (March/April), 40–49.

Matthiessen reports on his journey to the Black Mountains of Bhutan to view a wintering flock of black-necked or Tibetan cranes (*Grus nigricollis*).

C118. "Foreword." In *Thinking Green! Essays on Environmentalism, Feminism, and*

Nonviolence. Petra K. Kelly. Berkeley, CA: Parallax Press, pp. [ix]–xv.

A tribute to Petra Karin Kelly and her companion Gert Bastian. Matthiessen fondly remembers his encounters with Kelly, founder of the German Green Party and an unceasing and passionate peace, human rights, and environmental activist.

C119. "Great River (Peconic Bay, New York)." In *Heart of the Land: Essays on Last Great Places.* Ed. Joseph Barbato and Lisa Weinerman. Foreword by Barry Lopez. New York: Pantheon Books, pp. 273–280.

Eulogistic remembrances of his earlier years hunting, fishing, and living on the East End of Long Island, his "home country," which continues to restore him. The natural beauty and wildlife of the area — already seriously diminished in the years between his own youth and that of his grandson — is in danger of being irretrievably lost unless man realizes that "in a respectful attitude toward Earth lies true prosperity."

C120. "Gujarat and Rajasthan." In *The Nature of Nature: New Essays from America's Finest Writers on Nature.* Ed. William H. Shore. New York: Harcourt Brace & Co., pp. 65–84.

With Victor Emanuel, Matthiessen accompanies a group of travelers to northwestern India, during a period of rioting between Hindus and Muslims, to observe the rare birds and wildlife of the region. Of particular interest is the Indian wild ass (*Equs hemonius khur*), one of the last species of wild horses on earth, and four species of cranes: sarus (*Grus antigone*), Eurasian (*Grus grus*), demoiselle (*Anthropoides virgo*), and the Siberian (*Grus leucogeranus*), perhaps the world's most endangered crane species.

C121. "Koan of the Nine Marshes." *Outside,* 19 (May), 146–150, 152, 154, 156.

A pilgrimage with Victor Emanuel to the Poyang lakes region of China which has the greatest variety and concentration of wintering cranes on Earth. It is the only known winter home of the rare eastern white Siberian crane (*Grus leucogeranus*). Despite a severe drought, in one remarkable day, all four of the area's species of cranes are seen: the white-naped (*Grus vipio*), the hooded (*Grus monacha*), the Eurasian (*Grus grus*), and the eastern Siberian white crane. For Matthiessen, the cranes "are spirit and metaphor for the vanishing clean water, air, and earth in these last wild lands where the birds live."

1995

C122. "At Crystal Mountain." In *Words From the Land: Encounters with Natural History Writing.* Edited and with an introduction by Stephen Trimble. Expanded edition. Reno: University of Nevada Press, pp. 244–263.

Excerpts from *The Snow Leopard.* *See* **A22** and **C82.**

C123. "The Cranes of Hokkaido." *Audubon,* 97 (July/August), 36–47, 90–91. Photography by Masahiro Wade.

A craning expedition is made to Hokkaido, the northern-most island of Japan, to observe the red-crowned crane (*Grus japonensis*) or *tancho*, the largest of the world's great cranes.

C124. "Forest Elephants In Equatorial Africa." In *Saving Wildlife: A Century of Conservation.* Donald Goddard, gen'l. ed. New York: Harry N. Abrams, Inc., in association with The Wildlife Conservation Society, pp. 198–202.

Reprint, in part, of **C87.** *See also* **C125–C126.**

C125. "Foreword." In *Saving Wildlife: A Century of Conservation.* Donald Goddard, gen'l. ed. New York: Harry N. Abrams, Inc., in association with The Wildlife Conservation Society, pp. 24–25, 27.

Matthiessen recounts his association with The Wildlife Conservation Society over the years and his own interest and involvement in wildlife and environmental projects and concerns.

See also **C124** and **C126.**

C126. "From 'Epilogue'." In *Saving Wildlife: A Century of Conservation.* Donald Goddard, gen'l. Ed. New York: Harry N. Abrams, Inc., in association with The Wildlife Conservation Society, pp. 203–204.

A brief excerpt from *African Silences.* See **A28**. See also **C124–C125**.

C127. "A Hard Life." In *Ocean Planet: Writings and Images of the Sea.* Original text by Peter Benchley. Ed. Judith Gradwohl. New York: Harry N. Abrams, Inc., pp. 61–65.

An excerpt from *Men's Lives.* See **A27**.

C128. "From *The Snow Leopard.*" In *Writing Nature: An Ecological Reader for Writers.* Carolyn Ross. New York: St. Martin's Press, pp.

The entries dated November 3rd, 9th, and 14th are followed by four questions for "Considerations of Meaning and Method" and two "Possibilities for Writing" exercises. See **A22**.

C129. "In the Land of Mustang by Caravan to a Hidden Valley." *Shambhala Sun,* 3 (July), 18–25.

An excerpt from *East of Lo Monthang.* See **A32**.

C130. "Mean Spirit." *Outside,* 20 (October), 41–46, 48, 145.

Matthiessen rebuts Scott Anderson's use of erroneous and prejudicial terms in his portrait of Leonard Peltier and the presentation of the facts of his case. He also offers a passionate defense of himself in response to Anderson's attempt to discredit *In the Spirit of Crazy Horse* and to defame Matthiessen and present him as a "myth merchant" who is ultimately harming Peltier's quest for freedom. He believes that Anderson presents a hatchet job and is mean spirited in the extravagance of his attacks upon Matthiessen's professional integrity and personal honesty.

See **H157**. See also **H156, H158, H161–163**.

C131. *Meeting the Buddha: On Pilgrimage In Buddhist India.* Ed. Molly Emma Aitken. New York: Riverhead Books, pp. 19–21, 107–108.

Two separate brief excerpts from *The Snow Leopard*: "Lumbini" and "The Bodhi Tree."

See **A22**.

C132. "Survival of the Hunter." *New Yorker,* 71 (24 April), 67–77.

Matthiessen visits with Inuit whale hunters in Greenland and examines the ethical/moral questions of the traditional people's whaling for subsistence purposes while the environmental movement and the western nations attempt to dictate whaling policy.

Reprinted in **C134**.

1996

C133. "Accidental Sanctuary." *Audubon,* 98 (July/August), 44–55, 106–107. Photography by Greg Girard.

The Korean Demilitarized Zone and South Korea's Civilian Zone are a de facto wildlife refuge providing one of the last bastions of "wilderness" in Korea. The buffer zone offers food and protection to myriad species, including two of the world's rarest cranes: the red-crowned and white-naped cranes (*Grus vipio* and *Grus japonensis*). The sanctuary is now threatened by plans for development within the zone.

C134. "Survival of the Hunter." In *A Hunter's Heart: Honest Essays on Blood Sport.* Ed. David Peterson. New York: Henry Holt and Co., Inc., pp. 299–309.

An abbreviated version of **C132**.

1997

C135. "The Last Wild Tigers." *Audubon,* 99 (March/April), 54–63, 122–125.

A report on the tiger reserves of India and the Russian Far East, providing a brief natural history of tiger species and their status within the reserves and the ongoing problem of poaching.

Incorporated into **A34**.

C136. "Our Far-Flung Correspondents: Tiger in the Snow." *New Yorker*, 72 (6 January), 58–62, 64–65.

The endangered Amur, or Siberian tiger (*Panthera tigris altaica*), the largest of the great cats, is found almost exclusively in the Primorski Krai of eastern Siberia. Despite the establishment of the Siberian Tiger Project in 1992 to save the species from extinction, epidemic poaching has drastically reduced the number of tigers. The people are ambivalent regarding the Sikhote-Alin International Biosphere Reserve, the largest wildlife sanctuary in the Far East. Economically hard pressed, they are willing to sacrifice their natural resources for money and their own sustenance. Matthiessen observes that "the spiritual and mythic resonance of a creature as splendid as any on earth can only be removed from man's environment at a terrible cost."

Incorporated into **A34**.

C137. "Shey Monastery." In *Traveler's Tales Nepal*. Collected and edited by Rajendra S. Khadka. San Francisco: Traveler's Tales, Inc., pp. 175–187.

An excerpt from *The Snow Leopard*. Three additional brief, one paragraph excerpts also occur in the book.

See **A22**.

1998

C138. "The True Story: An Unsolved Murder." *Audubon*, 100 (November/December), 38.

A sidebar to an excerpt from *Bone by Bone* provides the bare known facts concerning the unsolved murder of Guy Bradley, Florida's first warden, on July 8, 1905.

1999

C139. "Foreword." In *Rebel With a Conscience*. Russell W. Peterson. Newark: University of Delaware Press, pp. 15–19.

Russell Peterson, a former Du Pont executive and governor of Delaware, is an independent citizen who can not be restricted by labels. As governor, he was instrumental in instituting prison reform and in protecting the state's coastal waters from heavy industrial development. He understands the connection between environmental problems and social problems. He has been active in various capacities for environmental and social progress.

C140. "Fur Countries and Forest Lakes." In *Bright Stars, Dark Trees, Clear Water: Nature Writings from North of the Border*. Selected and edited by Wayne Grady. Boston: David R. Godine, pp. [211]–220.

Reprint of **C106**.

C141. "Get Down to Earth. Are We Citizens or Mere Consumers?" *The Guardian*, 30 October, p. 3.

The earth is our home, and we can not be separate from it. It is not a simple question of man versus nature. This century will be remembered for the relentless and accelerating degradation of the human habitat. Our politicians provide little real leadership and few answers; they are interested only in "greenwash," causes that provide them good media opportunities. The real change must begin at the local level in an attempt to clean up politics. We must work toward a "fundamental shift of consciousness and attitude."

C142. "Global Corporate Power — Resist It If You Can." *Financial Times* [London], 29 May, "Off Centre," p. 9.

The effects of globalization worsen the "most intractable of our earthly woes." Global corporations and financial institutions, driven by greed and profits, have turned their economic power into political power and are exacerbating the destruction of the earth's life support systems and increasing the gap between rich and poor. There are the beginnings of a shift in public consciousness with an increasing segment of the population beginning to act locally to rally support and effect change. Disparate activists must begin to act together to oppose

globalization. Increased public awareness and activism are the keys to necessary reform. The political process and national policies can be influenced to prevent the homogenization of the world for the benefit of corporate greed.
See **H207**.

C143. "The Island at the End of the Earth." *Audubon*, 101 (September/October), [98]–107.

In January 1998 Matthiessen arrives at the island of South Georgia in the farthest region of the South Atlantic as part of a nature tour to Antarctica. South Georgia is home to "one of the greatest concentrations of seabirds and mammals anywhere on earth." A description of the island is given as well as a brief history of its role in whaling and seal hunting. Ernest Shackleton's voyage from Elephant Island to South Georgia in an attempt to rescue the crew of the *Endurance* is also recounted. Matthiessen comments on the myriad wildlife he observes, including penguins, elephant seals, fur seals, humpback whales, petrels, and albatross.

C144. "'Jungle Book' Fever." *Salon*, 23 (March). <http://www.salon.com/mwt/feature/1999/03/cov_23feature.html>. (18 June 1999).

Matthiessen remembers most fondly Rudyard Kipling's tales being read to him as a boy. Instinctively, he feels that these stories are very near the source of his lifelong fascination with wild animals and wild places. Kipling's stories are permeated with a feeling of the withheld and the unfathomable.

C145. "The Last Cranes in Siberia." In *The Gift of Birds: True Encounters with Avian Spirits*. Ed. Larry Habegger and Amy Greimann Carlson. San Francisco: Travelers' Tales, Inc., pp. 275–286.
Reprint **C116**.

C146. "Mindful of Unity." *Parabola*, 24 (Spring), 32–34.
An excerpt from *The Snow Leopard*.
See **A22**.

C147. *100 Voices for a Free Tibet*. <http://www.tibet.org/Tibet100/voices/matthiessen.html>. (9 August 1999).

A brief statement. It is difficult to imagine any thoughtful person who has truly acquainted himself with Tibet's culture and with its systematic destruction and pollution by China, as well as the Tibetan people's violent repression and imprisonment, not taking an active part in the world's outrage. People must act before it is too late to persuade their governments to act on behalf of Tibetan autonomy. The loss of Tibet is imminent.

C148. "Rachel Carson." *Time*, 153 (29 March), 187–188, 190.

A profile of the naturalist who "inspired a generation of activists." Matthiessen focuses upon the development of her work on the sea and the publication of *The Sea Around Us* and her early warnings against DDT and other insecticides which resulted in *Silent Spring*. Her ideas were initially rejected by the popular press, and she was attacked by the chemical corporations. Carson was an "intelligent and dedicated woman who rose heroically to the occasion."

C149. "Under Montauk Light." In *The Beach Book: A Literary Companion*. Ed. Aleda Shirley. Louisville, KY: Sarabande Books, Inc., pp. 114–129.
An excerpt from *Men's Lives*.
See **A27**. See also **C155**.

2000

C150. "Foreword." In *Crackers in the Glade: Life and Times in the Old Everglades*. Rob Storter. Edited and compiled by Betty Savidge Briggs. Athens: University of Georgia Press, p. xi.

Matthiessen reminisces about his visits with Captain Rob Storter, a delightful and gentle man with a phenomenal memory of the pioneer life in southwest Florida. It was from Storter that he received "perhaps the best description" of Edgar Watson. Storter's paintings of the region, including one owned by Matthiessen, *The Watson Cane Farm as I Remember It—1910*, are marked by freshness and provide a true historical document.

C151. "In Search of the Snow Leopard." In *Dharma Rain: Sources of Buddhist Environmentalism*. Ed. Stephanie Kaza and Kenneth Kraft. Boston: Shambhala Publications, Inc., pp. 319–322.

Abbreviated versions of the entries for November 11th, 12th, and 14th from *The Snow Leopard*.
See **A22.**

C152. "Pa-Hay-Okee: The Everglades." *Women's Hands*. <http://www.womens hands.com/artisans/florida/related_pay_ hay_okee.htm>. (2 May 2000).

A brief history of the destruction of the natural environment of the Everglades by exploitation, corporate greed, and mismanagement. Present efforts to restore, preserve, and protect this unique ecosystem are also discussed. Because all of its ecological components are still in place, although they are severely reduced, there is still hope that the Everglades will not be forever lost.

C153. "Peter Matthiessen on the Seminoles." *Women's Hands*. <http://www.wo menshands.com/artisans/florida/related_ betty.htm>. (2 May 2000).

A concise history of the Seminoles and their relationship with the federal government is presented. Through the three Seminole wars and the government's attempt to forcibly remove them to the Oklahoma territory, the Seminoles went into hiding, settling in remote locations in the Big Cypress and the Everglades. Unable to defeat them, the governement reclassified them out of existence as a distinct group. Two major groups of Seminoles remain — the Miccosukee and the Muskogee — although traditional differences and long-standing suspicions keep them separate.

C154. "Tigers in the Snow." *The Independent* [London], 5 March, pp. 22–23, 25–26.

Excerpt from *Tigers in the Snow*.
See **A34.**

C155. "Under Montauk Light." In *American Sea Writing: A Literary Anthology*. Ed. Peter Neill. Foreword by Nathaniel Philbrick. NY: The Library of America, pp. 569–582.

An excerpt from *Men's Lives*.
See **A27.** *See also* **C149.**

C156. "United States v. Leonard Peltier." With E. L. Doctorow, Kurt Vonnegut, Jr., and William and Rose Styron. *New York Review of Books*, 47 (July 20), 56.

This is a letter to the editor in support of Leonard Peltier's request for parole and in response to the Leavenworth parole officer's denial of parole on the grounds that Peltier's version of events at Pine Ridge doesn't coincide with that of the F.B.I. The letter appeals to the U. S. Parole Commission to act positively to commute the case.

D. Sound Recordings

1987

D1. *Peter Matthiessen Interview with Kay Bonetti.* Columbia, MO: American Audio Prose Library. 1 sound cassette (58 minutes); analog; 1⅞" ips; 2 track mono.

Recorded May, 1987 at the Fales Library in New York City.

See **H88.**

D2. *Peter Matthiessen Reading The Snow Leopard (excerpts) and On the River Styx (short story).* Columbia, MO: American Audio Prose Library. 1 sound cassette (78 minutes); analog; mono.

1989

D3. *The Snow Leopard.* Newport Beach, CA: Books on Tape. 8 sound cassettes. Read by John MacDonald.

D4. *The Tree Where Man Was Born.* Newport Beach, CA: Books on Tape. 7 sound cassettes (630 minutes); 1⅞" ips; analog.

1991

D5. *At Play in the Fields of the Lord.* New York: Random House Audiobooks. 2 sound cassettes (180 minutes). Read by John Lithgow.

An abridgement of the novel.

D6. *Killing Mister Watson.* Prince Frederick, MD: Recorded Books. 12 sound cassettes (1020 minutes); 1⅞" ips; analog. Narrated by various artists.

D7. _____. Washington, D. C.: Library of Congress. 7 sound discs; 9"; 8 rpm; analog. National Library Service for the Blind and Physically Handicapped.

1992

D8. *At Play in the Fields of the Lord.* Prince Frederick, MD: Recorded Books. 11 sound cassettes (16 hours); analog. Narrated by George Guidall.

1993

D9. *African Silences.* Newport Beach, CA: Books on Tape. 8 sound cassettes (60 minutes each); 1⅞" ips; analog. Read by John MacDonald.

D10. *The Naturalists.* Larkspur, CA: Gang of Seven. 1 sound disc; 4¾"; digital.

Recorded March–November 1992.

Matthiessen reads from *Sand Rivers*; the length of his segment is 9 minutes and 12 seconds.

D11. *No Boundaries.* Larkspur, CA: Gang of Seven. 1 sound cassette (71 minutes and 55 seconds); analog.

Recorded at Sear Sound, NY in December of 1992.

Contents: Introduction / The curious need to write / *The New Yorker* / Zen practice / The Himalayas / Om mani padme hum / Leonard Peltier / About Indian country / Mongoose story / Cesar Chavez / Inochi, life integrity

See **D12** and **D16.**

D12. _____. Larkspur, CA: Gang of Seven. 1 sound disc (71 minutes and 58 seconds); 4¾"; digital, stereo.

See **D11.**

1994

D13. *PLA President's Program: Author Peter Matthiessen, Laureate of the Wild.*

[Chicago]: American Library Association. 2 sound cassettes; analog.

Sponsored by the Public Library Association. The session was recorded at the 113th annual conference of the American Library Association held June 23–30, 1994, in Miami Beach, Florida.

D14. *Peter Matthiessen & Gary Snyder.* [San Francisco, CA]: City Arts of San Francisco. 1 sound recording (59 minutes); analog.

Recorded live at the Herbst Theatre on February 23, 1994 as part of the City Arts & Lectures, Inc. series. Hosted by Maya Angelou. Matthiessen and Snyder discuss environmental ethics and read from their works. Moderated by Jack Hicks.
See **D15**.

1996

D15. *Peter Matthiessen & Gary Snyder.* Petaluma, CA: Pacific Vista Productions. 1 sound cassette (59 minutes).

A reissue of **D14**.

1997

D16. *No Boundaries.* San Bruno, CA: Audio Literature. 1 sound cassette (72 minutes); analog.

A reissue of **D11**.

1998

D17. *Bearing Witness: Reflections on a Zen Retreat at Auschwitz.* Berkeley, CA: Conference Recording Service, Inc. 1 sound cassette (85 minutes).

Recorded at the San Francisco Zen Center as part of the "Buddhism at Millennium's Edge" series, January 31–November 14, 1998.

Matthiessen begins with an account of his participation in street retreats in New York City as part of the incorporation of social action into American Zen Buddhist practice. An extension of this concept of bearing witness retreats was a week long retreat at Auschwitz. At this "symbol of all the century's evil," Matthiessen identifies with the vast humanity who died there and gains clarification of his own personal grief. He experiences a "miraculous phenomenon" or something mysterious there: a strange exhilaration at the realized truth of the human species.

D18. *The Long Journey: Zen and the Writing Life.* Berkeley, CA: Conference Recording Service, Inc. 4 sound cassettes.

Recorded at the San Francisco Zen Center as part of the "Buddhism at Millennium's Edge" series, January 31, 1998–November 14, 1998.

An entertaining, humorous, and varied presentation on his career as a writer and as a practitioner of Zen. He speaks about his beginnings as a writer, presents anecdotes about himself and his Zen teachers, and talks about the association between writing and Zen. The focus here is really more upon Matthiessen's work, writers and writing than upon Zen.
See **D23**.

D19. *Lost Man's River.* Prince Frederick, MD: Recorded Books. 19 sound cassettes (27 hours and 25 minutes); analog. Narrated by George Guidall.

D20. *Writers & Company.* Toronto: Canadian Broadcasting Corporation, CBC Radio One. Date of broadcast, January 11, 1998. 1 sound cassette, mono.

A conversation with Eleanor Wachtel on various aspects of his work, particularly his nature writing and the Watson trilogy.

1999

D21. *Bone by Bone.* Prince Frederick, MD: Recorded Books. 16 sound cassettes (22 hours and 5 minutes); analog. Read by George Guidall.

D22. *To the Best of Our Knowledge: Conservation Stories.* [Madison, WI]: Wisconsin Public Radio. Date of broadcast, February 28, 1999. 1 sound cassette, mono.

Segment Two includes a conversation with Matthiessen by Jim Fleming. He discusses his travels to Asia to observe cranes and his interest in the species. The segment with Matthiessen is 12 minutes long.

D23. *Zen and the Writing Life*. San Anselmo, CA: Audio Wisdom. 2 sound cassettes (140 minutes); 1⅞"; analog.

An edited version of **D18**.

E. Video Recordings

1990

E1. *Lost Man's River—An Everglades Journey with Peter Matthiessen.* New York: Mystic Fire Video. 1 videocassette (VHS) (56 minutes); ½"; sound, color. A film by Noel Buckner and Rob Whittlesey. Part of the PBS television series, "Adventure."

Mattthiessen and his friend Randy White take a week long trip through the Ten Thousand Island area of Florida, fishing, meeting the people, exploring the area, and searching for the American crocodile.

1992

E2. *Killing Mister Watson ... Continued.* Fort Myers, FL: Edison Community College. ECC/USF Learning Resources Television. 1 videocassette (105 minutes); ½"; sound, color.

Taped live at the twelfth annual Southwest Florida's Writers's Conference.

1999

E3. *Peter Matthiessen in Conversation with Howard Norman.* Santa Fe, NM: Lannan Foundation. 1 videocassette (VHS) (77 minutes); ½"; sound, color.

Matthiessen is interviewed by Howard Norman on November 21, 1996 in Los Angeles and reads from *Killing Mister Watson* and *Lost Man's River.*

F. Adaptations

1992

F1. *At Play in the Fields of the Lord.* Universal City, CA: MCA Home Video. 2 videocassettes (VHS) (186 minutes); ½", sound, color.

Based on the novel. Originally produced as a motion picture in 1991. Director, Hector Babenco; producer, Saul Zaentz; screenplay, Jean-Claude Carriere and Hector Babenco.

F2. _____. Universal City, CA: MCA Home Video. 2 videodiscs (laser optical) (186 minutes); 12"; sound, color.

1994

F3. *Men's Lives.* New York: Dramatists Play Service, Inc. Adaptation by Joe Pintauro.

Originally developed and produced by the Bay Street Theatre Festival, Sag Harbor, New York, July 29, 1992.

F4. *The Young One.* Santa Monica, CA: Connoisseur Video Collection. 1 videocassette (VHS) (95 minutes); ½"; sound, black & white.

"Inspired by Peter Matthiessen's story *Travelin' Man.*" Originally produced as a motion picture in 1960 in Mexico by Producciones Olmec. Screenplay, H. B. Addis and Luis Buñel. Released in Great Britain with the title: *Island of Shame.*

G. Miscellany

1953

G1. [As Pierre Conrad]. Translation of "The Pantin Cemetery" by Henry de Montherlant. *The Paris Review*, no. 1 (Spring), [68]–77.

1954

G2. Translation of "Assunta Speaks" by Claude-Antoine Ciccione. *The Paris Review*, no. 6 (Summer), 53–63.

1964

G3. Gardner, Robert. *Dead Birds*. Salem, MA: Peabody Museum. 3 reels (83 minutes); sound; color; 16 mm. Released by Contemporary Films.

Robert Gardner, photographer, editor, and writer; Michael Rockefeller, sound recording; Jarius Lincoln and Joyce Chopra, sound editing; Karl G. Heider, photographic assistant; Jan Brockhuyse and Matthiessen, advisers.

A film account of the Harvard-Peabody New Guinea Expedition to study the Dani people, February 1961 to November 1963.

See **A14**.

1974

G4. *Fighting for Our Lives: The United Farm Workers' 1973 Grape Strike*. Keene, CA: National Farm Workers Service Center. 1 videocassette (VHS) (59 minutes); ½"; sound, color. Photographed and edited by Glen Pearcy.

Narration written by Glen Pearcy, Matthiessen, and Luis Valdez.

1976

G5. "An Indulgence of Author's Self-Portraits." *The Paris Review*, no. 67 (Fall), 129 [116–129].

Matthiessen self-portrait.
Reprinted in **G6**.

G6. "My Face (before my parents were born)." In *Self-Portrait: Book People Picture Themselves*. From the collection of Burt Britton. New York: Random House, p. 134.

Same as **G5**.

PART II

WORKS ABOUT
PETER MATTHIESSEN

H. Books and Articles

1953

H1. Styron, William. "The Paris Review." *Harper's Bazaar*, 87 (August), 122–123, 173.

A brief essay on the beginning of *The Paris Review* and a description of Matthiessen's involvement in its inception.

1954

H2. Wood, Anne, comp. "New Creative Writers." *Library Journal*, 79 (February 15), 374–375 [370–377].

A brief biographical sketch of Matthiessen is included in a survey of forty-eight first novelists.

1959

H3. Styron, William. "Introduction." In *Best Short Stories from The Paris Review*. New York: E. P. Dutton & Company, Inc., pp. [9]–16.

A report of the birth of *The Paris Review* in Paris in the early 1950s and the intent of its founders. Little is offered regarding Matthiessen and his participation in the magazine; a better, albeit brief, essay concerning Matthiessen's part is **H1**.

1963

H4. Talese, Gay. "Looking for Hemingway." *Esquire*, 60 (July), 44–45, 106, 108, 110.

This is an account of the founding and early years of *The Paris Review* and the people surrounding it, particularly George Plimpton but including Matthiessen and his first wife. It is not a particularly flattering portrait of "The Tall Young Man" who founded the magazine and the social "crowd" that orbited it. Matthiessen's wife reflects that "the whole life seemed after a while to be utterly meaningless." There was "something very manqué about them."

1964

H5. Montgomery, Ruth. "WLB Biography: Peter Matthiessen." *Wilson Library Bulletin*, 38 (March), 573–574.

A profile of "a most unusual phenomenon in the literary scene." This elementary review of Matthiessen's life and career emphasizes the Conradian influence in his first two novels and the extent of his keen observation in his works of non-fiction.

1966

H6. Cook, Roderick. "Mr. Cook Replies." *Harper's Magazine*, 232 (January), 12.

In response to complaints about his review of *At Play in the Fields of the Lord*, Cook apologizes for "reporting the plot as I did" and to Matthiessen and his publishers. Appalled that he blundered so carelessly, he refers readers to better informed reviews of the book.

See **I125** and **H7–H8**.

H7. Penn, Arthur and Stuart Miller. "Reviewer Reviewed." *Harper's Magazine*, 232 (January), 12.

A letter stating how amazed and appalled the writers are by the review of *At Play in the Fields of the Lord* by Roderick Cook. Because of his "muddle-headed plot inventions," Cook could only have thumbed through the book.

See review and **I125**, **H6** and **H8**.

H8. Styron, William. "Reviewer Reviewed." *Harper's Magazine*, 232 (January), 10, 12.

A letter in response to the review of *At Play in the Fields of the Lord* by Roderick Cook complaining that he failed to grasp the basic outline of the story. Based on Cook's "supercilious dismissal of so fine a book," Styron raises the question of whether the book was actually read by the reviewer. *See* **I125, H6–H7.**

1968

H9. Fiedler, Leslie A. *The Return of the Vanishing America.* New York: Stein and Day. Pp. 169–175 passim.

A brief discussion of *At Play in the Fields of the Lord* as an example of a novel of "Higher Masculine Sentimentality" which represents a conviction that the Indian way of life is a preferable one. While there is much that is "palpably false" in the novel, Matthiessen renders Moon's downward progress with real convincingness.

Reprinted in **H10.**

1969

H10. Fiedler, Leslie. "The Higher Sentimentality." In *The American Novel Since World War II.* Ed. Marcus Klein. Greenwich, CT: Fawcett Publications, Inc. Pp. 229–235 passim.

Reprint of **H9.**

1970

H11. Love, Deborah. *Annaghkeen.* New York: Random House, 1970.

While not specifically about Matthiessen, this account of his and his second wife's summer spent on Annaghkeen Island with his son Luke, then 12, and her daughter Rue, age 7, is an interesting and revealing portrait of the dynamics of their relationship at the time, and of Matthiessen as a man, a husband, and a father.

The book contains three untitled poems by Matthiessen.

1972

H12. Reilly, John M. "Matthiessen, Peter." In *Contemporary Novelists.* Ed. James Vinson. London: St. James Press; New York: St. Martin's Press. Pp. 852–854.

Following a set format, a listing of relevant biographical information is given followed by a basic but incomplete enumerative bibliography and a critical sketch which focuses upon the first four novels. Matthiessen's non-fiction offers a historical record of ecological disaster while his fiction provides a representation of "the disabled American character" that has wrought so much of the natural destruction. In *At Play in the Fields of the Lord*, his fiction and non-fiction become one in purpose.

See also **H21, H52, H136,** and **H179.**

1974

H13. "Matthiessen, Peter 1927– ." In *Contemporary Authors: A Bio-Bibliographical Guide to Current Authors and Their Works.* Ed. Clare D. Kinsman and Mary Ann Tennenhouse. Detroit: Gale Research Company. Pp. 584–585.

A minimal listing of basic information under the categories of Personal, Career, Writings, and Sidelights.

See also **H73.**

H14. Plimpton, George [G. A. P.]. "The Craft of Fiction in *Far Tortuga.*" *The Paris Review*, 15 (Winter), [78]–82.

A brief interview concerned with the development and structure of *Far Tortuga.* Matthiessen speaks of the novel's genesis in his sea turtle fishing voyage off Nicaragua and of the influences upon the book's experimental narrative form, including Japanese *sumi* painting. A facsimile of a manuscript page from the novel is included.

1975

H15. "Matthiessen, Peter." In *Current Biography*, 36 (October), 21–24.

A good biographical entry which also briefly traces the critical response to some of his major work, particularly *Far Tortuga*. Reprinted in **H19**.

H16. "Matthiessen, Peter." In *World Authors 1950–1970*. Ed. John Wakeman. New York: H. W. Wilson Company. Pp. 956–958.

A brief overview of Matthiessen's first four novels — which are generally too literal and explicit in their moral concerns — and of his early non-fiction work follows a concise but interesting and noteworthy autobiographical sketch.

H17. "Peter Matthiessen Goes Fishing for Turtle and Boats a Rare Best-Seller." *People Weekly*, 4 (4 August), 36–39.

A profile of Matthiessen on the occasion of *Far Tortuga*, a "haunting account" in a new form of the novel. A brief summary of his life and work is presented following a cursory discussion of the book.

1976

H18. Clark, C. E. Frazer. "Peter Matthiessen, 1927– ." In *First Printings by American Authors*. Series Editor, Matthew J. Bruccoli. Detroit: Gale Research Company. Vol. 1, pp. 249–250.

Reproductions of the title pages of the first four novels and *Wildlife in America* accompany title page information from twelve other books by Matthiessen.

H19. "Matthiessen, Peter." In *Current Biography 1975*. Ed. Charles Mortiz. New York: H. W. Wilson Company. Pp. 267–269.

Reprint of **H15**.

H20. "Matthiessen, Peter 1927– ." In *Contemporary Literary Criticism*. Ed. Carolyn Riley, Phyllis Carmel Mendelson. Detroit:

Gale Research Company. Vol. 5, pp. 273–275.

Brief excerpts from one review of *Blue Meridian*, two reviews of *The Tree Where Man Was Born*, and six reviews of *Far Tortuga*.

H21. Reilly, John M. "Matthiessen, Peter." In *Contemporary Novelists*. 2nd ed. Ed. James Vinson. New York: St. James Press. Pp. 920–923.

An expanded bibliographic listing with a slightly revised essay including a new paragraph on *Far Tortuga*.

See **H12, H52, H136,** and **H179**.

1977

H22. Clarke, Gordon W. "*Partisans*." In *Survey of Contemporary Literature*. Revised Edition. Ed. Frank N. Magill. Englewood Cliffs, NJ: Salem Press. Vol. 9, pp. 5750–5752.

A non-evaluative summary and critical analysis of the novel.

H23. "*The Cloud Forest*." In *Survey of Contemporary Literature*. Revised Edition. Ed. Frank N. Magill. Englewood Cliffs, NJ: Salem Press. Vol. 2, pp. 1319–1322.

This evaluation and summary of a book, "which may easily become a classic of its kind," is full of praise and admiration for Matthiessen and his work. His style is disciplined and straightforward "with the images strategically placed for the greatest appeal to sensations of sight, sound, and feeling." Matthiessen brings to his nature writing the same sense of scene, imagination, and passion for realistic detail that mark his fiction.

H24. Donovan, Alan. "*At Play in the Fields of the Lord*." In *Survey of Contemporary Literature*. Revised Edition. Ed. Frank N. Magill. Englewood Cliffs, NJ: Salem Press. Vol. 1, pp. 428–431.

An appreciative appraisal of the novel as well as a digest of it. While Matthiessen's themes are familiar, they are not clichés, and the effect of the novel is unique and totally moving. His style is lucid and well-paced. The character of Lewis Moon has such great appeal that he overshadows the other characters, and the reader is always awaiting his return to center stage.

H25. Payne, Alfred C. "*Sal Si Puedes.*" In *Survey of Contemporary Literature.* Revised Edition. Ed. Frank N. Magill. Englewood Cliffs, NJ: Salem Press. Vol. 10, pp. 6606–6609.

This assessment of the book is a medley of information on Matthiessen, the book, Cesar Chavez, his life, and the reaction to and results of his work. Matthiessen is a good biographer and should be commended for showing Americans the inhumanity that surrounds them.

H26. "*Raditzer.*" In *Survey of Contemporary Literature.* Revised Edition. Ed. Frank N. Magill. Englewood Cliffs, NJ: Salem Press. Vol. 9, pp. 6222–6226.

Matthiessen is "a novelist of considerable talent and distinction." This is a respectful evaluation of the novel. Despite its flaws the book becomes superior to its faults.

H27. "*Under the Mountain Wall.*" In *Survey of Contemporary Literature.* Revised Edition. Ed. Frank N. Magill. Englewood Cliffs, NJ: Salem Press. Vol. 12, pp. 7874–7877.

This book lies in "some undetermined region of reportage between the great books of exploration ... and the scientific studies of Franz Boas and Margaret Mead." The work is uniquely and superbly Matthiessen's own. A summary of this "vigorous, compelling narrative" is provided.

H28. Walters, Thomas N. "*Far Tortuga.*" In *Survey of Contemporary Literature.* Revised Edition. Ed. Frank N. Magill. Englewood Cliffs, NJ: Salem Press. Vol. 4, pp. 2462–2466.

"A restless writer of prodigious energies and talents," Matthiessen has brilliantly designed a new framework for what might have been merely another sea yarn. He has,

instead, created a poem of the Caribbean. It is a memorable and beautiful declaration of the human spirit. The novel's plot is summarized.

1978

H29. Allen, Henry. "An Improbable Bestseller: Matthiessen's *Snow Leopard.*" *Springfield Republican* [MA], December, p. 18.

Reprint of **H30**. Not verified. Cited in Nicholas, **H37**.

H30. _____. "Quest for the Snow Leopard's Secret." *Washington Post*, 13 December, "Style," pp. D1, D5.

This profile, based on a visit to Matthiessen's home in Sagaponack and the publication of The Snow Leopard, is predisposed toward the otherworldliness surrounding him: his "drudicial intensity" and the strangeness of the universe and its mysterious significances. He is "everything the American writer is supposed to be." With every book he moves further into his quest for experience.

Reprinted in **H29** and **H31**.

H31. _____. "What a Writer Who Has Done It All Does Next." *San Francisco Chronicle*, 31 December, "PUN," p. 7.

Reprint of **H30**. Not verified. Cited in Nicholas, **H37**.

1979

H32. Eldridge, Roger S. "On Target." *Audubon*, 81 (July), 123.

A letter voices delight at the often vehement letters in the May issue responding to Matthiessen's article on the GO road. Such strong reaction usually indicates that the article is "right on target."

See **C54** and **H39**.

H33. Freese, Sigrid H. "A Bed of Boughs." *Audubon*, 81 (May), 122.

This letter writer is shocked by Matthiessen's practice of cutting fern fronds and evergreen boughs to sleep on. *Audubon* replies that the area in question had not been traveled in decades and Matthiessen's act had a minimal impact on the area. It also notes the low-impact nature of Matthiessen's equipment and treks.

H34. Fremont-Smith, Eliot. "25 for '78." *Village Voice*, 1 January 1979, pp. 72–73.

Brief evaluations are given for the 25 books nominated for the National Book Critics Circle Awards. *The Snow Leopard* is a stunning account; it is a grand mix of astonishing travelogue, scientific curiosity, and spiritual pilgrimage.

H35. Grove, James P. "Pastoralism and Anti-Pastoralism in Peter Matthiessen's *Far Tortuga. Critique*, 21 (no. 2), 15–29.

Far Tortuga is the most successful portrayal of the prevailing pastoral-anti-pastoral pattern in Matthiessen's fiction. Raib's attempted escape to the pastoral ideal of Far Tortuga is a means to judge society's evils, but the pastoral dream is only valid for as long as it is not confused with reality. It does not represent a legitimate alternative to modern civilization. Speedy is the only character within the book who bridges the gap between the pastoral and anti-pastoral, between the old and modern times. He possesses old fashioned qualities but can also cope with the realities of the modern world.

H36. "Matthiessen, Peter 1927– ." In *Contemporary Literary Criticism.* Ed, Dedria Bryfonski. Detroit: Gale Research Company. Vol. 11, pp. 358–362.

Excerpts from seven reviews of *The Snow Leopard*.

H37. Nicholas, D. *Peter Matthiessen: A Bibliography: 1959–1979.* Canoga Park, CA: Orirana Press.

This is a fine early effort at an enumerative bibliography of primary material with an excellent listing of book reviews. It also contains a biographical outline.

H38. Patteson, Richard F. "*At Play in the Fields of the Lord*: The Imperialist Idea and

the Discovery of the Self." *Critique*, 21 (no. 2), 5–14.

This is an interesting and seminal discussion of *At Play in the Fields of the Lord.* The lack of critical attention paid to the novel is indicative of the widespread failure to recognize how ambitious the novel is. Matthiessen successfully unites two literary traditions to achieve the book's richness and complexity: the solitary American hero's search for himself and the imperialist-explorer's search for savage worlds to civilize and possess. He uses the conventions of the adventure literature of the late Victorian era ("the imperialist romance") to explore particularly American literary themes. These two traditions are seen in the character of Lewis Moon as a man who belongs neither with his Indian past nor with his present life as a white man. Matthiessen's prevailing vision is ecological, not moral. He is critical of the imperialistic exploits, but he does not present the life of the wild as a place of prelapsian primal innocence.

H39. "Return to the GO Road." *Audubon*, 81 (May), 119–120, 122.

Five letters in response to Matthiessen's article, one of which, printed anonymously, compliments him on it. The other four are all critical of him and his presentation of the information within the article.

F. W. Godrey, the Executive Manager of the Del Nortre Municipal League, calls the article fiction. Matthiessen was either misinformed or deliberately lied. The article is an attack on the free enterprise system.

James Zander believes the article is a disservice to the environmental movement. Common sense must be used to find a middle ground between preservation and wise use.

Gerard R. Griffin, Director of Corporate Communications for Louisiana-Pacific Corp., says the article is a biased and heavy-handed assault. He says the company's printed material is quoted out-of-context in an attempt to portray it as single-mindedly opposed to the wilderness. *Audubon* replies that Griffin is guilty of misquoting the company's ad and believes the ad's real message rings clear in Matthiessen's article.

Information Forester for the Western Timber Association Richard G. Reid, states that while he understood Matthiessen's position would be opposing the road, he felt it would be an opportunity to present the forest industry's point of view. Unfortunately, Matthiessen lacks journalistic ethics. He distorts Reid's title and qualifications and misquotes what he said. *Audubon* and Matthiessen briefly reply that Reid's statement was verified and accurately quoted. *See* **C54**, **H32**, and **H40**.

H40. "Stop and GO." *Audubon*, 81 (March), 122–123.

Two letters in response to "Stop the GO Road." Jan R. Seils is shocked by Matthiessen's "shabby journalistic tricks" to ridicule, malign, and discredit the U.S. Forest Service and its employees. Matthiessen replies and apologizes for referring to a young forester as a "boy" but emphasizes that he *was* very young looking; he looked younger than Matthiessen's son. He reiterates that all the Forest Service people he met were courteous and friendly.

Chris Stronsness, the Conservation Chairman of the Mount Shasta Area Audubon Society, seeks to correct "a few inaccuracies" in the article. *See* **C54**, **H32**, and **H39**.

H41. Styron, Nell Joslin. "The Snow Leopard." In *Magill's Literary Annual 1979*. Ed. Frank N. Magill. Englewood Cliffs, NJ: Salem Press. Vol. 2, pp. 685–688.

This is an extended summary of a book which is rewarding on many levels. The style lends itself to the beauty and introspection of the subject.

H42. Styron, William. "Introduction." In *Peter Matthiessen: A Bibliography: 1951–1979*. D. Nicholas. Canoga Park, CA: Orirana Press. Pp. xiii–xvii.

A tribute to his friend and a remberance of their introduction in Paris in 1952 when Matthiessen's appartment was the center of music, food, drink, and literary conversation. Matthiessen and his first wife, Patsy, introduced Styron to the pleasures of the city and its people. When they returned to the United States, they began a tradition of reading each other's manuscripts. As good as his first three novels were, they were merely forerunners to the "genuine stature" of *At Play in the Fields of the Lord*. Matthiessen has also produced a unique body of work of natural history reflecting his mingling of poet and scientist. His fiction and non-fiction prove him to be a writer of phenomenal scope and versitility.

Reprinted in **H53**.

H43. Young, James Dean. "A Peter Matthiessen Checklist." *Critique*, 21 (no. 2), 30–38.

This early listing focuses on enumerating Matthiessen's books and review citations. Brief and incomplete listings of short fiction, short nonfiction, miscellaneous items, and "critical comments" are also included.

1980

H44. Cobbs, John L. "Peter Matthiessen." In *American Novelists Since World War II*. Second Series. Ed. James E. Kibler, Jr. *Dictionary of Literary Biography*, vol. 6. Detroit: Gale Research Company. Pp. 218–224.

This essay is similar in content and approach to Cobbs's "Analysis" section of his entry in **H54**, but attention is also paid here to Matthiessen's non-fiction. Matthiessen's best works of fiction are *Far Tortuga* and *At Play in the Fields of the Lord*, while *The Tree Where Man Was Born* and *The Snow Leopard* are his best works of non-fiction. He is "one of the shamans of literature"; he puts his readers in touch with worlds and forces which transcend common experience.

H45. Schaller, George B. *Stones of Silence: Journeys in the Himalaya*. New York: Viking Press. Pp. 203, 205–222 passim, 225, 226, 227, 229, 230, 231, 232, 234, 235, 236, 242, 243, 244, 246–254 passim.

An account of Schaller's travels over a six year period in the mountains of the Himalaya. Matthiessen accompanied him on a trip to Nepal in 1973; this trip was the basis for *The Snow Leopard*. Schaller provides his own account of their trip to Crystal Mountain. There is not a great deal of specific information about Matthiessen, but Schaller provides an interesting and entertaining account of their travel together and the every day experiences, including problems with porters and the whether.

H46. White, Randy. "The Travels of Peter Matthiessen." *Outside*, 5 (April/May), 18–20, 22, 67–71.

An engaging profile of Matthiessen which reveals more of the individual rather than the writer or explorer. White and Matthiessen take a week long journey into the last stronghold of coastal and mangrove wilderness, into The Ten Thousand Islands area and Everglades National Park of Florida. They explore the area, including the foundation of the old Watson house, and meet its people. White shows the simple joy Matthiessen derives from being outside and observing, his enthusiasm for birding, his skills at fishing, as well as commenting on his preoccupation with traditional peoples and his writing.

1981

H47. Condini, Nereo E. "American Writers Look Inward." *National Catholic Reporter*, 17 (18 September), 11.

The Snow Leopard is one of several books discussed as evidence of American writers' desire to "find out about their inner selves, to probe deeply into their drives and apprehensions." Matthiessen sets out to prove that "religion is simply the appreciation of the infinite in every moment." He provides a haunting meditation on Buddhism and death's meaning.

H48. Heim, Michael. "The Mystic and the Myth: Thoughts on *The Snow Leopard*." *Studia Mystica*, 4 (Summer), 3–9.

Heim places *The Snow Leopard* within the genre of spiritual search and examines Matthiessen's conflict between his roles as the mystic and the artist. The free flights of awareness attained by the mystic in search of spiritual fulfillment transcend the verbal structures of the journalist/artist in his naturalistic and geographic descriptions of the literal journey. The literal account of the journal notes does not attain the level of actual learning. Only after the closing of the journal account is the true instruction realized.

H49. "Matthiessen on Africa." *Audubon*, 83 (May), 123.

Three letters from Maggie Burns, Jack P. Maloney, and Margaret Rusk in response to "Peter Matthiessen's Africa. Book One: Botswana." Burns and Rusk praise and support Matthiessen, but Maloney rebuts his "arrogant exclusion of South African whites" as "Africans." Matthiessen's sweeping condemnation of "white civilization" is as racist as the conditions he criticizes.
See **C62** and **H50**.

H50. "Nature and Politics." *Audubon*, 83 (March), 125.

A letter from K. E. Pletcher regarding "Peter Matthiessen's Africa. Book One: Botswana." The writer disagrees with Matthiessen's "gratuitous comments" about South Africa and criticizes his use of a literary effort as a political platform.
See **C62** and **H49**.

1982

H51. Devereux, Ellen. "Sand Rivers." In *Magill's Literary Annual 1982*. Ed. Frank N. Magill. Englewood Cliffs, NJ: Salem Press. Vol. 2, pp. 737–741.

A summary of the background of the book and of the safari to the Selous Game Reserve is given. No evaluation of the merits of the book itself is given.

H52. Reilly, John M. "Matthiessen, Peter." In *Contemporary Novelists*. 3rd edition. Ed. by James Vinson. New York: St. James Press, pp. 441–442.

Additions are made to the biographical and bibliographical listings and the essay from the second edition is reprinted.
See also **H12**, **H21**, **H136**, and **H179**.

H53. Styron, William. "Peter Matthiessen." In his *This Quiet Dust and Other Writings*. New York: Random House. Pp. 249–252.

Reprint of **H42**.

1983

H54. Cobbs, John L. "Peter Matthiessen." In *Critical Survey of Long Fiction*. English Language Series. Ed. Frank N. Magill. Englewood Cliffs, NJ: Salem Press. Vol. 5, pp. 1822–1833.

Basic information is provided within set sections of "Other Literary Forms," "Achievements," "Biography," and "Analysis," the longest section. Matthiessen's first three novels are seen as accomplished but unextraordinary. *At Play in the Fields of the Lord* and *Far Tortuga* are major works, however, and each is discussed at length. No other contemporary nature writer approaches Matthiessen's depth and his poetic command of the language.

See **H44** and **H121**.

H55. Karl, Frederick R. *American Fictions, 1940–1980*. New York: Harper & Row. Pp. 57–59.

Both *Far Tortuga* and *At Play in the Fields of the Lord* are evidence of Matthiessen's interest in the pursuit of edens and dispossessed gardens. *At Play in the Fields of the Lord* is a significant cultural document, a prophecy of the decade that will emerge. The only comparable novel to deal with such crucial issues is Saul Bellow's *Henderson the Rain King*. Lewis Moon's movement into the primitive is not a sentimental quest for simplicity but an essential course for life.

H56. Patteson, Richard F. "Holistic Vision and Fictional Form in Peter Matthiessen's *Far Tortuga*." *Rocky Mountain Review of Language and Literature*, 37 (no. 1–2), 70–81.

This is an interesting and important discussion of *Far Tortuga*. Matthiessen's work provides the "most striking literary articulation" of the holistic view of nature — the idea of man as part of, and dependent upon, an interconnected system larger than himself. *Far Tortuga* is Matthiessen's most ambitious fictional attempt at portraying this holistic vision. The central conflict is not between an ideal "then" and a corrupt "now" but between a state in which man is not separated from nature and a fallen state in which man separates himself from nature and consequently from his fellow human beings. Attention is paid to the conflicts among Raib, Brown, and Speedy and to these conflicts as indicative of the larger, mythic oppositions within the novel concerning Far Tortuga itself. The possible influence of oriental thought on Matthiessen's shaping and presentation of the book is also examined.

H57. "S. Dak. Governor Sues Viking, Three Bookstores for Libel." *Publishers Weekly*, 223 (17 June), 20.

A discussion of the inclusion of three bookstores in the lawsuit filed by William Janklow against Viking Press as a result of their refusal to stop selling *In the Spirit of Crazy Horse*. Viking is countersuing Janklow claiming that his actions violate the publisher's First Amendment rights and is causing it economic harm.

H58. "Viking Asks Dismissal of Janklow Libel Suit." *Publishers Weekly*, 224 (8 July), 21.

Viking Press filed a notice asking for the dismissal of William Janklow's libel suit against it and three South Dakota bookstores concerning *In the Spirit of Crazy Horse*. If the suit is not dismissed, Viking seeks to have the action moved to the U. S. District Court in Manhattan. Viking's grounds for dismissal are based on the doctrine of neutral reportage.

H59. Weyler, Rex. "Peter Matthiessen: The Search for Truth." *New Age*, 9 (August), 28–33, 36.

Various aspects of *In the Spirit of Crazy Horse* are discussed: how he came to write it and why, its critical reception, and the F.B.I.'s reaction to it. A question concerning the possible parallels between American Indian spirituality and the Buddhist contemplative tradition leads to a series of questions on his practice of Zen Buddhism.

that *In the Spirit of Crazy Horse* defames him is given.

1984

H60. Bender, Bert. "*Far Tortuga* and American Sea Fiction Since *Moby-Dick*." *American Literature*, 56 (May), [227]–248.

This is an important assessment of the novel which, following an overview of the tradition and influence of American sea fiction, admiringly discusses *Far Tortuga* within the context of that tradition. The character of Raib is a "contemporary representative man at sea" and a medium by which the traditional elements of sea fiction are "simultaneously infused." The novel is presented as being responsible for a renewed vitality in American sea-fiction.
See **H78.**

H61. Gleason, Judith. "Reclaiming the Valley of the Shadows." *Parnassus*, 12 (Fall), 40–43 [21–71].

Within this essay/review the Native American artist Jimmie Durham's opinion of *In the Spirit of Crazy Horse* is presented. He believes it presents a false situation since Leonard Peltier's story is isolated in a linear sense making it more important than it really is. Making Peltier the "hero with the thousand faces" is in keeping with western ego structures, not Indian narrative structures. Gleason, however, finds the book impressive in its commitment to research and the writing of the story. In writing the book Matthiessen grounds himself and commits himself to battle. Rather than Peltier, Leonard Crow Dog is the truly fascinating character in the book.

H62. Pell, Eve. *The Big Chill: How the Reagan Administration, Corporate America, and Religious Conservatives are Subverting Free Speech and the Public's Right to Know.* Boston: Beacon Press. P. 176.

A brief discussion concerning William Janklow's unique legal tactics of suing three South Dakota bookstores as well as Matthiessen and Viking Press over his charges

1985

H63. Alcosser, Sandra. "Celebration: Literature and the Land — Babb, Matthiessen, Smith, Lopez." *AWP Newsletter*, September, pp. 10–11.

An account of a panel discussion on literature and the land. Matthiessen calls for writers to be more socially and politically active by writing on controversial issues and/or topics of public welfare. Each poet and fiction writer must be the occasional journalist to investigate and expose the injustices within his environment.

H64. Bishop, Peter. "The Geography of Hope and Despair: Peter Matthiessen's *The Snow Leopard*." *Critique*, 26 (Summer), 203–216.

The Snow Leopard's mixture of personal philosophizing and empirical observation make it difficult to categorize; it is neither a conventional work of fiction nor a straightforward factual text. Bishop reverses the prevailing critical perspective and views Matthiessen's "travel fantasies" as drawing their inspiration from his fictional imagination. *The Snow Leopard* fits coherently into Matthiessen's fictional work. Thematic similarities are developed among *The Snow Leopard* and Matthiessen's novels, particularly *At Play in the Fields of the Lord* and *Far Tortuga*. The latter part of the essay centers upon what Bishop sees as the two primary trajectories of the story: a gradual ascent through the Himalayas representing, in part, Matthiessen's spiritual quest, and a psychological descent through memory. The book's "essays" provide the connection between the ascending landscape route and the descending route of the psyche.

H65. Harrison, Jim. *Esquire*, 104 (August), 81.

A brief quote accompanying the story "On the River Styx" and a photograph of Matthiessen. Matthiessen's work is an obsession of Harrison's. He has an interest in things other than himself and owns a "peculiar savagery of conscience and consciousness."

H66. Swan, Gladys. "Keynote Address: Matthiessen's Landscape." *AWP Newsletter*, September, pp. 10, 12.

A report on Matthiessen's keynote address at the AWP Conference. The year's theme was "Literature and the Land," and Matthiessen read his story, "On the River Styx."

1986

H67. Bishop, George. "Peter Matthiessen." In *Beacham's Popular Fiction in America*. Ed. Walton Beacham. Washington, DC: Beacham Publishing. Vol. 3, pp. 917–924.

Basic information is provided within the set categories of "Publishing History"; "Critical Reception, Honors, and Popularity"; "Analysis of Selected Titles"; "Related Titles"; "Other Titles"; and "Additional Sources." Under "Analysis of Selected Titles" *At Play in the Fields of the Lord* and *Far Tortuga* are discussed under the headings of "Socal Concerns/Themes," "Characters," "Techniques," and "Literary Precedents."

See also **H67**, **H169–H170**, and **H172**.

H68. Holladay, Hal. "*Far Tortuga*." In *Masterplots II: American Fiction Series*. Ed. Frank N. Magill. Englewood Cliffs, NJ: Salem Press. Vol. 2, pp. 521–526.

Information is presented in a standardized format of "The Novel," "The Characters," "Themes and Meanings," "Critical Context," and a brief three item "Sources for Further Study."

See also **H217**.

H69. Knudson, Thomas J. "'They Can Come Back.'" *New York Times Book Review*, 22 June, p. 30.

A sidebar accompanying the review of *Men's Lives* and based on an interview with Matthiessen. He recalls his own years on the East End of Long Island and his work as a

commercial fisherman as well as the writing of the book.

H70. Otten, Robert M. "*At Play in the Fields of the Lord*." In *Masterplots II: American Fiction Series*. Ed. Frank N. Magill. Englewood Cliffs, NJ: Salem Press. Vol. 1, pp. 65–70.

Extended plot summary and character descriptions are followed by brief comments on "Themes and Meanings" and "Critical Context." While acknowledging the Conradian nature of the work, it is noted that Matthiessen moves beyond Conrad in his anthropologist's goal of objectivity and naturalist's instinct for appreciation. The novel's central theme is the irreconcilable nature of the cultures which fatally interact. This novel signals the merging of Matthiessen's two interests: the literary and the anthropological.

See also **H219**.

H71. Smith, Wendy. "Peter Matthiessen [PW Interviews]." *Publishers Weekly*, 229 (9 May), 240–241.

This is not a true question and answer interview but rather a profile of and a discussion with Matthiessen on the occasion of the publication of *Men's Lives* and *Nine-Headed Dragon River*. Matthiessen's ability to capture the fishermen's language and his view of the fishermen of the East End of Long Island as one of the traditional peoples who are closer to the earth are discussed. He speaks of his hesitancy concerning the publication of *Nine-Headed Dragon River* and his not wanting to be perceived as pushing his personal interest in Zen. He views nonfiction as a means by which he can write fiction and desires to return to writing fiction, which he finds exhilarating and revitalizing.

1987

H72. Cooley, John R. "Waves of Change: Peter Matthiessen's Caribbean." *Environmental Review*, 11 (Fall), 223–230.

Far Tortuga and "To the Miskito Bank" provide a record of a vanishing species and a disappearing economy. They mirror the cultural issues and changes of Grand Cayman Island and the western Caribbean during the 1960s. Some historical information is provided about the turtle fishing industry in the area, and the difference between how the article and the novel reflect the changes taking place in the Caribbean is also examined. Raib Avers is representative of the people caught between worlds — caught during the period of social change. While Matthiessen's works convey an emotional fondness for the old ways of the undeveloped Caribbean, they do not sentimentalize nor give a false promise of their return.

H73. "Matthiessen, Peter 1927– ." In *Contemporary Authors*. New Revision Series. Ed. Deborah A. Straub. Detroit: Gale Research Company, Inc. Vol. 21, pp. 278–283.

This entry provides basic biographical and bibliographical information with an essay (or "sketch") by Anne Janette Johnson offering an overview of Matthiessen's career and its critical reception. Particular attention is given to *Far Tortuga* and *At Play in the Fields of the Lord*.
Reprinted in **H74**. Expanded and revised in **H177**.

H74. _____. In *Major 20th-Century Writers*. Ed. Bryan Ryan. Detroit: Gale Research Company, Inc. Vol. 3: L–Q, pp. 1935–1940.
Reprint of **H73**.

H75. Wiebe, Bruce. "Men's Lives." In *Magill's Literary Annual 1987*. Ed. Frank N. Magill. Pasadena, CA: Salem Press. Vol. 2, pp. 547–552.

A summary and analysis is provided. This is a book of loving tenderness and attentiveness. It does not blindly glorify or idealize a fading way of life.

1988

H76. Bawer, Bruce. "Nature Boy: The Novels of Peter Matthiessen." *New Criticism*, 6 (June), 32–40.

A seminal and interesting, albeit ultimately misleading, critical view of Matthiessen's work. Matthiessen's unique ability as a writer is his capacity to combine his talents as a naturalist and storyteller. *Far Tortuga* and *At Play in the Fields of the Lord*, his best novels, draw extensively upon his work as a naturalist and anthropologist and his travel experiences. However, his fiction and nonfiction also have a shared weakness: his romanticization of the lives of "people more primitive than himself" and his reverence of their oneness with nature and their closeness with God. Matthiessen uses this celebration of primitivism as an indictment of Western civilization generally and of the United States specifically, magnifying the United States into a symbol of "fatuous, menacing power." His "powerful antagonisms" toward Western civilization, America, and the Christian god also inform his nonfiction, must notably in the "truly pathetic" *Nine-Headed Dragon River*, a 'tiresome and dismaying experience." Bawer suggests that these antagonisms seem rooted in an antagonism toward fathers, which, while not explicit in either *Far Tortuga* or *At Play in the Fields of the Lord*, is an important theme in each. This hypothesis of father-related conflict transference is supported by a review of Matthiessen's three "terrible" earlier "apprentice" novels which exhibit a filial rebellion against comfort, pleasantness, and "good family." In the two more recent novels the much resented father figure becomes subsumed into America, Western civilization, and the Christian god. An uncritical reverence for nature replaces Matthiessen's "absorption in an inordinately puerile self."
This essay is the most consistently negative assessment of Matthiessen's work.
Reprinted in **H140**.

H77. Begley, Sharon and Tessa Namuth. "'Crazy Horse' Rises Again." *Newsweek*, 111 (1 February), 47.

A review of the legal action taken against Matthiessen and Viking Press by F.B.I. agent David Price and former South Dakota governor William J. Janklow as a result of *In the Spirit of Crazy Horse*. The U. S.

District Court has dismissed Price's suit, upholding Matthiessen's right to publish "an entirely one-sided view of people and events."

H78. Bender, Bert. "*Far Tortuga.*" In his *Sea-Brothers: The Tradition of American Sea Fiction from Moby-Dick to the Present.* Philadelphia: University of Pennsylvania Press. Pp. [212]–224.

This is essentially a reprint of Bender's discussion of the novel in his 1984 article but without the first section which provides a synopsis of the tradition of sea-fiction in American literature.

See **H60** and **H79**.

H79. Bender, Bert. "Peter Matthiessen and the Tradition in Modern Time." In his *Sea-Brothers: The Tradition of American Sea Fiction from Moby-Dick to the Present.* Philadelphia: University of Pennsylvania Press. Pp. [199]–211.

Several of Matthiessen's stories and novels derive their meaning from the sea, culminating in "his masterpiece," *Far Tortuga,* "one of the greatest sea novels of all time, in any language." While attention is paid to Matthiessen's use of the sea in *Race Rock,* it is *Raditzer* which shows his preliminary efforts to create the great sea book. Matthiessen's own direct involvement with the sea as a commercial fisherman provides him with the profoundly truthful presentation of sea life he achieves in *Far Tortuga.* He is the most accomplished naturalist in the tradition of American sea-fiction.

See **H78.**

H80. Blaustein, Arthur I. "Novel Giving: Gift Ideals for the Holidays." *Mother Jones,* 13 (December), 49.

At Play in the Fields of the Lord is among the twelve books recommended as gifts. It is an exceptional novel which exposes the moral posturing of American missionaries.

H81. "Five Authors Aid Matthiessen, See Litigation As Censorship." *Publishers Weekly,* 233 (18 March), 12.

William Styron, Kurt Vonnegut, Alfred Kazin, John Irving, and Susan Sontag filed a friend-of-the-court brief supporting a motion of summary judgment brought by Matthiessen and Viking Press seeking dismissal of William J. Janklow's libel action concerning *In the Spirit of Crazy Horse.* They believe that Janklow is attacking Matthiessen's right to present the historical record and that the threat of litigation costs result in authors avoiding controversial subjects. The writers believe that the courts must stand as the guardians of freedom of expression.

H82. Hassan, Ihab Habib. "The Spirit of Quest in Contemporary American Letters." *Michigan Quarterly Review,* 27 (Winter), 17–37.

After a general examination of the idea of quest — of a person inviting risk — in contemporary American literature, five "exemplary" texts are cited and briefly discussed as examples of the genre. Among the five is *The Snow Leopard.* Matthiessen's journey contains several "symbolic dimensions," including horizontal, vertical, cultural, and spiritual.

This idea is more fully developed and presented in **H104.**

Reprinted in **H127** and **H160.**

H83. "A *Newsday* Conversation: Poisons in the Wind: A Cure in the Trash?" *Newsday,* 7 February, "Ideas," p. 4.

An edited conversation between Matthiessen and Barry Commoner, the noted biologist and environmental activist. They discuss environmental issues on the East End of Long Island, including farmers' use of pesticides; the development of farm land; the conflict between commercial and sport fishermen, particularly the question of striped bass; and dioxin produced by incinerators. The craft of writing is also briefly touched upon.

H84. Model, F. Peter. "Eye on Publishing." *Wilson Library Bulletin,* 62 (March), 63 [62–63].

A brief notice of the new Vintage editions of *Race Rock, Far Tortuga,* and *Men's Lives.* The dismissal of former F.B.I. agent Dennis Price's law suit against Matthiessen is also mentioned.

H85. Schnitzer, Deborah. "'Ocular Realism': The Impressionist Effects of an 'Innocent Eye.'" In her *The Pictorial in Modernist Fiction from Stephen Crane to Ernest Hemingway.* Ann Arbor, MI: UMI Research Press. Pp. 55–60 [7–62].

Far Tortuga is one of several works discussed in regard to Impressionist art and the relationship between the visual and verbal arts. In the novel's opening chapters, Matthiessen experiments with multiple technical styles to visualize his subject. He utilizes Impressionistic methods to create illusions of depth through linear and atmospheric perspectives. He is concerned with making an art of surfaces, and this evocation of shallowness is similar to the effects of Impressionistic art. Matthiessen maintains a faithfulness to the perceptual present and emphasizes the relativity of vision that all Impressionist serials approach. The first chapter of *Far Tortuga* is among "the finest examples of literary Impressionism in Modernist fiction."

H86. "Viking and Matthiessen Prevail in Libel Suit." *Publishers Weekly,* 233 (29 January), 314.

A federal judge dismissed former F.B.I. agent David Price's libel claims concerning *In the Spirit of Crazy Horse.* The judge ruled that the content of the book is opinion and therefore cannot be the basis of libel, and that Matthiessen "took considerable care in writing the book." The article also provides a brief summary of the history of the suits brought by Price and former South Dakota governor William J. Janklow as a result of the book.

1989

H87. Atlas, James. "To the Ends of the Earth." *Condé Nast Traveler,* 24 (October), 146–149, 219–220.

A profile of Matthiessen and a brief look at his various journeys and their resulting books. Atlas attempts to find the source of Matthiessen's obsessive need to travel and explore. The persistent theme that emerges in his work is "his deep yearning for enlight-enment." The real journey takes place within his head. Despite "his aspirations to some purer realm" he maintains his connections to the real world.

H88. Bonetti, Kay. "An Interview with Peter Matthiessen." *The Missouri Review,* 12 (no. 12), 109–124.

An extended and revealing interview covering a variety of topics, especially writing and Zen. *At Play in the Fields of the Lord* and *The Snow Leopard,* in particular, are discussed.

Reprinted in **H183.** See also **D1.**

H89. "Court Dismisses Janklow Suit Against Viking and Matthiessen." *Publishers Weekly,* 235 (16 June), 14.

The Circuit Court of the Second Judicial Circuit in Sioux Falls, South Dakota dismissed the $25 million libel action brought by former South Dakota governor William Janklow. Janklow charged that statements made about him in *In the Spirit of Crazy Horse* libeled him, but the Court found that "by no means" were the statements in the book "a reckless publication about a public official."

H90. Garbus, Martin. "The F.B.I. Man Who Cried Libel." *The Nation,* 249 (13 November), 564, 566–567.

On the occasion of the dismissal of David Price's libel suit against Matthiessen and Viking Press over *In the Spirit of Crazy Horse* by the U. S. Court of Appeals for the Eighth Circuit, the history of the case and the two sides' arguments are reviewed. The Court's decision, which relies upon the resurrection and expansion of the doctrine of neutral reportage privilege, is a "reaffirmation of the right of authors and journalists to criticize government officials." It is also a reversal of recent Supreme Court decisions which have placed restrictions on freedom of the press.

See also **H191.**

H91. "In the Workshop of Peter Matthiessen." *Esquire,* 111 (May), 118–119.

A description of the converted playhouse Matthiessen uses as a work place and the mementos on the walls and shelves. There is a perfectly evolved equilibrium between man and place. This brief article is accompanied by a photograph by Arnold Newman.

H92. Rea, Paul. "Causes and Creativity: An Interview with Peter Matthiessen." *RE: Arts & Letters*, 15 (Fall), 27–40.

Matthiessen discusses his practice of Zen and its connection to his writing, the novel he is currently working on (*Killing Mister Watson*), and, most extensively, the Leonard Peltier case, and the issues raised in *Indian Country*.

H93. Shnayerson, Michael. *Irwin Shaw: A Biography*. New York: G. P. Putnam's Sons. Pp. 199, 205, 209, 210, 211, 213, 214, 220, 246, 293, 337, 345, 371, 372, 407, 408.

Matthiessen is occasionally named as involved with various social activities with Shaw. The most sustained discussion is of Matthiessen and Shaw's relationship in Paris in the early 1950s when *The Paris Review* was being started and Shaw was being introduced to the writers surrounding it.

H94. "Viking, Matthiessen Win In Price Libel Suit." *Publishers Weekly*, 236 (1 September), 8.

The U. S. Court of Appeals for the Eighth Circuit granted summary judgment to Matthiessen and Viking Press in David Price's $25 million libel suit. The Court ruled that an author must be free to report charges and countercharges in a controversy involving a public figure, regardless of his or her own subjective beliefs.

H95. Winterowd, W. Ross. "Reading (and Rehabilitating) the Literature of Fact." *Rhetoric Review*, 8 (Fall), [44]–59.

In "Peter Matthiessen's Lyric Trek," pp. 52–59, Winterowd discusses *The Snow Leopard* as an example of a non-fiction work which provides the "immersion" of fiction. Factual texts can be as valuable and satisfying as fiction.

This essay is adapted as a chapter in Winterowd's book. *See* **H114**.

1990

H96. Blaustein, Arthur I. "Novels With a Moral Conscience." *Tikkun*, 5 (January/ February), 66–68.

At Play in the Fields of the Lord is included in a list of twenty-four "Socially Conscious Books." It reveals America's moral posturing for what it is and explodes the stereotype of the "helping" missionary.

H97. Churchill, Ward. "GOONs, G-Men, and AIM." *The Progressive*, 54 (April), 28–29.

The dismissal of David Price's law suit against Matthiessen and Viking Press for defamation of character resulting from the publication of *In the Spirit of Crazy Horse* occasions this partisan review of the incidents at Pine Ridge between 1973 and 1976 which led to the deaths of the two F.B.I. agents and, ultimately, Matthiessen's book.

H98. _____. "In the Spirit of Crazy Horse." *Index on Censorship*, 19 (no. 1), 15–16.

Churchill, who is affiliated with the American Indian Movement, briefly discusses the court decision against F.B.I. agent David Price and former South Dakota governor William Janklow in their civil action against Matthiessen and Viking Press concerning the publication of *In the Spirit of Crazy Horse*. Churchill calls the suit possibly "the most virulent quasi-official manipulation of the US legal system for purposes of censorship in recent memory." The book's true significance and the reason why officials tried to suppress it is because Matthiessen reveals the events which took place at Pine Ridge Reservation between 1973 and 1976 and the government's covert war against AIM.

H99. Dawidoff, Nicholas. "Earthbound in the Space Age: Peter Matthiessen Explores the Wild and the Majestic." *Sports Illustrated*, 73 (3 December), [119–120], [122], [124].

A profile of Matthiessen as explorer and naturalist, his celebration of natural beauty and his denunciation of those who threaten it. Matthiessen makes some interesting remarks about his reluctance as a traveller.

H100. E. G. "Spring Mister Peltier." *San Francisco Review of Books*, 15 (Summer), 32.

This is an update on the Leonard Peltier case and the campaign for a new inquiry into the killings at the Pine Ridge Reservation as a result of Matthiessen's interview with the "real culprit" and the reissue of *In the Spirit of Crazy Horse*.

H101. Gabriel, Trip. "The Nature of Peter Matthiessen." *New York Times Magazine*, 10 June, pp. 30–31, 42, 94, 96, 98.

A nicely balanced and revealing profile of Matthiessen on the occasion of the publication of *Killing Mister Watson*.
Reprinted in **H102**.

H102. _____. "The Nature of Peter Matthiessen." *The New York Times Biographical Service*, 21 (June), 560–563.
Reprint of **H101**.

H103. "The Great Bears." *Outside*, 15 (November), [18].

Two letters from Harold Brink and William E. Rideg in response to Matthiessen's article on grizzly bears. One letter praises the article, while the other is critical of Matthiessen's romanticized and softened image of the grizzly.
See **C91** and **I84**.

H104. Hassan, Ihab. "Peter Matthiessen: The Fullness of Quest." In his *Selves at Risk: Patterns of Quest in Contemporary American Letters*. Madison: University of Wisconsin Press. Pp. 180–201.

An astute and admiring, albeit critical, examination and interpretation of Matthiessen's work within the context of quest literature. The expeditions Matthiessen participates in are meldings of personal, social, scientific, philosophic, and literary interests. The quests are allegories of failed existence between man and beast, civilization and wilderness. *The Snow Leopard*, a landmark in the literature of the quest, is especially

examined as Matthiessen's best work, although it is a flawed book. In it Matthiessen has combined several dimensions: the horizontal, vertical, temporal, cultural, generic, and spiritual. The book's triumph is that he does not write abstractly; the book is rooted in this world despite its spiritual virtues and intent. The quest motif is also found in *Far Tortuga* and *At Play in the Fields of the Lord*, and both are examined but to a lesser extent than is *The Snow Leopard*. It is in *At Play in the Fields of the Lord* and in *The Snow Leopard* that Matthiessen comes closest to realizing the form of quest — the ideal of selves at richest risk.
See also **H82**.

H105. "Hayduke Lives." *Outside*, 15 (December), 12, 14.

Four letters from Wanda Rokash, K. R. Peach, Dustin L. Martin, and Alan Blasenstein commenting on Matthiessen's article on the grizzly bears in Glacier National Park. While three of the letters praise the article, one questions the purpose in publicizing a secluded area free of bureaucratic interference and rangers.
See **C91** and **H103**.

H106. Howarth, William. "Getting Down to Earth: 20 Years Later." *Book World*, [*Washington Post*], 1 April, p. 1.

In observance of Earth Day, *The Snow Leopard* is one of several examples of nature writing briefly discussed.

H107. Jones, Malcolm, Jr. "A Murder in Paradise." *Newsweek*, 115 (11 June), [63]–64.

A profile of Matthiessen on the publication of *Killing Mister Watson*. Matthiessen defies easy categorization as a writer. He speaks about his interest in Watson and how a man is metamorphosed into a legend, as well as his love of backcountry Florida, and the balance he seeks among his fiction, nonfiction, and advocacy journalism.

H108. Matousek, Mark. "Call of the Wild." *Harper's Bazaar*, 123 (July), 18, 22.

A review/notice of *Killing Mister Watson* ("Matthiessen's powers have never been riper"), and a brief, generous (but superficial) profile of Matthiessen and his career.

H109. McDonald, William J. "*At Play in the Fields of the Lord.*" In *Cyclopedia of Literary Characters II.* Ed. Frank N. Magill. Pasadena, CA: Salem Press. Vol. 1, pp. 81–82.

Brief descriptions of thirteen characters from the novel.

Reprinted in **H193**.

H110. Nelson, John S. "*Far Tortuga.*" In *Cyclopedia of Literary Characters II.* Ed. Frank N. Magill. Pasadena, CA: Salem Press. Vol. 2, pp. 491–492.

Capsule descriptions of the eleven principal characters in the novel.

Reprinted in **H194**.

H111. Robertson, William K. "Legend About Killing Had 'Stuck in My Brain.'" *Miami Herald*, 24 June, "Viewpoint," p. 7C.

This interview was edited from a telephone conversation with Matthiessen and centers upon *Killing Mister Watson*, Matthiessen's knowledge of south Florida, and his research for the novel. His answers are generally very brief and to the point, whether from the editing or his own taciturnity.

H112. Von Drehle, Dave. "Zen and the Art of Writing." *Miami Herald*, 15 July, "Living Today," p. 1I.

An interesting and expansive profile of Matthissen and a chronicle of his career. Particular attention is paid to *Killing Mister Watson* and the people and country of Chokoloskee.

H113. Wick, Steve. "In the Spirit of Justice Peter Matthiessen Has Criss-Crossed the Country on Behalf of Leonard Peltier." *Newsday*, 15 August, Part II, p. 4.

An informative profile of Matthiessen and his activities on behalf of Peltier and the new edition of *In the Spirit of Crazy Horse* and to raise money for a planned documentary on Peltier's case.

H114. Winterowd, W. Ross. "Peter Matthiessen's Lyric Trek." In his *The Rhetoric of the "Other" Literature.* Carbondale: Southern Illinois University Press. Pp. 133–139.

A largely descriptive, although appreciative, account of *The Snow Leopard* as natural history, travel book, documentary, and philosophical novel. The total narrative unity of the work is contrasted to Barry Lopez's disunified *Arctic Dreams.* (*Arctic Dreams* is discussed separately within the chapter "Reading: Nature to Advantage Dress'd," pp. 119–139).

See **H95**.

1991

H115. Becker, Peter. "Zen and the Art of Peter Matthiessen." *M Inc.*, 8 (July), 54, 56–57.

Failing to get Matthiessen to agree to an interview about the publication of *African Silences*, Becker is invited to attend a meditation session at Matthiessen's zendo in Sagaponack. The focus of the article is more about Becker's uncomfortableness and inexperience during the ceremony, although a superficial portrait of Matthiessen as sensei and of the zendo itself is given.

H116. Bishop, George. "Peter Matthiessen." In *Beacham's Popular Fiction 1991 Update.* Ed. Walton Beacham, David W. Lowe, Katharine McLucas, and Charles W. Moseley. Washington, D.C.: Beacham Publishing, Inc. Vol. 2, pp. 819–822.

Killing Mister Watson is analyzed following set categories. The novel is a major advance for Matthiessen. It goes beyond his previous work in its thematic and formal complexity and maturity. It is an achievement of great originality.

See also **H67** and **H171**.

H117. "Books: What Writers Are Reading." *MS*, NS 2 (July/August), 83–84 [82–85].

A number of women writers provide brief statements concerning the books they are reading. Columnist Molly Ivins includes

Killing Mister Watson and comments on its extraordinary sense of place and Matthiessen's ability to make the reader feel and smell any place he writes about.

H118. Brown, Chip. "At Play in the Fields of Hollywood." *Esquire*, 116 (July), 110–[118].

The story of the more than twenty year attempt to bring *At Play in the Fields of the Lord* to the screen, complete with Hollywood machinations, logistical problems, and a cast of hundreds, including Paul Newman, Bob Rafelson, John Huston, Taylor Hackford, and, finally, producer Saul Zaentz and director Hector Babenco is examined.

H119. Carr, C. "Trail of Tears: One Hundred Years in the Life of the Lakota Sioux." *Voice Literary Supplement*, November, pp. 12–15.

In an essay reviewing the relationship between the federal government and the Sioux over the past 100 years, from the battle at Little Big Horn to the organization of the American Indian Movement and the shootout at Pine Ridge Reservation, *In the Spirit of Crazy Horse* is cited a number of times. People who read the book will find it difficult to argue against granting Leonard Peltier a new trial. The lawsuits brought against Matthiessen and Viking Press are briefly noted as is Matthiessen's epilogue in the reissued edition which concerns his interview with "X." In a sidebar accompanying the essay, "History Lessons," the book is listed among seven titles. It is a "powerful piece of advocacy journalism." Matthiessen's tone is even-handed even though one can sense his moral outrage. The racism and abuse of power he documents are "absolutely shocking."

H120. Catalfo, Phil. "Return of Crazy Horse." *New Age Journal*, 7 (May), 31–32, 98–99.

A review and discussion of the incidents at the Pine Ridge Reservation that led to the deaths of two F.B.I. agents and a Lakota man, and the subsequent trial and conviction of Leonard Peltier. The legal and political efforts on behalf of Peltier are examined.

The legal ordeal of Matthiessen and Viking Press over the law suits brought against *In the Spirit of Crazy Horse* and the new revelations in the epilogue of the revised edition of the book are also discussed.

H121. Cobbs, John L. "Peter Matthiessen." In *Critical Survey of Long Fiction*. English Language Series. Revised Edition. Ed. Frank N. Magill. Pasadena, CA: Salem Press. Vol. 5, pp. 2308–2320.

Essentially a reprint of **H54** with the addition of a brief note concerning *Killing Mister Watson*.
See also **H215**.

H122. Donnelly, John. "Mister Watson Author Plans to Revisit Character." *Miami Herald*, 13 November, "Local," p. 1B.

A brief report on Matthiessen's talk at the Miami Book Fair International where he spoke of his long time interest in the story of Edgar J. Watson and of his plans to complete the story with "one or two more volumes."

H123. Dowie, William. *Peter Matthiessen*. Boston: Twayne Publishers.

Remarkably, this is the only book length study of either Matthiessen's fiction or nonfiction. Fortunately, it is an excellent examination of his fiction through *Killing Mister Watson* and of his nonfiction through *Men's Lives*. It is a clearly written, perceptive, and fair-minded critical analysis. Dowie has structured his examination of the work by decades which allows him to easily show relationships among Matthiessen's writings and his social and ecological concerns.

H124. Gagnon, Deb. "*In the Spirit of …* Criticized by First Nations Editor." <http://www.dickshovel.com/giaggo.craz y.html>. (19 January 2000).

Tim Giago believes *In the Spirit of Crazy Horse* is a one-sided book which contains many errors as well as "outright lies." While glad that the courts upheld Matthiessen's First Amendment rights, Giago says that William Janklow certainly has a right to sue.

The "ultraliberal people" are trying to make Leonard Peltier a saint. Any comparison between him and Crazy Horse is ludicrous and embarrassing. Matthiessen only interviewed American Indian Movement members; he made no effort to interview those people that AIM made allegations and libelous charges against.

See **H125**.

H125. Giago, Tom. "Misguided Advocacy Journalism Twists Facts." *Lakota Times*, 12 February, p. A4.

Reacting to an editorial by Bob Hulteen in *Sojourners* which tries to "elevate Leonard Peltier to the status of a martyred saint," Giago suggests that he has taken a lot of his misinformation from *In the Spirit of Crazy Horse*. It is a book filled with inaccuracies and outright lies. All of the false accusations in the book have been "debunked" many times over. The focus of the article is on Hulteen rather than Matthiessen.

See **H124**.

H126. Graeber, Laurel. "As Elephant Goes …" *New York Times Book Review*, 18 August, p. 3.

A brief sidebar to the review of *African Silences*. In a telephone interview Matthiessen states his belief that the survey conducted with Dr. David Western was instrumental in the international ban on ivory, and he is hopeful that the wildlife will ultimately benefit. For him, the title of the book is elegiac but also celebratory.

H127. Hassan, Ihab Habib. "The Spirit of Quest in Contemporary American Letters."

In *Writers and Their Craft*. Ed. Nicholas Delbanco and Laurence Goldstein. Detroit: Wayne State University Press, pp. 364–383.

Reprint of **H82**. See also **H160**.

H128. Joyce, Lionel. "What Rasputin Said." *The New York Review of Books*, 38 (April 11), 61.

In response to Matthiessen's portrait of Valentin Rasputin in his article on Lake Baikal, Joyce questions the morality of the Russian writer based on his comments concerning homosexuality, as well as Matthiessen's defense of him as an illiberal but moral man.

See **C96**.

H129. Marvel, Mark. "Why Write Now?" *Interview*, 21 (May), 70.

Matthiessen is one of seven authors who respond to the question, "What did you get out of writing your book?" Getting *In the Spirit of Crazy Horse* republished is significant since it is the primary organizing tool to promote Leonard Peltier's story. Matthiessen believes Peltier's case is "the single most important example of human rights violations in this country since Sacco and Vanzetti."

H130. Muste, John M. "Killing Mister Watson." In *Magill's Literary Annual 1991*. Ed. Frank N. Magill. Pasadena, CA: Salem Press. Vol. 2, pp. 480–484.

A summary and analysis of the novel is given. The first half of the story moves slowly, but it gathers momentum and dramatic force. Matthiessen is fascinated by the character of Watson himself, but he also uses him to present a history of a particular time and place. This is not always a clear novel, but it is ultimately a memorable one.

H131. "Peter Matthiessen." In *Authors & Artists for Young People*. Ed. Agnes Garrett and Helga P. McCue. Detroit: Gale Research, Inc. Vol. 6, pp. 129–138.

A well balanced, straightforward overview of Matthiessen's life and career, especially his experience with Zen, drawn extensively from his own work and secondary sources.

H132. Peterman, Gina D. and Timothy C. Lundy. "Peter Matthiessen." In *Facts on File Bibliography of American Fiction 1919–1988*. Ed. Matthew J. Bruccoli and Judith S. Baughman. New York: Facts on File. Vol. 2, pp. 331–332.

A woefully incomplete and arbitrary bibliographic listing of primary and secondary sources.

H133. Shnayerson, Michael. "Higher Matthiessen." *Vanity Fair*, 54 (December), 114, 116, 120, 122, 124, 128, 130, 132.

A wide-ranging profile of Matthiessen on the occasion of the production of the film version of *At Play in the Fields of the Lord*. The article achieves a well balanced view between his professional and personal lives and relationships. It emphasizes his comparative lack of recognition and acclaim as a writer.

1992

H134. McNamee, Gregory. "The Books That Mattered." *Outside*, 17 (October), 182, 184.

The Snow Leopard is included within a list of fifteen books of nature, travel, and outdoor life that will endure. It is "an exquisite book of nature and travel writing, and more: a grand Buddhist parable."

H135. Okrent, Neil. "*At Play in the Fields of the Lord*: An Interview with Hector Babenco." *Cineaste*, 19 (no. 1), 44–47.

In an interview discussing the film adaptation of Matthiessen's novel, Babenco, the film's director, makes several belligerent comments regarding the book and Matthiessen's original intentions. He talks about the changes he sought to make in the film version of the story, particularly in the character of Lewis Moon.

H136. Reilly, John M. "Matthiessen, Peter." In *Contemporary Novelists*. 5th edition. Ed. Lesley Henderson. Chicago: St. James Press, pp. 614–616.

Expanded biographical and bibliographical listings accompany a reprint of the essay from **H52**.

H137. Richardson, John H. "Twofer." *Premiere*, 5 (April), 29–30.

An examination of the difficulties of bringing Leonard Peltier's story to the screen based on *In the Spirit of Crazy Horse*. A conflict developed between Robert Redford's plans for a documentary and Oliver Stone's interest in a motion picture. Though

only tangentially concerned with Matthiessen, he is quoted regarding Redford's involvement in the conflict.

H138. Shone, Tom. "A War of Attrition Against Their Own." *The Independent* [London], (May 30), 31.

A profile of Matthiessen that is primarily concerned with *In the Spirit of Crazy Horse* and the case of Leonard Peltier. Matthiessen wanted to avoid a strident polemic and let the facts of the case speak for themselves. The intent of the work was to win Peltier his freedom. Matthiessen would consider returning to the book if that happens to cut it by a third and achieve a more literary work.

1993

H139. Axelrod, Alan and Charles Phillips. "Matthiessen, Peter (May 22, 1927–)." In their *The Environmentalists: A Biographical Dictionary from the 17th Century to the Present*. New York: Facts on File, Inc. Pp. 149–150.

A superficial biographical and professional portrait focusing upon Matthiessen's non–fiction works. With *Wildlife in America* Matthiessen discovered his "true vocation as a writer," travelling to wild places, recording his impressions and shaping them into books. He is considered one of the 20th century's most important wilderness writers.

H140. Bawer, Bruce. "Peter Matthiessen, Nature Boy." In his *The Aspect of Eternity*. St. Paul, MN: Graywolf Press, pp. [36]–50.

Reprint of **H76**.

H141. Harrison, Jim. "Pie in the Sky." *Esquire Sportsman*, 2 (Fall/Winter), 33–34.

The rereading of *Wildlife in America* inspires the idea that if every member of Congress would read it along with *Sand County Almanac*, *Desert Solitaire*, and *Practice of the Wild*, then there would be no need for an environmental movement. These books contain the restorative power of knowledge. *Wildlife in America* is a gorgeously written, seminal book calling people to action. Harrison calls for everyone to make a concerted effort to act locally, concerned that no one in Congress actually reads books.

H142. [Houy, Deborah]. "A Moment with Peter Matthiessen." *Buzzworm*, 5 (March/April), 28.

A brief but revealing interview.

H143. Iyer, Pico. "Laureate of the Wild." *Time*, 141 (11 January), 42–44.

A profile of Matthiessen, the "practical rebel," as writer, environmentalist, and Zen practitioner. Nearly all of his books "simply trace the dialogue of light and dark," but his fiction is often more demanding than his nonfiction; it is daunting, punishing, and ambitious. Despite his obvious gifts as a writer, Matthiessen's various interests and genres may work against his achieving the reputation and audience he otherwise might. Reprinted in **H186.**

H144. Lopez, Ken. "Collecting Peter Matthiessen." <http://www.lopez.com/articles/matthies.html>. (5 June 1998).

This is an informative essay on the publication history of Matthiessen's work with some helpful distinctions made concerning issues of a number of his books.

H145. Sacharow, Anya. "Zoo Story." *Art News*, 92 (January), 20, 22.

A notice of the collaborative effort between Matthiessen and artist Mary Frank to produce *Shadows of Africa* and the origins of the project. The focus is more on Frank and her studies from animals in zoos rather than from Africa itself.

H146. Shainberg, Lawrence. "Emptying the Bell: An Interview with Peter Matthiessen." *Tricycle*, 3 (Fall), 42–47.

All aspects of this interview are related to Zen and Zen practice as it pertains to Matthiessen's life, his work as a writer, and literature in general.

H147. Wiener, Jon. "Murdered Ink." *The Nation*, 256 (31 May), 747–748 [743–750].

In an essay about why and how publishers "kill" books, *In the Spirit of Crazy Horse* is one of the six books discussed. The circumstances surrounding the book are briefly reviewed. Viking Press acquiesced to William Janklow's lawsuit by destroying the warehouse copies of the book and withdrawing it from publication. Matthiessen was unaware of the destruction of the copies and disagreed with Viking's "overcautious" decision to keep the book out of print. While large publishers might be expected to defend their books vigorously, they seem often to be motivated by fear and greed than a commitment to their authors, their readers, and the First Amendment.

1994

H148. Adamson, Shawn. "Interviewing Mister Matthiessen." *Proteus* [Southampton College, Long Island University], 66–78.

An interesting and informative interview with Matthiessen providing expansive answers to a wide-ranging (if sometimes predictable) array of questions.

H149. Cooley, John. "Matthiessen's Voyages on the River Styx: Deathly Waters, Endangered People." In his *Earthly Words: Essays on Contemporary American Nature and Environmental Writers*. Ann Arbor: The University of Michigan Press. Pp. 167–192.

Matthiessen uses the River Styx, either directly or indirectly, as a trope in *The Cloud Forest, At Play in the Fields of the Lord, Far Tortuga,* "On the River Styx," and *Killing Mister Watson.* Each of these works is concerned with the "often-neglected margins," areas of rapid change and human and environmental degradation. The ecological and social issues of each work are examined with extended discussions of *Far Tortuga* and *Killing Mister Watson.* While Matthiessen employs elements of the pastoral in these works, his tone is that of pastoral irony, and his form is that of pastoral fragmentation. Habitat destruction is dramatized but Matthiessen does not offer models of resolution nor does he embrace a particular ecological vision.

An introductory biographical essay (pp. 165–166) prefaces the essay.

H150. Cutts, David. "Profiles: Peter Matthiessen's Life and Works." *Proteus* [Southampton College, Long Island University], 31–34.

A succinct overview of Matthiessen's career. The combining of fact and fiction in *Killing Mister Watson* seems to be representative of his career as a powerful and versatile writer.

H151. Koger, Grove. "All At Sea." *Wilson Library Bulletin*, 69 (December), 38 [36–39].

In an article concerned with the best sea literature in print, *Far Tortuga* is included in the list of essential titles and briefly discussed as an intense, poetic drama. With *Moby-Dick* and *The Sea Wolf*, it is one of the masterpieces of American sailing fiction.

H152. Raglon, Rebecca. "Fact and Fiction: The Development of Ecological Form in Peter Matthiessen's *Far Tortuga*." *Critique*, 35 (Summer), 245–259.

Matthiessen's career and, in particular, *Far Tortuga* demonstrate that underlying any ecologically concerned writer's work is the perception of the interrelatedness of all life. *Far Tortuga* and Matthieesen's work are examined for the means by which he attempts to reconcile the conflict between humanity and nature, and for the influence of Zen upon his approach. The roles of Raib, Speedy, and Desmond are discussed at some length.

H153. Revkin, Andrew. "Roasting Mr. Matthiessen." *New York Magazine*, 27 (7 March), 30.

Matthiessen is named the subject of the annual roast to raise money for The Rainforest Alliance. He will be roasted by George Plimpton, E. L. Doctorow, and William Styron among others despite his "considerable reluctance."

H154. White, Jonathan. "Inochi, Life Integrity." In his *Talking on the Water: Conversations About Nature and Creativity*. San Francisco: Sierra Club Books. Pp. [229]–245.

An interview with Matthiessen focusing upon his experiences and relationships with the land, the wild, and the native peoples he has written about. The case of Leonard Peltier and *In the Spirit of Crazy Horse*, as well as the writing process are also discussed. *See also* **H155** and **H168**.

H155. _____. "Talking on the Water: Wisdom about the Earth, Dispersed from a Floating Podium." *Sierra*, 79 (May/ June), 73 [72–75].

Two questions and answers from White's interview are presented. *See* **H154**.

1995

H156. Anderson, Scott. "The Crumbling Conspiracy Theory." *Outside*, 20 (November), 22, 24.

Anderson replies to Matthiessen's rebuttal of his original article. He refutes the foundation of Matthiessen's conspiracy-theory pyramid concerning Leonard Peltier's arrest and conviction. He answers the arguments that Matthiessen presents in replying to the original article. *See* **C130** and **H157**.

H157. _____. "The Martyrdom of Leonard Peltier." *Outside*, 20 (July), [44]–55, 120–126.

A reexamination of the events leading to the conviction of American Indian Movement (AIM) member Leonard Peltier for the murders of two F.B.I. agents on the Oglala Sioux Pine Ridge Reservation in South Dakota in 1975. *In the Spirit of Crazy Horse* is widely accepted as the definitive account of the events at Pine Ridge, but Anderson believes it is a "curious book" whose story is casually documented. Matthiessen presents an unsubstantiated "über-conspiracy" concerning the government's wish to destroy Peltier and AIM to gain access to uranium deposits on the reservation. He stretches the truth of the case to fit his theory.

Although not the primary focus of the article, the latter part discusses Matthiessen's involvement with the Peltier case and the writing of *In the Spirit of Crazy Horse*. Matthiessen is one of the primary architects of the Peltier myth. The book was instrumental in revitalizing the free Peltier movement and focusing attention on him as a martyr and international cause-celebre rather than as a man. Matthiessen's interview with the now discredited X, the confessed killer of the agents, is also discussed in the context of an interview with Dino Butler, one of the defendants in the original case.

See **A24, H156, H158,** and **H161–H163.**

H158. "Character Witnesses." *Outside,* 20 (November), [28].

Two letters from Doug Peacock and Victor Emanuel supporting the integrity of Matthiessen as a writer and as a person in light of Anderson's article on the Leonard Peltier case.

See **H157.**

H159. Flag, Johnny. "Banned Books, 1995." *The Ojibwe News,* September 29, p. 8.

Within an article discussing banned books, William J. Janklow's attack against *In the Spirit of Crazy Horse* and the three South Dakota bookstores who sold the book is cited.

H160. Hassan, Ihab Habib. "The Spirit of Quest in Contemporary American Letters." In his *Rumors of Change: Essays of Four Decades.* Tuscaloosa: The University of Alabama Press, pp. [187]–207.

Reprint of **I82.**

H161. "Lawyers, Guns, and Martyrdom." *Outside,* 20 (October), 18, 22.

William M. Kunstler, E. K. Caldwell, and Laurel Berger respond in three letters to "The Martyrdom of Leonard Peltier." Kunstler and Caldwell dispute Anderson's representation of Dino Butler's view of

Matthiessen and *In the Spirit of Crazy Horse.* Berger writes in support of Matthiessen's personal intergrity.

See **H157.**

H162. "The Making of Leonard Peltier." *Outside,* 20 (September), 20.

Four letters from the Leonard Peltier Defense Committee, Randy Wayne White, Frederic Alan Maxwell, and Rick Telander in response to Scott Anderson's article on the Leonard Peltier case. The Peltier Defense Committee and White letters specifically defend Matthiessen's intergrity and work on behalf of Peltier and refute the idea that he is a liar.

See **H157.**

H163. Peltier, Leonard. "Since I'm the Object of So Much Discussion, I Believe It's My Turn to Speak." *News From Indian Country,* 10 (December 31), 17A.

Peltier responds to Scott Anderson's articles in *Outside* regarding him and his case. He also addresses what he believes to be Anderson's attempt to demean Matthiessen's character. He and "many Indian people" are outraged over this. Peltier claims that *In the Spirit of Crazy Horse* is one of the "finest and most professionally researched and footnoted reports of any historical event."

See **H157.**

H164. "Peter Matthiessen, New York State Author." *New York State Writers Institute.* <http://www.albany.edu/writers-inst/matthisn.html>. (25 February 1999).

A brief biographical and professional profile noting Matthiessen's being awarded the New York State Edith Wharton Citation of Merit for fiction writers and serving as New York State Author for two years. A seminar and reading by Matthiessen in Albany, New York is announced.

H165. "Peter Matthiessen State Author, 1995–1997." *New York State Writers Institute.* <http://www.albany.edu/writers-inst/matsnsa.html>. (25 February 1999).

A concise overview of Matthiessen's work.

H166. Powers, William F. "The Magazine Reader." *Washington Post*, 20 June, "Style," p. E7.

A notice of the July 1995 issue of *Outside* magazine which goes after "two cultural demigods" in Matthiessen and Leonard Peltier. A brief review of Peltier's case, Matthiessen's involvement, and Anderson's article is given. Matthiessen's piece in *Audubon* on the red-crowned cranes of Japan and in *Shambala Sun* on his journey to a valley near the Tibet-Nepal border are also cited and briefly discussed.

See **C123**, **C129** and **H157**.

H167. _____. "The Magazine Reader." *Washington Post*, 26 September, "Style," p. E7.

A notice of Matthiessen's rebuttal to Scott Anderson's article in *Outside* with a brief overview of the "battle" between to the two.

See **C130** and **H157**.

H168. White, Jonathan. "At Home In the World: An Interview with Peter Matthiessen." *The Sun*, no. 229 (January), 4–10.

An excerpt from **H154**.

1996

H169. Bishop, George. "At Play in the Fields of the Lord." In *Beacham's Encyclopedia of Popular Fiction*. (Analyses Series). Ed. Kirk H. Beetz. Osprey, FL: Beacham Publishing Corporation. Vol. 1, pp. 218–221.

A reprint of **H67** with a brief one paragraph discussion of the film adaptation and a series of "Ideas for Group Discussions."

H170. _____. "Far Tortuga." In *Beacham's Encyclopedia of Popular Fiction*. Ed. Kirk H. Beetz. (Analyses Series). Osprey, FL: Beacham Publishing Corporation. Vol. 3, pp. 1357–1360.

An "Ideas for Group Discussions" section has been added to a reprint of **H67**.

H171. _____. "Killing Mister Watson." In *Beacham's Encyclopedia of Popular Fiction*.

Ed. Kirk H. Beetz. (Analyses Series). Osprey, FL: Beacham Publishing Corporation. Vol. 4, pp. 2274–2277.

A reprint of **H116** with an "Ideas for Group Discussions" section added.

H172. _____. and Robert J. McNutt. "Peter Matthiessen 1927." In *Beacham's Encyclopedia of Popular Fiction*. (Biography Series). Ed. Kirk H. Beetz. Osprey, FL: Beacham Publishing Corporation. Vol. B2, pp. 1216–1221.

The "About the Author" section by McNutt provides a brief biographical overview. The section entitled "Publishing History, Critical Reception, Honors, and Popularity," is a reprint of the respective sections from **H67**.

H173. Dowie, William. "Peter Matthiessen." In *American Novelists Since World War II*. Fifth Series. Ed. James R. Giles and Wanda H. Giles. *Dictionary of Literary Biography*, vol. 173. Detroit: Gale Research. Pp. 132–147.

A well presented overview of Matthiessen's life and career. He has produced a body of work "distinguished by its quanity, breadth, commitment, and style." *Far Tortuga* and *The Snow Leopard* represent Matthiessen's best fiction and non-fiction of his career so far.

H174. Flowers, Charles. "Totch Brown, 76, Dead." *Seminole Tribune*, 18 (May 31), 1.

An obituary of Loren "Totch" Brown who "taught" Matthiessen about "Bloody" Ed Watson, and whose recollections, among others, formed the basis for *Killing Mister Watson*.

H175. Hale, Frederick. "Peter Matthiessen's Displaced Cheyenne Vision Quest." *European Review of Native American Studies*, 10 (no. 1), 37–42.

Hale examines the character of Lewis Moon from *At Play in the Fields of the Lord* as an example of Matthiessen's early sympathetic treatment of Native Americans. Of particular importance is Moon's ayahuasca induced version of the Plains Indian vision quest and its importance within the novel and to the development of Moon's character as he comes to terms with his own ethnic legacy. Hale places Matthiessen's depiction of Moon's vision quest within an anthropological and historical review of the Cheyenne vision quest and Matthiessen's own use of hallucinogens. Some brief remarks are also made concerning the differences between the novel and the film adaptation's portrayal of Moon and the vision quest.

H176. Harvey, Miles. "The Outside Canon: A Few Great Books." *Outside*, 21 (May), 78 [66–76, 78, 80].

Within a listing of fiction and poetry, "Outside Lit 101," *At Play in the Fields of the Lord* is listed as a "gripping" novel and as a prophetic warning about the razing of the rainforest.

H177. "Matthiessen, Peter 1927– ." In *Contemporary Authors*. New Revision Series. Ed. Pamela S. Dear. Detroit: Gale Research. Vol. 50, pp. 301–307.

A revised and expanded sketch from **H73** including a discussion of *Killing Mister Watson* and the legal controversy surrounding *In the Spirit of Crazy Horse*. *See* **H73**.

H178. Payne, Daniel G. "Peter Matthiessen." In *American Nature Writers*. Ed. John Elder. New York: Charles Scribner's Sons. Vol. 2, pp. 599–613.

This is an excellent overview of Matthiessen's life and career. It is composed of discussions of major works of fiction and nonfiction, including *Wildlife in America, The Cloud Forest, At Play in the Fields of the Lord, Under the Mountain Wall, Far Tortuga*, Matthiessen's fascination with Africa and the works that have resulted from it, and *The Snow Leopard*. There is a surprisingly brief account of his social criticism. The brevity of this section is accounted for by the assessment that, with the exception of *Men's Lives*, Matthiessen's social criticism is generally not the equal of his best works of other nonfiction.

H179. Reilly, John M. "Matthiessen, Peter." In *Contemporary Novelists*. 6th ed.

Ed. Susan Windisch Brown. New York: St. James Press, 670–672.

The essay remains unchanged from the previous edition. Items have been added to the biographical and bibliographical listings. *See* **H136**.

H180. Worthington, Peter. "Commentary on Peltier — Still in Prison, and Still Innocent." *News From Indian Country*, 10 (April 15), 14A.

In a review of Peltier's case and the movement for executive clemency, Scott Anderson's *Outside* article is briefly discussed as is Matthiessen's rebuttal arguing that no critic has made a substantial dent in the documentation that he presents to show that Peltier was railroaded. *See* **C130** and **H157**.

1997

H181. Baringer, Sandra K. "Indian Activism and the American Indian Movement: A Bibliographical Essay." *American Indian Culture and Research Journal*, 21 (no. 4) 229–230 [217–250].

In the Spirit of Crazy Horse is the leading work on the case of Leonard Peltier. It is the most comprehensive and well-researched book available on the history of AIM at Pine Ridge Reservation. While it is controversial and detailed to a fault, it is thorough enough to allow readers to come to their own conclusions.

H182. Barry, John. "Welcoming Mr. Matthiessen." *Miami Herald*, 8 November, "Living," p. 1G.

A report on Matthiessen's trip to Chokoloskee Bay after the publication of *Lost Man's River* discusses the people's reaction to the story of Edgar Watson. It also examines Matthiessen's relationships with the people of the area and their lives, what he admires about them despite their "political" differences with him. His attraction to the Watson story and the development of the trilogy from "a mountainous, handwritten draft" which he had originally intended to be a novel about the whole Everglades is reviewed.

H183. [Bonetti, Kay]. "Peter Matthiessen." In *Conversations with American Novelists: The Best Interviews from The Missouri Review and the American Audio Prose Library*. Ed. Kay Bonetti, Greg Michalson, Speer Morgan, Jo Sapp, and Sam Stowers. Columbia: University of Missouri Press, pp. 142–152.

Reprint of **H88**.

H184. Carroll, Jerry. "Writer's Restless Mind Keeps Him Working." *San Francisco Chronicle*, 22 November, p. D1.

The publication of *Lost Man's River* occasions this profile of Matthiessen. The focus of the article is on the dual pull of fiction and nonfiction in his career. While acknowledging his intense curiosity and restless mind, Matthiessen insists that he only began writing nonfiction to support his family. Though fiction is his first love, he is presently working on two more nonfiction projects.

H185. Cryer, Dan. "Talking with Peter Matthiessen: A Traveler Home From the Swamp." *Newsday*, 14 December, "Currents & Books," p. B11.

After some brief biographical information, the primary focus of this profile is Matthiessen's interest in the Edgar Watson story and the ongoing trilogy. There is some discussion about the division between his fiction and nonfiction work.

H186. Iyer, Pico. "Peter Matthieseen: In Search of the Crane." In his *Tropical Classical: Essays from Several Directions*. New York: Alfred A. Knopf. Pp. [110]–114.

Reprint, with an alternate title, of **H143**.

H187. Jones, Amanda. "Favorite Travel Books: The Snow Leopard." *Salon*, 8 July. <http://www.salonmagazine.com/july97/wanderlust/matthiessen970708.html>. (18 June 1999).

Given a cheap copy of the book by a Sherpa accompanying her on a trek on Kanchenjunga, the third tallest mountain in the world, Jones reads it on her journey down the mountain. She finds that Matthiessen's words and experiences begin to resonate with her, and the book springs to life.

H188. Keiser, Ellen. "Book to Film." *Dan's Papers* [Bridgehampton, New York], 1 August, pp. 29, 56.

A casual account of Matthiessen's particpation in a discussion series on film adaptations and of his own less than satisfying experiences with Hollywood and film projects. The article includes brief references to Hector Babenco's film of *At Play in the Fields of the Lord* and the failure to make a film based on *In the Spirit of Crazy Horse*.

H189. "PW's Best Books '97." *Publishers Weekly*, 244 (3 November), 52 [50–60].

Lost Man's River is selected as one of the best books of fiction. It is a "haunting jeremiad to the ecological and cultural depredation of the region."

H190. Ross-Bryant, Lynn. "The Self In Nature: Four American Autobiographies." *Soundings*, 80 (Spring), 83–104.

The Snow Leopard is one of four works used to "re-image" the relationship between the self and environment in autobiography. Matthiessen does not see himself as separate from nature but as a particpant in the world. His journey is not apart from nature or the world. This view seems to strike Ross-Bryant as odd, and she is uncomfortable with the fact that Matthiessen seems comfortable with not having found total resolution; she questions whether he truly sees the "incongruities between the self and its world and the self and itself." Matthiessen fails to address "the 'problem' of the metaphysical self." She cites the influence of Asian religions on his view of the world. Ross-Bryant tries to force Matthiessen into her pre-existing ideas of the self and its relationship to autobiographical models. (The other writers included in the essay are Annie Dillard, William Least Heat Moon, and Terry Tempest Williams).

1998

H191. Garbus, Martin with Stanley Cohen. *Tough Talk: How I Fought for Writers, Comics, Bigots, and the American Way.* New York: Times Books, pp. 139–155.

Garbus, the attorney who represented Matthiessen and Viking Press in the libel suits brought by William J. Janklow and David Price over the publication of *In the Spirit of Crazy Horse,* discusses the cases and the seven years of litigation. He provides the legal background of the cases, their merits, differences, and the First Amendment ramifications. He comments on the people involved, both directly and indirectly. He has particular admiration for the judges in both cases.

See also **H90**.

H192. Knight, Heather. "LIer Patsy Southgate, 70; Writer, Poet, Theater Critic." *Newsday,* 26 July, p. A41.

Matthiessen provides several brief comments regarding his first wife and their life together in Paris.

H193. McDonald, William J. "*At Play in the Fields of the Lord.*" In *Cyclopedia of Literary Characters.* Revised Edition. Ed. A. J. Sobczak. Pasadena, CA: Salem Press. Vol. 1, pp. 107–108.

Reprint of **H109**.

H194. Nelson, John J. "*Far Tortuga.*" In *Cyclopedia of Literary Characters.* Revised Edition. Ed. A. J. Sobczak. Pasadena, CA: Salem Press. Vol. 2, p. 624.

Reprint of **H110**.

H195. "'New Yorkers Aren't Interested in Stories About Swamp People': Peter Matthiessen: The Books Interview." *Observer,* 10 May, p. 17.

A wide-ranging interview. The questions and spare responses touch briefly upon his background, the environment, drug usage, and the Watson trilogy.

H196. Schupack, Adam. "Mathiessen [sic] Takes Audience On a Wildlife Adventure." *Herald Sphere* [Brown University], 6 March. <http://www.theherald.org/herald/issues/030698/lecture.f.html>. (26 July 1999).

A report on Matthiessen's President's Lecture at Brown University. He talked of his trips to Asia to observe cranes and tigers, and of his life-long interest in conservation.

H197. Seal, Jeremy. "On the Shelf." *Sunday Times,* 31 May, 8–9.

In search for the perfect safari book, *The Tree Where Man Was Born* provides a memorable evocation of East Africa's true wild places. It has been overshadowed by *The Snow Leopard,* but it may be the better work of the two. There is a sense that Africa is the one place that truly engages Matthiessen. His unflinching eye provides "a learned, poetic and profoundly moving portrait." The book is a wonderful and effortless mix of natural history, travelogue, anthropology, and personal reflection.

H198. Short, Carroll Dale. "Lost Man's River." *Magill's Literary Annual 1998.* Ed. John D. Wilson. Pasadena, CA: Salem Press. Vol. 2, pp. 530–533.

A brief overview of Matthiessen's interest in the story of Edgar Watson and the background of the planned trilogy precedes a discussion of the plot of the book. Matthiessen has the eye and ear of a born writer; his rendering of the various dialects is a marvel.

H199. Thomas, Robert McG., Jr. "Patsy Southgate, Who Inspired 50's Literary Paris, Dies at 70." *New York Times,* 26 July, p. 37.

The obituary of Matthiessen's first wife discusses their years together in Paris, the people they knew, and the inception of *The Paris Review.*

H200. "To Film *Men's Lives.*" *The East Hampton Star,* 4 June, p. I-1.

Producer James D'Ambrosio plans to film an adaptation of *Men's Lives* in East Hampton, and Matthiessen has served as a consultant on the project. Few specific details of the production are given, however.

1999

H201. "American Environmental Literature: Selected Classics and Recent Favorites." *Environment*, 41 (March), 8–9.

The Snow Leopard is one of 31 books listed. It is one of "the most vibrant and suspenseful examples of this genre."

H202. Clements, Andrew. "Wild at Heart." *The Guardian*, 26 October, p. 14.

This is an interesting profile that doesn't break any new ground but nicely coordinates and presents brief comments regarding Matthiessen's life and work.

H203. Dillingham, Thomas F. "Matthiessen, Peter." In *Encyclopedia of American Literature*. General editor, Steven R. Serafin. New York: Continuum. Pp. 732–733.

A succinct overview of Matthiessen's career. While he is best known for *The Snow Leopard*, *Men's Lives* is justly praised for its powerful evocation of a dying culture. His best fiction is to be found among *At Play in the Fields of the Lord*, *Far Tortuga*, and *Killing Mister Watson*.

H204. Gibson, James William. "Expert's Picks: Places." *Book World [Washington Post]*, 5 December 1999, p. 5.

Within a brief article on the documentation of lost places by American writers and photographers, *Bone by Bone* is one of the five works cited for its "brilliant meditation on frontier violence."

H205. "I Love Paris in the Fifties." *The Paris Review*, no. 150 (Spring), [320]–335.

Excerpts from a panel discussion on Paris in the 1950s held in Sag Harbor during the summer of 1998. Matthiessen was a participant and comments upon his years in Paris with his first wife, the starting of *The Paris Review*, and the people he knew, including James Baldwin, Terry Southern, and Irwin Shaw.

H206. Kahn, Joseph P. "A Writer's Wide, Wide World." *Boston Globe*, 1 June, "Living," p. C1.

A profile of Matthiessen on the occasion of *Bone by Bone*'s publication. He discusses the trilogy and his desire to one day reconstruct the original manuscript without "the scaffolding," his flirtations with the bestseller lists, the need to help publishers promote books, and, briefly, a few terrifying moments during his various trips.

H207. Kemasang, A. R. T. "China Can Make a Big Difference." *Financial Times* [London], 5 June, p. 10.

A letter in response to "Global Corporate Power," **C142**, which points out that China, by virtue of its population, could make a big difference even acting alone. China has missed an opportunity to act, and it is surprising that Matthiessen fails to refer to China in his article.

H208. "Matthiessen, Peter, 1927– ." In *Contemporary Authors*. New Revision Series. Ed. Daniel Jones and John D. Jorgenson. Detroit: The Gale Group. Vol. 73, pp. 313–319.

The essay from **H177** is condensed and information concerning *Lost Man's River* has been added to it. Minimal additions have also been made to the biographical and bibliographical listings.

H209. McCandless, Bruce. "Peter Matthiessen's Obsessions Continue." *Austin Chronicle*, (5 November). <http://www. auschron.com/issues/dispatch/1999-11-05 /books_feature3.html>. (2 May 2000).

A brief profile focusing upon the Watson trilogy.

H210. McNamara, Mary. "Creating a Killer Who's Larger Than Life." *Los Angeles Times*, 29 June, p. 1.

A discussion with Matthiessen while on tour promoting *Bone by Bone*. The character of Edgar Watson may be unique in the devotion and utter absorption he has received from a single author. None of Matthiessen's previous work resembles the scope, detail, and ambition of the Watson trilogy. The real challenge for him was to take the character of Watson and make him sympathetic, to make readers recognize the shared human condition even if they did not like him.

H211. Norman, Howard. "Peter Matthiessen: The Art of Fiction, CLVII." *The Paris Review*, no. 150 (Spring), [186]–215.

Not much new ground is explored in this interview other than Matthiessen's comments on the now completed Watson trilogy. The discussion covers his early career, the writing of fiction and nonfiction and his thoughts on each, and the taking of risks in life and in writing. *The Snow Leopard, Far Tortuga*, and *At Play in the Fields of the Lord*, in particular, are discussed.

H212. O'Briant, Dan. "Pioneer, Presley Have the Winning Touch." *The Atlanta Constitution*, 5 August, p. F2.

A brief announcement that *Bone by Bone* is the fiction winner of the Southern Book Awards presented by the Southern Book Critics Circle.

H213. Streitfeld, David. "Book Report." *Book World* [*Washington* Post], 9 May, p. X13.

A discussion with Matthiessen at the time of *Bone by Bone*'s publication. He talks briefly about his relative obscurity as a fiction writer, about his interest in Edgar Watson, as well as the resulting trilogy. Matthiessen sees Watson as a sympathetic figure: "he was only a criminal of the law." Part of the story's appeal to him is that it is about the destruction of the environment at the time when its despoliation is becoming widespread.

2000

H214. Berger, Laurel. "How We Met: Peter Matthiessen and Leonard Peltier." *The Independent* [London], 5 November, p. 86.

Matthiessen and Peltier briefly comment on how they became involved in each other's life and what that involvement has meant to each of them. Matthiessen admires Peltier's stoic quality and states that he will never walk away from him. Peltier believes

Matthiessen has "been a saviour to me," attracting attention to his course with *In the Spirit of Crazy Horse* and never asking for anything in return. He finds Matthiessen "probably more Indian in his heart than a lot of 'real' Indians."

H215. Cobbs, John L. Updated by Charles A. Gramlich. "Peter Matthiessen." In *Critical Survey of Long Fiction*. Second Revised Edition. Ed. Carl Rollyson, Pasadena, CA: Salem Press, Inc. Vol. 5, pp. 2205–2216.

A slightly revised version of **H121**, updated with an analysis of the Watson trilogy.

H216. Gatta, John. "Peter Matthiessen 1927– ." In *American Writers: A Collection of Literary Biographies*. Supplement V. Ed. Jay Parini. New York: Charles Scribner's Sons. Pp. 199–217.

A comprehensive biographical and critical overview with good discussions of both his fictional and non-fictional work; particular attention is paid to *The Snow Leopard* and the Watson trilogy. The completion of the trilogy with what may be Matthiessen's greatest work, *Bone by Bone*, will enhance his reputation as one of the late twentieth century's leading novelists.

H217. Holladay, Hal L. "Far Tortuga." In *Masterplots II: American Fiction Series, Revised Edition*. Ed. Steven G. Kellman. Pasadena, CA: Salem Press. Vol. 1, pp. 119–124.

Other than an expanded bibliography, this is a reprint of **H68**.

H218. Jones, Jane Anderson. "Bone by Bone." In *Magill's Literary Annual 2000*. Ed. John D. Wilson. Pasadena, CA: Salem Press, Inc. Vol. 1, pp. 82–85.

This is a synopsis of the novel with little, if any, evaluative comment. In the third book of the Watson trilogy, Edgar Watson's narration "moves outside the very real communal and ecological concerns" in *Killing Mister Watson*. This book focuses on Watson's psychological makeup and the historical context that helped shape it.

H219. Otten, Robert M. "At Play in the Fields of the Lord." In *Masterplots II: American Fiction Series, Revised Edition.* Ed. Steven G. Kellman. Pasadena, CA: Salem Press, Inc. Vol. 2, pp. 782–787.

Reprint of **H70** with a new six item bibliography.

H220. Sims, Michael. "A Series of Tiny Astonishments: An Interview with Peter Matthiessen." *Bookpage* (February), <http://www.bookpage.com/0002bp/peter_matthiessen.html>. (2 May 2000).

This is not a true question and answer interview, but Matthiessen's comments made during a telephone interview are incorporated into a profile of him that is primarily concerned with *Tigers in the Snow* and the Watson trilogy.

I. Book Reviews

RACE ROCK

I1. Baro, Gene. "During a Hectic Storm-Ridden Week End at Shipman's Crossing." *New York Herald Tribune Book Review*, 4 April, 1959, p. 3.

This is one of the more appreciative reviews of Matthiessen's first novel. The characters are handled with a certain sureness and an easy authority, and the dialogue has the ring of authenticity. There is some curious organizing, but the novel is absorbing and well paced. It is a first novel of undoubted merit.

I2. Berkman, Sylvia. "The Reluctant Adults." *New York Times Book Review*, 4 April 1954, p. 5.

An excessively admiring review. The book immediately places Matthiessen as "a writer of disciplined craft, perception, imaginative vigor and serious temperament." He has a gift of "flexible taut expression which takes wings at times into a lyricism beautifully modulated and controlled."

I3. *The Booklist*, 50 (February 15, 1954), 230.

A brief descriptive notice. The book is emotionally complicated and subtle.

I4. Brown, Karl. *Library Journal*, 79 (March 15, 1954), 551.

The novel is filled with striking imagery. It demonstrates more power in technique than in narrative.

I5. Cranston, Maurice. *London Magazine*, 2 (June 1955), 99–101.

An extravagantly appreciative notice within an omnibus review. The book's style is vigorous, fresh, and personal. In "its passion and pessimism, its moral guts and psychological knowledge, its eloquence and its humanity" this work is close to that of

Joseph Conrad. There is no American novelist of Matthiessen's age or younger who has written anything so good as this book.

I6. Fuller, Edmund. "Yankee Violence." *Saturday Review*, 37 (10 April 1954), 20–21.

This is a rather indifferent, non-committal assessment of Matthiessen as a novelist. He is a peripheral member of the current literary cult of violence. While he is effective in the sketching of harsh scenes and handles the characters' situations with skill, his intent in the story is not entirely clear.

I7. Hartman, Carl. "Technique and Theme in 1954." *Western Review*, 19 (Autumn 1954), 72–73 [72–80].

Part of an omnibus review. The novel is competent and well made. Matthiessen uses several modern techniques well, but he doesn't have a particularly moving, interesting, or powerful story to tell.

I8. Jackson, Joseph Henry. "Mixed Up Generation." *San Francisco Chronicle*, 9 April 1954, p. 19.

While his moral may be made too obvious, Matthiessen is a fine novelist who will survive and prevail over some "flashier" young writers. He writes admirably and knows how to construct a story.

I9. *Kirkus Reviews*, 22 (January 15, 1954), 44.

A brief, descriptive notice. The book is an effective, if somber, fusion of memory and reality.

I10. McLaughlin, Richard. *Springfield* [MA] *Republican*, 2 May 1954, p. 9C.

Not verified. Cited in *Book Review Digest* 1954.

I11. Molloy, Robert. "Strained View of Three Worthless Characters." *Chicago Sunday Tribune*, 11 April 1954, p. 4.

A highly critical review. Matthiessen's prose is strained, inflexible and a thin composition of constantly unpleasant metaphor. Any good popular suspense writer could surpass him in dramatic tension and many could also teach him something about psychology.

I12. "Search for Maturity." *The Nation*, 178 (10 April 1954), 312.

This is a strong novel that suffers from technical defects. The flashback technique is occasionally awkward and ineffective, but the conventional narration is interesting. It might have made a stronger and more effective novella or short story.

I13. Weeks, Edward. "The Peripatetic Reviewer." *Atlantic*, 193 (June 1954), 74 [72, 74].

Matthiessen is an able young writer, but this is not an agreeable book. He is beyond his depth in certain places of the novel. He clutters up the book with similes and metaphors, which he handles very unsurely, producing a self-consciousness.

I14. *Wisconsin Library Bulletin*, 50 (May 1954), 137.

A brief review. The book is easy to read, but it is hard to classify and to summarize, although it is impossible to put aside.

PARTISANS

I15. Adams, Robert Martin. "Fiction Chronicle." *Hudson Review*, 8 (Winter 1956), 631 [627–632].

Part of an omnibus review. The melodrama and the theme are occasionally stagy, but the book's real weakness is caused by the flashbacks which choke the story's progress and test the reader's credulity. While this is a good, brave book, it is too dully rendered. It is totally absent of wit. Matthiessen is destined to write a fine novel, but this isn't it.

I16. Barrett, Mary L. *Library Journal*, 80 (August 1955), 1696.

This "highly recommended" book is notable for its integrity and dramatic quality.

I17. *The Booklist and Subscription Book Bulletin*, 52 (November 1, 1955), 103.

This is a novel of ideas which is told dispassionately and objectively. Its economical style helps create suspense.

I18. "Brief Notices." *Chicago Review*, 10 (Spring 1956), 128.

The story is suspense filled but inconclusive. It features perhaps the most stupid hero in modern writing.

I19. "Briefly Noted." *New Yorker*, 31 (8 October 1955), 191–192.

Matthiessen has provided "an admirably whole picture" of a man struggling through confusion to reach a better future.

I20. Cooperman, Stanley. "Selected New Books." *The Nation*, 181 (19 November 1955), 446.

A very brief notice. There is some fine handling of scene and narration, but Matthiessen does not convey the sense that he knows where he is going, leaving the reader lost as well.

I21. Finn, James. "A Modern Quest." *Commonweal*, 63 (28 October 1955), 102–103.

This is a novel of ideas that does not quite succeed. Matthiessen inadequately handles the ideas which concern his protagonist. Too many situations seem contrived. The characters fail to emerge "from the dialectic in which they are involved." Despite the problems, "there is much to be commended in the novel." The writing has a nervous energy suitable to its subject and exciting in itself.

I22. Goyen, William. "Underground Quest." *New York Times Book Review*, 2 October 1955, p. 4.

At times brightly written, this novel is sluggishly constructed and the characters are not fully realized. The book lacks "authentic magic, it lacks voice." It is a discursive and youthful treatment.

123. Hogan, William. "Political Chase Through the Paris Underground." *San Francisco Chronicle*, 10 October 1955, p. 23.

The story reads like an early Graham Greene interpreted by Arthur Koestler. This is not a major work, but it places Matthiessen among the most interesting of young American novelists.

124. Johnson, George. "New & Noteworthy." *New York Times Book Review*, 3 January 1988, p. 22.

A very brief notice of the Vintage paperback edition.

125. Stone, Jerome. "Wanderer in the City of Light." *Saturday Review*, 38 (3 December 1955), 48.

Matthiessen seems uncomfortable with his subject. Some of the writing is forced and, at times, awkwardly naïve. Generally, the book is without vigor or imaginative grasp.

WILDLIFE IN AMERICA

126. Ames, Alfred C. "An Impressive Memorial to Vanishing Wildlife." *Chicago Tribune*, 18 October 1959, "Magazine of Books," p. 8.

The declining and extinct animals of North America have received an impressive and beautiful memorial. The book's virtues are its thoroughness and style. The writing is vigorous and resourceful. Matthiessen is a man of feeling, but he is never sentimental or unfair. The book contributes to our knowledge, appeals to our emotions, and presents a reasonable argument for sensible conservation practices. This is a sad story beautifully told.

127. *The Booklist and Subscription Books Review*, 56 (January 1, 1960), 260.

A brief, essentially nonevaluative review.

128. *Booklist*, 84 (November 15, 1987), 522.

The book remains an impressive record of the deaths of animals at the hands of man.

129. Brooks, Rae. "Books in Brief." *Harper's Magazine*, 219 (November 1959), 118 [114–121].

Matthiessen is a writer with grace, sureness, and often a wry humor. He reveals a genuine love for every creature he writes about, a sorrow over their loss, and an anger at the waste of natural resources. No one can remain indifferent to the subject after reading this book.

130. Carr, Archie. "The Need to Let Live." *New York Times Book Review*, 22 November 1959, p. 38.

This is a fair and balanced assessment of the book. Matthiessen never succumbs to sentimentality or over-documentation. He does not rant or rave. If anything, he is perhaps too restrained "for good propaganda" in his explanation for the need for conservation. The book is a delight to read, skillfully told in a clean, strong prose. He provides a unique account of the relationship between man and wildlife in North America, and if the book is as widely read as it should be, future generations will be in his debt.

131. Foell, Earl W. "Early Immigrants to the American Wild." *Christian Science Monitor*, 19 November 1959, p. 16.

The book is briefly discussed within an omnibus review. Matthiessen is not the doctrinaire angry naturalist. He credits man when credit is due and places blame fairly. The book is written with the skill of a novelist and a zoologist's accuracy.

132. Gorner, Peter. "Exploring All the Different Worlds of Land, Sea and Sky." *Chicago Tribune*, 6 December 1987, "Books," p. 8.

A very brief mention of the revised, updated edition within an omnibus review. The book's return is something to rejoice about.

133. Necker, Walter. *Library Journal*, 85 (January 15, 1960), 291–292.

This "fascinating" account should be required reading for everybody.

134. *New Yorker,* 35 (24 October 1959), 190–191.

Matthiessen recognizes that the greatest destructive force of wildlife is the willful ignorance in the name of progress that encourages the wanton destruction of our natural resources. This is "an excellent book — hardnosed, warm-hearted, and high-spirited — and it cannot be too strongly recommended."

135. Norman, Geoffrey. *Outside,* 13 (March 1988), 101.

The updated and expanded edition is disappointedly substantially neither. While Matthiessen's prose has grown over the years and there are passages of great lyrical force, there are also long stretches of "very tepid" prose. The book has the hallmark of Matthiessen's strength as a nature writer, "his calm good sense" without the self-righteous strut.

136. "Now in Paperback." *Los Angeles Times Book Review,* 13 September 1987, p. 22.

A brief appreciative joint review with A. Starker Leopold's *Wild California.*

137. Orenstein, Ronald I. *Science Books and Films,* 24 (September/October 1988), 15–16.

The reappearance of this classic of conservation literature is most welcome. Its impact has not been dimmed by more recent books on the subject, and it remains nearly unequalled in the breadth of its scope. The book is beautifully written — evocative and disturbing.

138. Peterson, Roger Tory. "Our Rich Heritage of Birds and Beasts." *New York Herald Tribune Book Review,* 8 November 1959, p. 6.

A flattering endorsement of a "handsome book." This should be the "first source volume" for everyone who embraces the philosophy of conservation, for every ethical person who thinks about the future. One's

wildlife education will not be complete without this book.

139. Poore, Charles. "Books of The Times." *New York Times,* 29 December 1959, p. 23.

The one objection to this superb history is Matthiessen's constant belaboring of the nation's past sins of rapacity. His writing has "a sharp, luminous and uncluttered style." The book contains "a thousand and one interesting commentaries." It should be sent to every member of Congress.

140. Rogers, Michael. "Classic Returns." *Library Journal,* 120 (May 1, 1995), 138.

A brief notice of the new paperback editions of *Wildlife in America* and *The Tree Where Man Was Born.*

141. S. A. "Some Wildlife Has Become Only a Living Curiosity." *San Francisco Chronicle,* 22 November 1959, "Christmas Books," p. 33.

The book is a well written account that will make unpleasant reading for anyone who wishes to forget the sins man has committed against wildlife.

142. "Saving the Species." *Times Literary Supplement,* no. 3062 (4 November 1960), 711.

A brief appreciative review of a "fascinating book" with an "admirably told story."

143. Skenazy, Paul. "Books in Brief." *Mother Jones,* 13 (January 1988), 52.

A brief notice. This is a vivid, compelling account of what once was a warning of what still could be.

144. Weeks, Edward. "The Peripatetic Reviewer." *Atlantic,* 205 (March 1960), 110, 112 [108, 110, 112].

This is the first modern and comprehensive record of our wildlife and of what the white man has done to eliminate them. Matthiessen's delight in the remaining wildlife and the crusading spirit with which he argues against the continuing destruction of our natural resources prevents this from being a bleak story of extermination.

145. *Wilderness*, 51 (Spring 1988), 68.

Wildlife in America is one of the central texts in the history of wildlife in the United States and by the far the most beautifully written. The updating and expansion is unfortunately flawed. Too much of the text still documents thirty year old assumptions. This limits the book's usefulness as a tool for modern study.

RADITZER

146. "'Ain't I Human.'" *Newsweek*, 57 (6 February 1961), 85–86.

A brief descriptive review. The novel does not achieve the Conradian reverberations of evil that Matthiessen seems to be striving for. The language is "tidy" and the story moves.

147. Baro, Gene. "In the Society of Men at Sea A Romantic Comes to Self-Knowledge." *New York Herald Tribune*, 29 January 1961, "The Living Arts," p. 30.

Matthiessen is an immensely talented writer, and this book is a substantial achievement. He has a sensitivity to the values of language that distinguishes him from his "flashier contemporaries." He strives for exactness. At his best, he reminds the reader of Joseph Conrad's work.

148. *The Booklist and Subscription Books Bulletin*, 57 (December 15, 1960), 241.

Brief. This is an unusual story that deals compellingly with the brother's keeper theme. The writing is finely wrought and understated.

149. Boroff, David. "The Tyranny of Weakness." *New York Times Book Review*, 5 February 1961, pp. 4, 36.

Matthiessen writes with "athletic vigor and ease," but the book has an exasperated earnestness. The main character is too equivocal to fulfill "the metaphysical role assigned to him."

150. "Briefly Noted." *New Yorker*, 37 (22 April 1961), 178–179.

The story retreats into "symbolistic country" and reaches "a singularly unimpressive climax." Matthiessen has a clear, pointed style and is able to convey a sense of atmosphere.

151. Greenberg, Martin. "Fiction Chronicle." *Partisan Review*, 29 (Winter 1962), 149. [149–152, 154, 156, 158].

An omnibus review. This is a perfectly good idea, but it isn't developed into a story. Raditzer falls short of the kind of reality needed, and the other characters are nonexistent. The failure of the characters, however, is dependent upon the failure of the story itself.

152. "Hell Let Loose." *Times Literary Supplement*, no. 3131 (March 2, 1962), 141.

Reviewed with two other books. Matthiessen is unerring in execution but much mistaken in his theme. Raditzer is denied the elementary privilege of flesh and blood, and the reader's understanding of Charlie Starks is not increased through his relationship with Raditzer.

153. Hicks, Granville. "The Real and the Surreal." *Saturday Review*, 44 (28 January 1961), 14.

A comparative review with Egon Hostovsky's *The Plot*. Matthiessen's ideas are not original, but he is able to give an old theme new life. The struggle he portrays between Raditzer's evil and Stark's good is beautifully dramatic.

154. Houlihan, Thomas F. *Library Journal*, 86 (January 1, 1961), 114.

It is a tautly written novel recommended for all fiction collections.

155. Jackson, Katherine Gauss. *Harper's Magazine*, 222 (February 1961), 106.

This is a remarkable tour de force and morality play. It is a moving idea almost successfully realized. The violence of the final scene is embarrassing and the reader is left as an onlooker rather than as the participant he has been up to this point.

156. Johnson, George. "New & Noteworthy." *New York Times Book Review*, 3 January 1988, p. 22.

A very brief notice of the Vintage paperback edition.

157. Klausler, Alfred P. "Mostly Top-Notch ." *Christian Century*, 78 (13 September 1961), 1082.

A brief discussion within an omnibus review. The work is a strangely moving and well written story of man's dual nature.

158. *Kirkus Reviews*, 28 (November 15, 1960), 978.

A brief, tentative assessment of a "curious" book which is "not easily likeable." Raditzer has a "weird, uncomfortable power" as a symbol of guilt.

159. Mayne, Richard. "Messrs Universe." *New Statesman*, 63 (2 March 1962), 309.

An omnibus review. This is a short bitter book, vibrant with multiple meanings. Although it turns "sour" in the end and the characters are actualized symbols, the book can wear its defects honorably.

160. McLaughlin, Richard. "'Raditzer' Shows Torment of Soul." *Springfield* [MA] *Republican*, 12 February 1961, p. 4D.

This is a grimly fascinating story that is packed with excitement and suspense despite its brevity. It is Conradian in tone, taut and sparely written.

161. Nordell, Rod. "Grim Gadfly." *Christian Science Monitor*, 2 Feburary 1961, p. 7.

Matthiessen spells things out rather than allowing the reader to attribute his own meanings. This labeling damages the work as a novel while not improving it as a tract. The book is generally not worth plowing through, but it does provide an indication of Matthiessen's literary promise.

162. Poore, Charles. "Books of The Times." *New York Times*, 28 January 1961, p. 17.

This review is primarily descriptive rather than evaluative. Raditzer is one of the most astonishing scoundrels in recent memory.
See **163.**

163. ____. "Character with a Conradian Touch." *San Francisco Chronicle*, 7 February 1961, p. 27.

An abbreviated version of **162.**

164. Price, R. G. G. "New Novels." *Punch*, 242 (7 March 1962), 406 [405–406].

A brief, multi-title review. This may have made a more effective longer short story. It trails off at the end, and the central theme has to carry the worn props of the American war novel.

165. Raskin, Alex. "Now in Paperback." *Los Angeles Times Book Review*, 20 December 1987, p. 14.

The story is taut and gripping without being ponderous. It is packed with ideas that demand reflection.

166. Southern, Terry. "Christ Seen Darkly." *The Nation*, 192 (25 February 1961), 170–171.

While the general tenor of the review is positive and admiring, Southern finds too many forced elements that mar the novel. The dialogue is wooden, the secondary characters are dull and inconsequential, and the work is almost totally lacking in outward drama or suspense. An excellent and updated Christ story is to be found in the novel, but it is best read as a character portrayal, not as an allegory. Raditzer is that rarity in literature, an original that possesses both uniqueness and verisimilitude.

167. "Universal Heel." *Time*, 77 (27 January 1961), 78.

Matthiessen has succeeded in producing something more than just a war novel. Raditzer and the Raditzer-Stark amalgam are evocative and thought provoking.

168. Warnke, F. J. "Some Recent Novels: A Variety of Worlds." *Yale Review*, 50 (Summer 1961), 627–628 [627–633].

Part of an omnibus review. This is a serious and careful piece of work with a valid and provocative theme, but the style is labored, at times nearly pretentious. Matthiessen tends to explain at length the significance of his incidents and symbols. "He's no Melville."

169. Zane, Maitland. "And Three More From the States." *Time & Tide* [London], 15 March 1962, p. 37.

Reviewed with Vance Bourjaily's *The Violated* and Harvey Swados's *Nights in the Garden of Brooklyn*. None of the novels break any new ground or make the reader care deeply. While there is humor, intelligence, and sympathy displayed, there is also a reliance on stock situations and stock characters. It is a direct, crisp story, which is enormously moving in the end.

THE CLOUD FOREST

170. Adams, Phoebe. "Potpourri." *Atlantic*, 208 (November 1961), 192.

To too great of an extent, Matthiessen is a careful, precise observer who suppresses his own sentiments and personality. He becomes a disembodied observer.

171. Bagg, Donald B. "'The Cloud Forest.'" *Springfield* [MA] *Republican*, 29 October 1961, p. 4D.

A descriptive account of the book. No evaluation is provided.

172. Bates, Marston. "Fortune Smiled on the Traveler in an Unmapped Part of the Earth." *New York Times Book Review*, 15 October 1961, pp. 3, 30.

Among American writers on South America, Matthiessen is unique. He has gotten to parts of the continent usually not seen by North Americans, and he has gotten it right. He is the master of a clean, dry, straightforward prose which is often vivid and aptly picturesque as well. Interested in everything, he has extraordinary perception. This is a delightful book.

173. *The Booklist and Subscription Books Bulletin*, 58 (September 1, 1961), 19.

Brief. Matthiessen views the world around him with genuine interest and appreciation rather than superficial curiosity.

174. Bush, Monroe. "South of the Border." *American Forest*, 68 (January 1962), 30.

This is an admiring and appreciative review. "Matthiessen is a modest, unselfconscious naturalist with a gift for poking and prying." He has an impressive childlike sense of surprise, humor, and a "marvelously simple acceptance of the wholeness of creation." He gives new dimension to our understanding of wilderness.

175. Crow, John A. "Red Carpets and Wild Rapids." *Saturday Review*, 44 (18 November 1961), 42–43.

Reviewed with Sacheverell Sitwell's *Golden Wall and Mirador*. The book is a beautifully written and disturbingly honest account which provides astute commentaries on and detailed observations of the people and wildlife of the Amazon basin. Matthiessen admires the wild freedom, grace, and animal skills of the tribal Indians. He laments that the tribe which allows contact with the white man on the white man's terms is condemning itself to extinction.

176. Foster, Thomas. "A South American Wilderness Journey." *New York Herald Tribune*, 8 October 1961, "Books," p. 3.

A largely descriptive review. Matthiessen's chronicle is exciting and evocative. His narrative skill makes the reader feel he is participating first-hand in the discovery of this relatively unknown area. The book deserves a long life along with the records of earlier naturalists, such as Darwin and Bates, who also studied South America.

177. Gould, Gordon. "Heart Quickening Account of Jungle Adventures." *Chicago Tribune*, 29 October 1961, "Magazine of Books," p. 13.

Matthiessen can persuade you that he is chatting with you over a good drink by a comfortable fire. He writes with a soft, bemused manner. His descriptions of the wildlife have a poetic lucidity. The ability to recreate the wonder of the jungle is his great strength.

178. Haycraft, Colin. "White and Blue." *New Statesman*, 64 (21 September 1962), 371.

An omnibus review. The book is fresh and exciting despite a slow start and some orinthological longueurs. Matthiessen studiously downplays all dangers and wonders that he encounters.

179. Hegen, E. E. *Hispanic American Historical Review*, 42 (August 1962), 449.

A brief, odd, disparaging review.

180. Hogan, William. "Stirring Account of South American Wilds." *San Francisco Chronicle*, 16 October 1961, p. 41.

Matthiessen is a daring and, at times, fool-hearty explorer. He is an articulate and disciplined writer, and this is probably his best book yet. It is a superior blend of adventure and reflection, and ranks with the classics of the genre.

181. "In Brief." *Natural History*, 71 (March 1962), 7.

The style is urbane, and his observations are clear and evocative. As with the best of explorers, Matthiessen seems led on by something below and beyond the surface of things.

182. Johansson, Bertram B. "To Share What They Saw, How They Felt." *Book World*, [*Washington Post*], 19 October 1961, p. 11.

An appreciative review of "one of the more authentic wilderness books on South America." Matthiessen writes with poetic vividness and a deep appreciation for wilderness. He is an acute observer and is at the height of his descriptive prose when he becomes the active adventurer.

183. *Kirkus Reviews*, 29 (August 1, 1961), 720.

This is an excellent book, an adventure story of the highest order. "Fiction has never topped this."

184. M. B. "Literary Appraisals." *Mexican Life*, 38 (April 1962), 34.

An admiring notice of a "completely delightful book." Matthiessen is unique among American writers on South America. He has extraordinary perception, and the book is without a false note. He is the master of a clean, dry, straightforward prose that is also vivid and aptly picturesque.

185. Matthews, William H., Jr. *Library Journal*, 86 (November 15, 1961), 3953.

While Matthiessen writes voluminously and interestingly of everything he experiences, he gives the impression of callowness and a lack of comprehension. Harry A. Franck did a better job in his acuteness of observations and the breadth and depth of his descriptions.

186. "New in Paperback." *Book World*, [*Washington Post*], 22 March 1987, p. 12.

A very brief notice of the Penguin Travel Library edition.

187. O'Conner, Patricia T. "New & Noteworthy." *New York Times Book Review*, 18 January 1987, p. 34.

Brief notice of the new paperback edition.

188. Poore, Charles. "Books of The Times." *New York Times*, 19 October 1961, p. 33.

Matthiessen possesses three indispensible qualities for a writer: a sense of style, a sense of humor, and an ungovernable curiosity. All three are brought into play in this excellent book. He has an admirable lack of pompousness toward adventure.

189. Price, R. G. G. "Vicarious Discomforts." *Punch*, 243 (19 September 1962), 432–433.

Brief. Reviewed with *The Great Saharan Mouse-Hunt* by Miggs Pomeroy and Catherine Collins. The original reason for Matthiessen's journey is not clear. However, despite his hopping around, the book cumulates as a solid picture of South America's biology, geology, and social structure.

190. *Publishers Weekly*, 189 (27 June 1966), 105.

Brief. Vivid descriptions of the natural environment and Indians are mingled with "often dangerous feats of exploration."

191. Seaborn, Richard G. *Canadian Geographical Journal*, 66 (June 1963), x–xi.

As a naturalist, Matthiessen prevails in the book, but when he speculates on the future, he weakens it and digresses into material better left for his novels. What separates this book from other travel accounts in his recounting of his trip though the rain (cloud) forest of the eastern Peruvian Andes. Here the book becomes an adventure story and will linger in the mind of the reader to be enjoyed again.

192. "The Subtle Explorer." *Newsweek*, 58 (9 October 1961), 105.

While Matthiessen is an able stylist who is full of "splendid moments," he never achieves the "exuberance of the Victorian writer-explorer." Nothing seems exciting or wild enough for the sophisticated twentieth-century man. Not only the jungle, but "the great, green greasy Limpopo of the spirit" is disappearing too.

193. Ternes, Alan. "A Plentitude of Paperbacks." *Audubon*, 71 (November 1969), 131 [131–135].

This is often an adventure story, but Matthiessen retains a naturalist's eye throughout. His reports of his surroundings are evocative.

194. "Through the Looking Glass." *Times Literary Supplement*, no. 3161 (September 28, 1962), 763.

A less than enthusiastic assessment of Matthiessen's journey and book. There is a persistent note of frustration and disengagement about the journey in spite of much brilliant observation and reflection. He has brought the jungle home with him and succeeds in passing along some bits of it to the reader.

195. Walker, Laurence C. *American Scientist*, 50 (September 1962), 304A.

A brief admiring account. This is not an ecological treatise or a description of the flora and fauna. It is a well written report of the people and their habits and habitats. The historical account and the geography are finely interwoven into a smooth fabric. He has a way with adjectives; he paints pictures without pigment.

UNDER THE MOUNTAIN WALL

196. Adams, Phoebe. "Reader's Choice." *Atlantic*, 210 (November 1962), 139–140 [134, 136, 138–144].

This is a strange book as a result of Matthiessen's description of the Kurelu as if neither he nor any other expedition member has ever interacted with them. His attempt to see everything but comment on nothing is courageous but unsuccessful since he is of necessity an alien sensibility. There is something spurious about all of the careful, calculated objectivity. He needs to admit his own existence and risk a little, honest bias. The book offers no support for the old "noble savage" legend, and it does not succeed in conveying the charm Matthiessen says he found in the Kurelu.

197. "Back to the Stone Age." *Times Literary Supplement*, no. 3229 (January 16, 1964), 51.

In his sympathetic observations, Matthiessen provides colorful details and effective evocations of personalities and atmosphere. He responds to the common humanity of the Kurelu but fails to convey what would be the concerns of an academically trained social anthropologist.

198. Bagg, Donald B. "Primitive Tribe Subject of Study." *Springfield* [MA] *Republican*, 4 November 1962, p. 4D.

A brief non-evaluative notice. The tribesmen's lives are objectively told in extensive factual detail.

199. *The Booklist and Subscription Books Bulletin*, 59 (November 1, 1962), 202.

Brief. Matthiessen writes with scientific detachment but reportorial skill.

I100. Bram, Joseph. *Library Journal*, 87 (December 15, 1962), 4556.

The book combines documentary value with a haunting literary quality. It is a precious record of a doomed way of life.

I101. Eiseley, Loren. "Miniatures of Ourselves." *New York Times Book Review*, 18 November 1962, pp. 3, 64.

This is a sensitively written book. Matthiessen has brought to the subject "the pity and insight that only a truly articulate observer can focus upon scenes so remote from the ordinary, and so barbaric." Through his powerful observation the hidden message of the book is revealed: the Kurelu are ourselves in miniature.

I102. Hogan, William. "A Voyage Into the Stone Age." *San Francisco Chronicle*, 2 November 1962, p. 33.

Despite Matthiessen's cool scientific approach, this is an often moving account of the Kurelu. It is an absorbing specialized book weighted with scholarship rather than adventure.

I103. Janeway, Elizabeth. "Vivid Chronicles of Adventures in Far Corners of the Earth." *Chicago Tribune*, 18 November 1962, "Magazine of Books," p. 4.

The interesting and effective technique employed by Matthiessen is to chronicle the life of the Kurelu as if he were reporting for a local newspaper. While he is an excellent and evocative writer, his method has the disadvantage of not adequately explaining the differences in thought, outlook, and emotional responses between his subjects and his readers. His intention is for readers to see the Kurelu as human beings, just like themselves, but they, in fact, remain puppets. Nonetheless, it is a worthwhile and interesting book.

I104. *Kirkus Reviews*, 30 (August 1, 1962), 752.

The overly sensitive may at first be fascinated but then revolted by the self-

inflicted, primitive suffering Matthiessen records. But he achieves a nearly impossible feat of characterization and motivation. He also provides infinite detail concerning the flora and fauna of New Guinea.

I105. *Library Journal*, 88 (July 1963), 2785.

This is a brief notice of an absorbing account.

I106. Metraux, Rhoda. "In Densest New Guinea." *New York Herald Tribune Books*, 11 November 1962, p. 12.

In this "exceedingly felicitous account," Matthiessen combines the talents of a novelist and a naturalist in his dual interest in biography and the scene itself. His descriptions of the environment have the clear sophistication of a trained and highly skilled naturalist, but he demonstrates great restraint in his depiction of the Kurelu by not attributing thoughts or words to them to which he would have no access. This book is a rare success in what it sets out to do and in awakening the readers.

I107. "New in Paperback." *Book World*, [*Washington Post*], 22 March 1987, p. 12.

A very brief notice of the Penguin Travel Library edition.

I108. O'Conner, Patricia T. "New & Noteworthy." *New York Times Book Review*, 18 January 1987, p. 34.

Brief notice of the new paperback edition.

I109. Pickrel, Paul. "The New Books." *Harper's Magazine*, 226 (February 1963), 102 [99–106].

There are some disadvantages to Matthiessen telling his account as if there is no white, outside observer impacting upon the Kurelu's behavior. It is not easy to understand who is fighting whom because there is little exposition of the tribal structures. Some facts remain hazy. These problems are outweighed by the advantages, the most important of which is that Matthiessen is simply a superb writer. The book should become something of a classic. It combines the scientist's precise observation with the artist's tact, grace, and sympathy.

I110. _____. "Reader's Guide." *Yale Review*, 52 (March 1963), xviii, xx.

Matthiessen is a perceptive and sensitive chronicler who presents the Kurelu as convincing human beings rather than as callous savages. He has written a masterful and compelling account.

I111. *Publishers Weekly*, 196 (8 September 1969), 58–59.

A very brief notice of an "absorbing and perceptive" account.

I112. Saal, Rollene W. "Pick of the Paperbacks." *Saturday Review*, 52 (27 December 1969), 33 [32–33].

This is a remarkably poignant account and an intensely human study which provides an important window into the past.

I113. Siegel, Bernard J. "Lost World." *Saturday Review*, 46 (5 January 1963), 73.

The work exhibits the advantages and disadvantages of the novelist's perceptions. The narrative flows with style and elegance, bringing a small island of mankind emotionally alive. Matthiessen catches the essential humanity of the people. From an anthropologist's viewpoint, however, the book provides no conceptual interpretation of the Kurelu and their culture, and it fails to place them in the succession of adaptations made by human groups worldwide.

I114. Southern, Terry. "Recent Fiction, Part I: 'When Film Gets Good ....'" *The Nation*, 195 (17 November 1962), 332 [330–332].

An omnibus review. This is an extraordinary and successful book. Matthiessen has conveyed the strange existence of the Kurelu in "a beautifully poetic way."

I115. Taylor, Nora E. "The Stone Age Family Next Door." *Christian Science Monitor*, 22 October 1962, p. 9.

Matthiessen is an eloquent writer whose work provides a warm, evocative look at the terrain. He has effectively excluded himself from the work and makes the Kurelu as understandable as the people down the street. This book is a welcome exception to the usual dry accounts of Stone Age peoples.

I116. Turnbill, Colin. *Natural History*, 72 (August/September 1963), 8–9.

While this work is powerful in places, it is marred by its total presentation as a book which separates the reader from the subject. The book's design destroys the effects of a potentially beautiful work. Matthiessen does not pretend to present a consistent enthnography but writes simply and without sentimentality of the people's day-to-day existence. When emotion does creep into his account, the story is even more powerful.

I117. Zwart, F. H. A. G. *Polynesian Society Journal*, 73 (no. 1, 1964), 98–99.

Matthiessen provides a popular but penetrating account of the Kurelu. His writing is sober and straightforward, yet often picturesque.

AT PLAY IN THE FIELDS OF THE LORD

I118. "Amazonian Advent." *Time*, 86 (19 November 1965), 133.

Matthiessen is "a doer who indefatigably does, and a writer who skillfully writes what he does." His two sides — scientist and artist — have collaborated to produce a large and powerful novel.

I119. *The Booklist and Subscription Books Bulletin*, 62 (January 15, 1966), 476.

A brief positive review. There is "magnificent writing" in this story which is "elevated into something remarkable by the author's ability to communicate mental suffering and the drive of Moon's search for identity."

I120. Broyard, Anatole. "Matthiessen, Innes, Jones." *New York Times Book Review*, 29 May 1977, p. 12.

This is Mattiessen's best book by far. The sense of place is flawless, and there are, easily, half a dozen first-rate characters. It is a book filled with beautiful epiphanies.

I121. Capouya, Emile. "The Bible and Bombs." *New York Times Book Review*, 7 November 1966, pp. 4, 66.

Matthiessen has the tendency to be over-explicit with easily intelligible ideas and occasionally sensationalistic, but, nevertheless, this is an extraordinary and "most unusual" novel. It is well conceived and beautifully written.

I122. *Carleton Miscellany*, 7 (Winter 1966), 114.

A brief dismissive review. The book can be put down at any time without any thought as to when the reader will be able to return to it.

I123. *Choice*, 3 (July/August 1966), 411.

While not an original theme, this is an exciting adventure novel with clever and poetic writing.

I124. Conley, John. "A Clutch of Fifteen." *Southern Review* NS, 3 (Summer 1967), 777–778.

An omnibus review. Read simply as an adventure story, the book might interest even somebody without romantic tastes. Rather than be satisfied with an uncomplicated story of romantic regeneration, Matthiessen has taken on too much. His apparent belief that wisdom is found only in the Indian way is greeted with some disdain by the reviewer.

I125. Cook, Roderick. "Books in Brief." *Harper's Magazine*, 231 (November 1965), 129–130 [128–133].

The plot of the book is misrepresented in this review. The best thing about the book is the background of the country and the insights into the natives. The book's most ambitious writing is when Moon works at his salvation by "going native." Otherwise, there is a lot of "post–Maugham and post–Greene clichés

about missionaries, sex, death, God, and guilt."

See **H6–H8**.

I126. Curley, Thomas. *Commonweal*, 83 (7 January 1966), 413–414.

While Lewis Moon is the main actor, he is less memorable than Martin Quarrier and is upstaged by him at times. The book is a serious and rich achievement.

I127. Davenport, John. "Exoticisms." *Observer*, 24 April 1966, p. 27.

Reviewed with Hortense Calisher's *Journal from Ellipsia*. Although Matthiessen writes with authority about the Amazon, the work is too long and fatally repetitive. The characters are almost all unbearably flawed. Moon is the only character with any weight, but his actions seem pointless and uncomprehensible.

I128. DeVoss, John. *Catholic World*, 202 (March 1966), 373–377.

Matthiessen has attempted a rare thing, a many-faceted novel: an adventure story, a study of comparative civilizations, a somber evaluation of misguided Christian missionaries, and an examination of man's relationship with God. Martin Quarrier is the novel's principal character and its central issue is the "'institutional' Christian's quest for a God more real and meaningful than the one conveyed by his individual system of beliefs." This is a well-handled story line with rich, unforgettable characters.

I129. Fleischer, Leonore. *Publishers Weekly*, 190 (18 November 1966), 62.

This is "a very, very good novel" which deals sympathetically and thought-provokingly with missionaries.

I130. Fremont-Smith, Eliot. "Once More, the Noble Savage." *New York Times*, 8 November 1965, p. 33.

The book is a close failure, but a failure nonetheless. Matthiessen has the intent and the tools but somehow misses the magic which transfers caring from author to reader. The work lacks a sense of quality, of necessity; it does not compel the reader. While one may be admiring or interested, one is never transported or engrossed.

I131. Gilmore, T. B. "Where Words End." *North American Review*, 2 (November 1965), 40–41.

While the characters are sometimes handled clumsily, the prose is, more often than not, lush. There are at least three unforgettable scenes in the book: Father Xantes at supper, Martin Quarrier's reaction to his son's death, and the book's final scene with Moon. Matthiessen's first-hand knowledge brings the jungle to life. This is far superior to most other novels.

I132. Harlan, Robert D. *Library Journal*, 90 (October 1, 1965), 4110.

The different elements provide the potential for an impossible story, but Matthiessen's talents hold the structure together. The story presents a compassionate and perceptive picture of people under stress.

I133. Hicks, Granville. "No Eden on the Amazon." *Saturday Review*, 48 (6 November 1965), 29–30.

This is a fascinating story told well. Matthiessen's evocation of the jungle is no less remarkable than his insight into his characters. Most of the review is a summary of the story.

I134. Hill, William B., S. J. "Fiction." ["America's Survey of Notable Fall Books."] *America*, 113 (27 November 1965), 690 [767–677, 680–686, 688, 690–692].

This "savage account" is "a slanted, unpleasant novel with an abundance of detail about sex lives of ignorant, abandoned people."

I135. "Innocents Abroad." *Christian Science Monitor*, 9 December 1965, p. 19.

A brief review. The book is all patterns and rounded designs. Is Matthiessen exploring the larger questions of life or merely manipulating the plot and props of a theological melodrama?

I136. Johnson, George. "New & Noteworthy." *New York Times Book Review*, 3 January 1988, p. 22.

Brief notice of a paperback edition.

I137. *Kirkus Reviews*, 33 (September 1, 1965), 942.

This is a marvelously exciting story with savage satire, telling comment, and great moments. Matthiessen has written "a flaming soul wringer."

I138. Kluger, Richard. "Heart of Darkness with a Big Beat." *Book Week*, 14 November 1965, pp. 5, 25.

Matthiessen has tried to combine the best of his two forms — the eloquent reportage of this nonfiction and the dramatic power of his fiction. The book is expertly crafted and, at times, deeply affecting. The writing is sensuously evocative and sometimes poetic without being overwrought. This is a serious and engaging work, reminiscent of Conrad. However, Matthiessen falls prey to the bias of the reviewer concerning the intent of contemporary literature. Kluger believes that the writers who have the most to say are the ones who "are daring to invent boldly, to outrage and mock the conventional-minded." They strike something more than merely real. Matthiessen has written a successful story; it is a realistic novel of adventure. But he is encumbered by his bondage to realism.

I139. Kugelmass, Harold. "Moving East of Eden." *Northwest Review*, 8 (Summer 1966), 123–126.

Most of this favorable review is a description of the plot and the main characters. The book is in the tradition of nineteenth-century romanticism and variants of the "academic" novel, yet it achieves its own unique and modern vision.

I140. "The Last Savage." *Newsweek*, 66 (8 November 1965), 114, 116.

Matthiessen is "the psalmist of the unblemished wilderness." This is a forceful but uneven novel. It contains passages of lyricism and poignancy. The best part is the last chapter.

I141. Lynch, William J. *America*, 113 (4 December 1965), 728.

Although the book lacks artistic evenness, as a whole, it conveys a remarkable impact. It moves forcefully and dramatically. The pauses in the narration for descriptive nature passages are the result of Matthiessen as sensitive explorer rather than mature artist. The Lewis Moon "subplot" detracts from the "more spiritually significant struggles of Quarrier and his family." This is an impressive work. Matthiessen has an instinctive sense of beauty in both man and nature, and he refuses to glorify the noble savage.

I142. Mathes, William. "Exciting Novel." *The Progressive*, 30 (January 1966), 42–43.

Matthiessen has written a popular novel that transcends its genre. The disarmingly conventional elements add up to an unconventional experience. The same elements in a less skillful writer's hands would have produced just another potboiler. The book works because Matthiessen is a philosopher and a searcher for life. He uses the novel as a means for esoteric and vital contemporary explorations. The real excitement of the book is in his philosophical base, in the book's search for the truth.

I143. Morse, J. Mitchell. "Madison Avenue Medicine Man." *The Nation*, 201 (13 December 1965), 475–477.

An insulting and pompous review. Matthiessen is an earnest novelist but not a serious one. He does not possess the necessary language to think seriously about elemental questions. His clumsy language fails him when he tries to use the techniques of modern novelists to derive order, meaning, and life. The novel is chiefly melodramatic action, persona-type talk, and exotic nature notes. There are occasional vivid images, but Matthiessen simply does not write well. (His writing is unfavorably compared to Samuel Beckett's prose.) While he obviously intended to be serious, he has unconsciously condescended to cheapness.

I144. Ostermann, Robert. "In Recent Fiction, Literary Satire and Neo-Conrad." *National Observer*, 8 November 1965, p. 22.

Matthiessen is testing his artistic ability in this long, rich novel. He repeatedly brings his characters to the brink of utter banality only to continue his dangerous path with surety. He is comparable to Joseph Conrad in his interest in characters under stress responding to profound moral temptations and in his knowledge and use of exotic, primitive areas. Like Conrad, he is a master of a superlative style.

I145. Pryce-Jones, Alan. "Vigor Tinctured With Shoddy Craftsmanship." *New York Herald Tribune*, 2 December 1965, p. 23.

Matthiessen is an original talent who writes with fine vigor and clarity; however, this is an odd book. Its framework is not particularly good. While the book leaves a powerful impress, the overall sense of it is as a series of set pieces. He fails to find a strong focus among any of the stories he could have made of the material, so it becomes a little of all of them. As a result, the characters are not clearly defined. The readers see them through "a kind of miasma."

I146. "Red Man's Burdens." *Times Literary Supplement*, no. 3346 (14 April 1966), 332.

This finely-shaped and complex novel powerfully evokes the Amazon basin. Lewis Moon and Wolfie are both brilliantly characterized.

I147. Robinson, Cecil. *Arizona Quarterly*, 22 (Summer 1966), 179–180.

The book's multitudes and ambitious scope result in occasional repetitiousness and unevenness of characterization, but Matthiessen freshly handles some perennial themes.

I148. Ternes, Alan. "A Plentitude of Paperbacks." *Audubon*, 71 (November 1969), 131 [131–135].

This is a superb novel. It contains powerful descriptions and is one of the few good books in English about the Indians of South America.

I149. Thompson, John. "Matthiessen and Updike." *New York Review of Books*, 5 (December 23, 1965), 20 [20–22].

Reviewed with Updike's *Of the Farm*. That Matthiessen has given us a good old-fashioned adventure story with ingenious plotting is the point repeatedly made.

I150. Tractenberg, Stanley. "Accommodation and Protest." *Yale Review*, 55 (Spring 1966), 447–448 [444–450].

This is a story in the Romantic tradition of primitive nobility corrupted by civilization. Moon's rebirth is to a new freedom which celebrates itself without comprehension and, consequently, conviction of its own worth.

I151. *Virginia Quarterly Review*, 42 (Winter 1966), ix–x.

The story is a thorough and interesting study of hopeless and fruitless careers. It may have benefited from being shorter, increasing its effectiveness and heightening its emotional impact.

I152. White, Richard C. "To Save the Savage." *Christian Century*, 82 (8 December 1965), 1514–1515.

Matthiessen shines as a naturalist and as a storyteller. His characters are well drawn and believable but pathetic. He strikes a telling blow at old-fashioned missionaries, but does he know anything about modern missionary approaches? This is good preparatory reading for any missionary candidates.

I153. Wordsworth, Christopher. "Snake-vines and Martinis." *Manchester Guardian Weekly*, 21 April 1966, p. 11.

The familiar characters are too obviously there to develop the story's "big" themes. The book's power comes from the authenticity of its setting and the mystery and suspense it evokes, not from its "jumbo moral excursions."

OOMINGMAK

I154. Crawhaw, H. B. *Horn Book*, 43 (August 1967), 487.

A brief notice. Matthiessen provides interesting information as well as a feel for Nunivak Island.

I155. Dahl, Patricia. *Library Journal*, 92 (June 15, 1967), 2462.

Matthiessen's respect and affection for the animals and for the traditional Eskimo culture are evident in this beautiful account.

I156. Goodwin, Polly. "Children's Book World." *Book World*, [*Washington Post*], 15 October 1967, p. 22.

Brief. This is a vivid and memorable account. Matthiessen seems to be fascinated by everything.

I157. *Kirkus Reviews*, 35 (May 1, 1967), 571.

Matthiessen writes with a simple affection for the Eskimos and with an easy authority about the island. He has a fellow-feeling for the animals.

I158. Morrison, Philip and Phyllis. "Books about Science for Young Readers." *Scientific American*, 217 (December 1967), 152 [140, 142–143, 145–148, 151–153].

Included in a list of books about "Exploration and Adventure," this is a "limpid, rhythmic and honest account."

I159. *Publishers Weekly*, 191 (10 April 1967), 78.

Brief. A fine picture of Nunivak Island is presented in this zestful account. Matthiessen is a skillful reporter of wildlife.

THE SHOREBIRDS

I160. *Antiquarian Bookman*, 40 (23 October 1967), 1465.

A brief notice of a beautiful and carefully realized book.

I161. Boland, Hal. "Nature Illustrated." *New York Times Book Review*, 3 December 1967, p. 10 [pp. 8, 10, 12].

Within a briefly annotated list of nature books, this is noted as "the most distinguished" title seen during the year. Matthiessen's text is of classic quality.

I162. *The Booklist and Subscription Books Bulletin*, 64 (January 1, 1968), 525.

Brief. The text provides an entertaining and informative natural history.

I163. *Choice*, 5 (April 1968), 218.

A generally negative assessment. The book compares badly to H. M. Hall's *A Gathering of Shore Birds*, which has a more knowledgeable text.

I164. Farb, Peter. "Nature Beneath the Tree." *Saturday Review*, 50 (25 November 1967), 44 [44, 46].

An omnibus review. A brief but hyperbolic review. This is "among the finest nature books ever" to be published in the United States and one which "will some day rank as an important document in natural history." Matthiessen's text is superlative and memorable. He is one of our time's three or four most important and impassioned nature writers.

I165. Glixon, David M. "Just the Facts Please." *Saturday Review*, 50 (18 November 1967), 41 [38–43].

A very brief entry within a listing of titles. The book is a superlative achievement. The text imparts knowledge in a Thoreauvian style.

I166. Harding, Walter. *Library Journal*, 92 (November 15, 1967), 4168.

Matthiessen's joy in his subject comes through on every page. His essay is fascinating. This is "a real treasure," one of the most important bird books of recent years.

I167. *Harper's Magazine*, 235 (December 1967), 128–129.

A brief, unimportant notice.

I168. Hay, John. *Natural History*, 77 (January 1968), 70.

This is "one of the finest books of natural history" ever seen by the reviewer. It has authentic unity and depth. The text has the deftness and balance of a fine writer. Matthiessen provides a "mosaic of fascinating information, of observation and of expertly placed description."

I169. Mengel, Robert M. "Haunting the World's Great Empty, Open Places." *Book World* [*Chicago Tribune* and *Washington Post*], 10 December 1967, p. 5.

At his best, Matthiessen achieves a flowing, poetic style suggestive of Daphne DuMaurier. His unflagging enthusiasm for his subject is remarkable for its sustained pitch. Despite the good deal of information he imparts, he is clearly not a trained biologist, and the text contains minor factual errors and conceptual near misses (with a few wider than others). The text is well documented and his opinions, which are not always sound, are clearly labeled. Concerning his prose style, when he is at his best, he is good. But he is at his best too rarely. He becomes preoccupied with words for their own sake. Still, he writes better than most scientists can or are willing to, and he has done a distinct service with this book.

I170. "'Of the Winged Dragon.'" *Christian Science Monitor*, 30 November 1967, p. B6.

An inconsequential notice.

I171. Perreault, John. "More Big 1967 Books." *The Nation*, 205 (25 December 1967), 698 [696–698].

Very brief. This is a book for the specialist, the naturalist, and the advanced bird watcher only. Its treatment contains a great amount of scientific detail.

I172. *Publishers Weekly*, 192 (31 July 1967), 50.

The book is a thing of beauty. Matthiessen provides a graceful and compact description of the birds he observes near his home.

I173. *Science Books*, 3 (December 1967), 244.

Matthiessen's text is a literary delight. This collaborative effort is an extraordinary "art book" and a treasure for ornithologists.

SAL SI PUEDES

I174. Anderson, David C. "César Chavez: Is He for Real?" *Wall Street Journal*, 13 February 1970, p. 8.

Matthiessen deliberately casts away any pretense to objectivity. This bias obscures understanding the strike's complexity and diminishes the book's real substance — a portrait of Chavez. The reader cannot be sure of the impression he is left with because Matthiessen has so evidently squandered his credibility as an objective reporter.

I175. *Best Sellers*, 33 (May 1, 1973), 71.

That the book is the fullest treatment of Chavez and the farm workers movement to date is the extent of this notice.

I176. Bongartz, Roy. "La Raza in Revolt." *The Nation*, 210 (1 June 1970), 664–666.

Reviewed with *Tijerina and the Courthouse Raid* by Peter Nabokov. Matthiessen makes no pretense at being objective, but he is a good and honest reporter who successfully brings the people to life.

I177. *The Booklist*, 66 (April 1, 1970), 943.

This is a powerful book which reflects Matthiessen's admiration for Chavez.

I178. *The Booklist*, 66 (April 15, 1970), 1038.

Very brief. This is a sympathetic account of Chavez and his movement.

I179. Buelna, Joseph L. *Library Journal*, 95 (March 1, 1970), 896.

Matthiessen allows his own personal bitterness toward the nation to interfere with his narrative. There is little historical or objective analysis and too often irrelevant points are introduced. The book does, however, produce a brilliant picture of the life of the migrant laborer.

I180. *Choice*, 7 (September 1970), 892.

Matthiessen has expanded his good *New Yorker* essay into a loose and disorgnaized conglomeration of fact and opinion strongly reflecting his bias against the country's farm labor policies.

I181. de Toledano, Ralph. "César Chavez — Fact and Fiction." *National Review*, 22 (March 24, 1970), 313–314.

Because he is a novelist, Matthiessen can not be blamed for lacking a reporter's ability to separate fact from fiction. He is also, commendably, a man of emotions, but he has allowed those emotions to come between him and a careful view of Chavez. The facts of Chavez don't warrant the superlatives Matthiessen applies to him. He is a rank fraud as a humanitarian and a failure as a union leader. Matthiessen should have investigated the situation in California and the outspokenly anti–Chavez pickers before interviewing Chavez. While Chavez is an unusual and fascinating man, Matthiessen has limited himself to too great of an extent on what Chavez and his followers have told him.

I182. D. G. "Idealist — Minus Ideology." *Christian Science Monitor*, 30 April 1970, p. 13.

Brief background information on Chavez and the United Farm Workers is given. No evaluative discussion of the book takes palce.

I183. Forest, John. "Rendering to Cesar." *The Critic*, 20 (May 1970), 72–77.

Matthiessen presents the written equivalent of the cinema verité. He records everything as it is happening and being said and does not apply ideologically selected filters. The great majority of this review/essay is not concerned with the book but rather with sharing some of Matthiessen's experiences with and observations of Chavez. Thus, it is more of an essay on Chavez than a review of the book.

I184. Gannon, Thomas M., S. J. "Home Scene." *America*, 122 (2 May 1970), 470.

A brief notice within a list of spring books. The book is highly readable and justifiably pro–United Farm Workers Organizing Committee.

I185. Gavin, Mortimer H. *America*, 122 (11 April 1970), 396–397.

Matthiessen provides "valuable, first-hand accurate documentation" in a simple, warm and very readable style. Those looking for the straight story of the United Farm Workers Organizing Committee's struggle will find it here. His account rings true.

I186. Gross, Robert. "The Chicanos." *Newsweek*, 75 (16 February 1970), 97–98.

Reviewed with *La Raza: The Mexican American* by Stan Steiner. Matthiessen's admiration for Chavez is understandable but a bit unbounded. The book never really achieves an understanding of the man. The study is diffuse and disorganized, and Matthiessen serves more as a Chavez amanuensis than interpreter.

I187. Jensen, Dorothy. *Library Journal*, 95 (April 15, 1970), 1665.

The rambling journalistic style limits the usefulness of the book. A number of strong statements concerning environmental problems associated with California's monolithic agri-business are made.

I188. *Kirkus Reviews*, 37 (December 1, 1969), 1303.

This is a fine study which conveys with passionate clarity the spirit and sense of *la Huelga*. Matthiessen is a sensitive observer who has pulled together the threads of the controversy well. The book has a few weak spots, but its major failure is with the presentation of Chavez himself. Matthiessen labors for too long "to establish and analyze [his] saintliness and charisma."
See **I189.**

I189. *Kirkus Reviews*, 37 (December 15, 1969), 1332.
Slightly abbreviated version of **I188.**

I190. Leonard, John. "Brown Power." *New York Times*, 3 February 1970, p. 41.

Reviewed with *La Raza: The Mexican Americans* by Stan Steiner. Both books are

"very good" and allow the people their own voices without filtering the facts through particular anthropological or ideological lenses. Matthiessen's portrait of Chavez is more convincing and because of his long-standing outrage concerning ecological questions, he has "earned his right to gloomy digressions."

I191. Mills, Nicolaus. "Mexican Americans." *Yale Review*, 59 (June 1970), 587–592 passim.

A review essay including *Tijerina and the Courthouse Raid* by Peter Nabokov and *La Raza: The Mexican Americans* by Stan Steiner. Matthiessen's Chavez often seems more like a religious figure than the head of a union. All three books fail to come to terms with the larger problems before them. They leave a series of questions that never get asked let alone answered.

I192. Nabokov, Peter. "Taking the Lid Off." *The Progressive*, 34 (June 1970), 40–41.

Reviewed with *La Raza: The Mexican Americans* by Stan Steiner. The book is superbly conceived and written. The portrait of Chavez emerges from a combination of relaxed discussions, impressions, skillful interviewing, and quietly worked descriptions. The suggestion of some critics that Matthiessen is idolizing Chavez is irrelevant. This is also a piece of consciously ecological reportage.

I193. "1970: A Selected List From Books of the Year." *New York Times Book Review*, 6 December 1970, p. 105.

Included among the year's best books in "Politics and Sociology."
Same as **I198.**

I194. Power, Keith. "The Way of Chavez." *Book World* [*Washington Post*], 7 June 1970, p. 7.

An unexpectedly flat notice of the work. Matthiessen's portrait of Chavez is graceful; his affection for the man does not dull his appreciation of the absurdities that surround Chavez.

1195. *Publishers Weekly*, 196 (24 November 1969), 41.

Brief. This is a vigorous and sympathetic portrait.

1196. Rechy, John. "No Mañanas for Today's Chicanos." *Saturday Review*, 53 (14 March 1970), 31–34.

A review essay with *La Raza: The Mexican Americans* by Stan Steiner. The broad scope of Matthiessen's intentions are marred by his awe of Chavez and the labyrinth and accumulation of detail he presents. The drama of the strike is lost at times because of his "staggering insistence on comprehensiveness." Matthiessen mistakenly tries to canonize Chavez, and despite his "honest outrage" the book is too idealistic, sweet and wistful in its depiction of Chavez and his movement.

1197. Roberts, Steven V. "Sal Si Puedes." *New York Times Book Review*, 1 February 1970, p. 8.

Curiously little is actually said about the book and Matthiessen's approach to Chavez other than to state that this is an "excellent new account" of Chavez and the United Farm Workers. The review is actually an admiring profile of Chavez.

1198. "A Selection of Recent Titles." *New York Times Book Review*, 7 June 1970, p. 43.

Very brief. The book is a perceptive portrait of Chavez.

1199. "Suffering for Others." *Time*, 95 (23 February 1970), 91.

In attempting to do justice to all the possibilities of his theme, Matthiessen has attempted too much. He fails to answer the question of who Chavez is; he never takes the clues to Chavez's character and composes a satisfactory portrait. He has found a hero in Chavez, and he refuses to take chances with his portrayal. In preserving the hero, he fails to reveal the man. The book is a "peculiarly frustrating failure of excellence."

1200. Torres, Ignacia. *Social Casework*, 52 (December 1971), 655.

Matthiessen is to be commended for focusing attention on Chavez and the plight of the migrant farm workers. However, the real, gut feelings of the strikers and Chavez are not revealed in this book. Chavez's portrait is painted in quick, light strokes. The pain, frustration, anger, and desperation of the people are passed over lightly.

1201. *Top of the News*, 26 (June 1970), 428.

A very brief and insignificant notice.

1202. Womack, John, Jr. "The Chicanos." *New York Review of Books*, 19 (August 19, 1972), 16 [12–18].

An omnibus review/essay. Matthiessen's is the "truest" of all the recent books on farm workers. This is a splendid and inspiring book. While not a biography in style or purpose, he has captured the man Chavez has become.

BLUE MERIDIAN

1203. "Best Books of 1971." *Library Journal*, 96 (December 15, 1971), 4161 [4157–4161].

This vividly reported "great adventure" is included among the year's best.

1204. *The Booklist*, 67 (July 15, 1971), 922.

The book is filled with diving and undersea lore and exciting and dramatic incidents. The final scene of the actual encounter with the great white shark seems anticlimatic.

1205. *Choice*, 8 (September 1971), 858.

Clear descriptions, frightening accounts, and perceptive insights make for a highly readable and interesting book.

1206. Diliberto, Gioia. "Paperbacks." *Chicago Tribune Books*, 29 June 1997, p. 8.

Very brief notice.

1207. Foden, Giles. "Papa's Boy?" *Times Literary Supplement*, no. 4817 (28 July 1995), 36.

This "part log-book memoir and part meditation" is compelling. The book is marked by a series of contradictions, such as between the subject matter and the fine writing used to express it as well as Matthiessen's own "primal, adventurous urges" and his "proto–Green ecological conscience." It is a record of an existential quest as well as a zoological one. He has produced a "splendid and vigorous book."

I208. Herrnkind, William F. "The Great White Hope." *Natural History*, 80 (May 1971), 95–96, 98, 100.

Rather than the usual dramaticized, romanticized and exaggerated shark-diving story, this is subdued, analytical, truthful and intimately personal. The prose sparkles. The book is interesting and praiseworthy, but the personal and moral questions raised by Matthiessen as well as his discussions of apartheid and whaling are inappropriate.

I209. *Kirkus Reviews*, 39 (Janaury 15, 1971), 92.

This is an agreeable miscellany. Its weakness (and the expedition's) is the long wait for the encounter with the great white shark. While Matthiessen offers some extraordinary diversions, they ultimately tend to cancel the excitement of the wait for the shark (and vice versa). *See* **I210**.

I210. *Kirkus Reviews*, 39 (March 1, 1971), 248.

Shorter version of **I209**.

I211. Lehmann-Haupt, Christopher. "White Monsters of the Deep." *New York Times*, 23 April 1971, p. 35.

The book is basically a very high-class advertisement for Peter Gimbel's film, *Blue Water, White Death*. It provides strong descriptive writing and high-tension scenes but an artificial climax. There is a subtle ambivalence to the book as a result of Matthiessen's realization of the connection between the thrill of danger and the relentlessness of human scavaging, leading to the while shark's eventual demise.

I212. Rogers, Michael. "Classic Returns." *Library Journal*, 122 (August 1997), 142.

Brief non-evaluative notice of the paperback reisssue.

I213. *Publishers Weekly*, 199 (4 January 1971), 56–57.

Matthiessen's "magnificent descriptive power" raises this book above the ordinary. It is a fascinating reading experience.

I214. Richie, Mary. "Underwater Terrors and Glories." *Book World* [*Washington Post*], 18 April 1971, p. 4.

This is a brilliant documentation of minds, means, and monsters. It is a very good, exciting, literate book.

I215. Robotham, John S. *Library Journal*, 96 (March 1, 1971), 849.

The hazards and hard work of making the film are made real by this finely written and intriguing book.

I216. Schmitt, Yvette. *Library Journal*, 96 (September 15, 1971), 2941–2942.

This is a well written report and a vivid account of the personalities and problems involved in making the film.

I217. "Shark Hunting." *National Observer*, 5 April 1971, p. 23.

A brief notice remarking on the book's "wonderful sensitivity to the natural world," followed by a slightly longer passage from the book itself.

I218. Weeks, Edward. "The Peripatetic Reviewer." *Atlantic*, 227 (March 1971), 109–110.

Most of this review is a descriptive account of Peter Gimbel's attempt to film the great white shark. Matthiessen writes in strong, graphic prose. His depiction of natural history, persistent courage, and the shark itself contribute to make memorable reading.

I219. Wolff, Geoffrey. "Man-Eater in the Deep." *Newsweek*, 77 (26 April 1971), 92, 94.

The book is a trove of shark lore, a suspenseful adventure yarn, and a decent man's report of how decent men behave when under great pressure. His account of how the great white looks beneath the ocean's surface is memorable.

SEAL POOL

I220. Babbitt, Natalie. "Picture Novels: Daughters & Sons." *New York Times Book Review*, Part II, 5 November 1972, p. 16.

A brief entry within an omnibus review. First-rate adult writers do not necessarily make first-rate writers for children. The book relies too much on whimsy. The theme is too thin for the complexities Matthiessen places upon it.

I221. *Bulletin of the Center for Children's Books*, 26 (January 1973), 80.

The story almost fails as a result of its dialogue too often verging on the cute or precious. The puns, latent content, and oblique references are too heavily laid on.

I222. Harmon, Virginia. *Library Journal*, 98 (February 15, 1973), 645.

Although the animals' conversations lack subtlety, this is a delightful fantasy and whimsical tale.

I223. *Kirkus Reviews*, 40 (July 1, 1972), 724–725.

The badinage among the animals can be corny and snobbish but "certain sophisticated children" will enjoy the predacious meditations of the owl, the rapid exchange of insults, and "the general contempt for man." The drawings have a more universal appeal than the text.

THE TREE WHERE MAN WAS BORN

I224. Barnett, S. A. "'Ostriches Have Charisma, Too.'" *Book World* [*Washington Post*], 14 January 1973, pp. 8–9.

Reviewed with *The Long African Day* by Norman Myers. This is an elegantly written book that conveys Matthiessen's intense feelings and affection for Africa. It transcends mere travelogue.

I225. "The Best of 1972 — For Giving and Getting." *Saturday Review*, 55 (2 December 1972), 84 [71–72, 78–80, 82, 84, 88–90].

Listed under "Nature & Ecology" is this "beautiful and heartbreaking portrait" by a superb naturalist-writer.

I226. *The Booklist*, 69 (September 1, 1972), 67.

A masterful depiction of the natural and human history of East Africa is presented in a richly detailed tapestry.

I227. _____. 69 (October 15, 1972), 172–173.

A very brief notice of no significant consequence.

I228. _____. 69 (November 11, 1972), 240.

A very brief notice.

I229. "Books Received." *Times Literary Supplement*, no. 3698, (19 January 1973), 73.

Brief. This is a stimulating book. Matthiessen is a shrewd observer, and he provides valuable insights on the people and attitudes of East Africa.

I230. Broyard, Anatole. "The Elephant in the Mire." *New York Times*, 17 October 1972, p. 39.

Even Matthiessen's extraordinary talents are "hard-pressed to squeeze any real juice" from this book. While there is splendor in both the prose and the photographs, "the *feel* of emergent Africa" remains unrevealed.

I231. Connolly, Cyril. "Carnage in Eden." *New York Review of Books*, 19 (January 25, 1973), 19–21.

A review/essay with *The Serengeti Lion* by George B. Schaller The joint product is warmly recommended. The text is admirable, accurate, original, scientific, and moving. The text and photographs should share the same title.

I232. "The Costs and Colors of Christmas." *Time*, 100 (4 December 1972), 73 [68–74].

Within a listing of selected books, this one is recommended as "desperate and elegiac and full of the urge to save" more wildlife from further catastrophe.

1233. Elisofon, Eliot. "A Four-Eyed View of Africa." *Natural History*, 81 (December 1972), 92–97.

The publisher has made an error in the idea of "separate identities" for the text and photographs. The text overwhelms the photographs and "neither contributes enough to the other." Matthiessen's writing on African prehistory and the origins of man is "outstanding," and no single photograph could match his rich and varied African experiences. He balances a wide range of subjects into a fascinating text. Approximately the first half of the review focuses on the text, and the second half on Porter's photographs.

1234. Fuller, Edmund. "Enthralling Africa and the Ancient Baobab Tree." *Wall Street Journal*, 7 December 1972, p. 28.

Reviewed with *The Long African Day* by Norman Myers. This is an absorbing study written with a fine style and reflective insights. Both books are opulent works and cries for help for the African wildlife and tribal people.

1235. Grumbach, Doris. "Books I've Enjoyed Hugely During 1971–1972." *Commonweal*, 97 (8 December 1972), 234–235.

Five books are briefly listed, including this literate and poetic account.

1236. Hoagland, Edward. "Eden Rediscovered — Just in Time." *Life*, 73 (27 October 1972), 24.

Matthiessen is a traveler possessed of scholarship and élan. This book is the rare occasion when words outshine the photographs. He is a "master of a rolling, old-fashioned, aloof rhetoric suitable for evoking a continent and its surging, migratory tribes." This "sweet, sweet, big book" is the centerpiece of Matthiessen's maturity.

1237. *The Horn Book Magazine*, 49 (April 1973), 170.

The mystery of East Africa emerges in magnificent magnitude in this book. Matthiessen's commentary is lively, and he provides a "glowing account" of his visit with Tindiga.

1238. Hughes, John. *Christian Science Monitor*, 18 April 1973, p. 11.

The text is perceptive but there is too much reliance on "old white hunters' tales" rather than research among the native peoples.

1239. *Kirkus Reviews*, 40 (August 15, 1972), 1004–1005.

Although he is only incidentally an ethnologist, Matthiessen has considerable narrative power. His prose is lush, and he views the landscape with awe and inexplicable sadness.

1240. McLellan, Joseph. "Paperbacks." *Book World* [*Washington Post*], 20 April 1975, p. 4.

Very brief. The combined effect of the photographs and Matthiessen's evocative text is uncommonly satisfying.

1241. Murray, Michelle. "Praise Be! The Best Gift Books Aren't the Costliest." *National Observer*, 2 December 1972, p. 25.

Within an article on books for the holiday season, this one is cited as the top choice. It is a beautiful and intelligent book and an overall excellent collaborative work.

1242. Prescott, Peter S. "The Pulse of Africa." *Newsweek*, 80 (30 October 1972), 103, 106.

Reviewed with *The Long African Day* by Norman Myers. Matthiessen is a fine writer who skillfully blends history and anthropology with precise observations. Both books are essential for anyone who cares about Africa.

1243. *Publishers Weekly*, 202 (4 September 1972), 50.

This is a deeply felt book that captures the sights, sounds and smells of Africa. It is a work of sympathy, understanding, and wonder.

1244. _____. 206 (30 September 1974), 61.

A very brief notice of the paperback edition repeating the comments of **1243**.

1245. R. F. G. *Best Sellers*, 32 (November 1, 1972), 355.

This is a fascinating book with a "smoothly written text." Matthiessen and Porter complement each other in their descriptions of the land and its people.

1246. Rasmussen, R. Kent. *Library Journal*, 97 (December 1, 1972), 3923.

There is little of intrinsic value here. The text is nothing but a lengthy impressionistic survey of man and nature in East Africa. Matthiessen's ignorance of Africa shows badly. The exceptional photographs are the book's only value, and the text should have been limited to something less ambitious in the same vein.

1247. Rogers, Michael. "Classic Returns." *Library Journal*, 120 (May 1, 1995), 138.

A brief notice of the new paperback edition in the Penguin Nature Classics series.

1248. *Saturday Review*, 55 (28 October 1972), 78–79.

This is one of the most stunning books of this or any year. Matthiessen and Porter have combined their passions and impressive talents "to evoke the human and natural history of East Africa." Matthiessen combines a gift for acute observation, a sense of African tribal history and myth, and a vivid personal account of this own encounter with Africa. The text is both informative and deeply moving; it ranks with Isak Dinesen's *Out of Africa*.

1249. "A Selection of Gift Books." *Christian Century*, 89 (22 November 1972), 1187.

Brief. One of the season's most worthwhile books is this "highest-class travelogue."

1250. Shepard, Paul. *New York Times Book Review*, 26 November 1972, pp. 31–32.

Reviewed with Norman Myers's *The Long African Day*. Matthiessen's text is a skillfully woven but disparate tapestry of travel fragments largely unrelated to the photographs. Porter's brilliant collection does not suggest Matthiessen's keen and troubled wanderlust. The publisher has made a pseudo-collaboration in pursuit of a profit. There is a plethora of information, perhaps too much. The reader has the feel of being a privileged, intelligent tourist.

1251. Simonds, C. H. "Big and Beautiful." *National Review*, 24 (December 8, 1972), 1361–1362.

In a listing of books for the holidays, this is the best of several available nature books on Africa. The juxtaposition of the formally independent text and photographs is an unusual and happy case.

1252. *Virginia Quarterly Review*, 49 (Spring 1973), xciii.

This collaboration is a joy to read and behold. Porter and Matthiessen are both poets. Whatever is eternal of Africa will be found in this book.

1253. Weeks, Edmund. "The Peripatetic Reviewer." *Atlantic*, 230 (November 1972), 125–126.

Matthiessen provides an illuminating text but he loses the reader in his speculation on human prehistory. One has to read with "a skipping eye" and discern the general truths. He is more engrossing in his observations of the native people, the wildlife, and the landscape.

THE WIND BIRDS

1254. *The Booklist*, 70 (October 1, 1973), 142.

A very brief non-evaluative notice.

1255. *The Bookwatch*, 15 (June 1994), 9

A brief inconsequential review.

1256. *Choice*, 11 (March 1974), 119.

Matthiessen is a master of prose, and the text is one great beauty. Yet he is an amateur naturalist, and biologists may find fault with his interpretations. His obvious passion, insight and knowledge, and delightful descriptive skills, however, make this a desirable book.

1257. *Kirkus Reviews*, 41 (June 15, 1973), 678.

A very brief recommendation.

1258. "On Birds." *Living Wilderness*, 38 (Spring 1974), 54.

A brief insignificant notice.

1259. Puleston, Dennis. *Quarterly Review of Biology*, 51 (March 1976), 153–154.

This is an exceptionally eloquent text. It gathers together fascinating facts about the shorebirds' biology and general behavior and presents them gracefully and passionately. Robert Gillmor's drawings are beautiful but cannot surpass Matthiessen's poetic touches in conveying the subjects' wild grace.

1260. Schneider, David. *Whole Earth Review*, no. 85 (Spring 1995), 28.

An extremely brief notice of the paperback edition with a one paragraph excerpt from the book.

1261. *Science Books*, 9 (March 1974), 308–309.

A brief review. The text provides a great wealth of information in an often poetic and occasionally wryly humorous style. It does contain a few errors.

FAR TORTUGA

1262. Allen, Bruce. *Saturday Review* NS, 2 (June 28, 1975), 24–25.

This interesting novel is "an adventurous failure." Matthiessen moves between "lucidly powerful impressionistic descriptions and a bewildering articulation of semi-bearable dialect." The novel's surface "exudes a magnificent and paradoxical radiance" but beneath it there is no discernable harmonious whole.

1263. B. R. "A Sea Story With Impact." *Yachting*, 138 (September 1975), 88.

It is an unusual novel. The dialogue becomes repetitive and monotonous, and the characters take a long time to develop as individuals. A sense of life aboard the schooner, however, is achieved with an almost physical impact.

1264. Bell, Pearl K. "Elusive Perfection." *New Leader*, 58 (June 9, 1975), 18 [17–18].

An omnibus review. The book is full of "unfortunate typographical experiments." It is bereft of any memorable words, deeds, or morals. It may be an ambitious book, but it goes genuinely wrong.

1265. *The Booklist*, 71 (July 15, 1972), 1162.

Very brief. The book is a stylistic tour de force.

1266. "Briefly Noted." *New Yorker*, 51 (19 May 1975), 118–119.

The exact significance of this book will have to be surmised, but it is a superb feat of storytelling. The book grows in resonance, and Matthiessen brings the story to stark and insistent life.

1267. Broyard, Anatole. "A Slow Boat to Symbolism." *New York Times*, 6 May 1975, p. 37.

This is an immensely disappointing book. Matthiessen's subject and characterizations silence the greater part of his talent. His use of dialect is a mistake; it presents no advantages in the telling of the story and is not in the least expressive. The characters are, for the most part, indistinguishable and the little action in the story seems arbitrary. In Broyard's view the book is damned by the greatness of *At Play in the Fields of the Lord*.

1268. *Choice*, 12 (October 1975), 1001.

This is a most unusual and unconventional novel. Matthiessen has successfully suffused the ingredients of the conventional adventure novel with a distinctly modern sensibility and a modern sense of form.

I269. Davis, L. J. "The Job of Experiment and a Case in Point." *National Observer*, 7 June 1975, p. 21.

Although some of its typographical effects are a bit affected, this experimental novel succeeds on the level of telling its story; it is both clear and beautifully controlled. While a striking and challenging attempt, the book fails totally on a deeper level. It remains a story of event and not of meaning. The reader is locked out of the story and remains an observer rather than a participant. The characters do not change and so the only movement is that of the plot. It is a well-used and time-tested one, the same as Melville used in *Moby-Dick*. He took an adventure story and made it poetry. Matthiessen has taken poetry and made it into an adventure story.

I270. "Editor's Choice." *New York Times Book Review*, December 28, 1975, p. 2 [1–2].

Far Tortuga is one of thirteen titles chosen. The book "risks a lot and demands considerable patience." But the originality of its form, the sustained rhythms and beauty of its language, and its precise and serious love of its subject outweigh its eccentric dialogue, occasionally self-indulgent and precious descriptions, and its pretension to myth.

I271. Edwards, Thomas R. "Adventures of the Deep." *New York Review of Books*, 22 (August 7, 1975), 34–35 [34–36].

There is an air of poetic self-consciousness about the book. The reader will readily know he is in Conrad and Melville territory as "significance" asserts itself, *but* the story is enthralling and Matthiesssen uses his method for character development, not self-display. The characters' voices sound remarkably right, and the story is not strained by literary means to make more of this acutely observed life than it makes of itself. It is a spare and sober story of great purity and intensity. But "one such book should be enough."

I272. Fremont-Smith, Eliot. "The Road to 'Far Tortuga.'" *Village Voice*, 2 June 1975, pp. 39, 41.

This is a meditation on reviewing and the review process as it relates to *Far Tortuga*. The first reviewer he assigned the book to returned it as pretentious and unreadable. Fremont-Smith has difficulty reading the book as well and feels guilt as a result of it. Finally, reading the book backwards provides him with "a feel for the seriousness" of it, and he is then able to go forward again. Despite Matthiessen's intentions, the book fails not because of its difficulties of dialect, slowness, or dramatic coincidence, but because it lacks the intelligence that "grows from character." The characters are all Matthiessen's mannequins; they do and say only what is needed to fulfill his destiny for them. His "design" is too evident in the book. The language is not natural, and the plot is predictable and completely thematic. The intent of the book may be admirable, but it is all "a little dumb, and not wrenching."

I273. Fuller, Edmund. "On a Turtle Boat in the Caribbean." *Wall Street Journal*, 23 June 1975, p. 10.

A well balanced and insightful review. Matthiessen is an innovator and an ambitious writer. The book is a fine, brave and striving work. The story is told almost completely in dialogue and there is the feel that his ear is phenomenally accurate; the dialogue is vivid and eloquent. There is a monotony to the devices used and to the dialogue, despite the skill with which they are rendered. The book seems to realize Matthiessen's intentions, however. It demands time and attention but may not be to everyone's liking.

I274. Gray, Paul. "Sea Changes." *Time*, 105 (26 May 1975), 80.

At first these pages of unattributed dialogue and white blank space seem too close to the works of lazy poets. But as the characters develop through their dialogue, unheard melodies emerge and the periodic descriptive passages possess a haunting beauty. Matthiessen has duplicated as thoroughly as possible his own earlier experience on a turtle boat and created "an uncommonly successful mixture of fact and fiction." He has stripped the novel bare of almost all fictional resources.

The review is followed by a profile of Matthiessen.

1275. Hill, William B. "Fiction." *America*, 133 (15 November 1975), 311.

A brief notice. The tedium of the voyage is sometimes as bad for the reader as it is for the crew. The ship and crew share an evanescence with the turtles. Matthiessen writes "sad and piercing comments in an absolutely melodious dialect."

1276. Kennedy, William. "Sea Spun Tale." *New Republic*, 172 (7 June 1975), 28–30.

While occasional confusion persists throughout the book concerning who is speaking, this is a virtuoso novel. It is the work of a mature writer with a poetic bent and a familiarity with the sea. His great achievement is in the realm of vast experience transformed. This is a work in which art prevails.

1277. *Kirkus Reviews*, 43 (March 1, 1975), 258.

This book is proof that the boldest writing is also the simplest and most universal. It is a sublime work of intense human drama.

1278. Larson, Charles R. "Another Voyage of the *Pequod*?" *The Nation*, 220 (31 May 1975), 661.

Far Tortuga is a fascinating book typographically, but by the end of it one must question how much has been gained by the innovations. They make it difficult for the characters or events to engage the reader. Although there are passages that are as fine as anything Matthiessen has written, this book is not the equal of his small masterpiece, *At Play in the Fields of the Lord*.

1279. Mahoney, Lawrence. "A Magnificent Novel of the Caribbean." *Miami Herald*, 22 June 1975, p. 7E.

A laudatory review of a "splendidly gifted novel" and a "visionary sea story." This is a sublime book that is so original it

is uncanny. The descriptions are wonderfully and sparsely done. In this book Matthiessen measures up to Melville and Conrad.

1280. McLellan, Joseph. "Paperbacks." *Book World* [*Washington Post*], 16 May 1976, p. L4.

This is a simple but beautifully written story. It is alive with "the slow pulse and mysterious green depths of the ocean."

1281. Mewshaw, Michael. "Tortuga's Complaint." *Texas Monthly*, 3 (August 1975), 46, 48.

The effect of the style and the design is cumulative and considerable. Matthiessen has found the perfect form for his multifarious talents and has flawlessly meshed his content with it. The novel's tone is elegiac, but the characters are never sentimentalized.

1282. Murray, John J. *Best Sellers*, 71 (July 1975), 89.

This quasi-novel is alternately rewarding and infuriating. While the idioms and Caribbean patios are generally authentic and a delight, there is too much wasted space. The characters don't seem to be distinct and are not easily differentiable. The story itself is not much of an adventure, and the details of shipboard life are boring. It is ultimately a tiresome read.

1283. "New & Noteworthy." *New York Times Book Review*, 4 November 1984, p. 42.

A brief positive notice of the paperback edition.

1284. "1975: A Selection of Noteworthy Titles." *New York Times Book Review*, 7 December 1975, p. 62.

A one line assessment: this is "a visionary novel of the sea."

1285. Prescott, Peter S. "The Last Turtles." *Newsweek*, 85 (19 May 1975), 85–86.

A laudatory review. This is "a beautiful and original piece of work, a resonant, symbolical story." It is a difficult yet successful undertaking, both moving and impressive.

1286. *Progressive*, 39 (August 1975), 45.

Matthiessen controls language, type, and design in a way to actively involve the reader. The book is both an adventure and a lament for the terrible waste and pollution of our resources.

1287. *Publishers Weekly*, 207 (17 March 1975), 80.

This is an extravagant assessment of the book. The novel is simply a work of brilliance. The comparisons to Conrad and Melville are completely justified. It is a story to experience on many levels; it is a book both worldly and otherworldly.

1288. *Publishers Weekly*, 209 (1 March 1976), 97.

A very brief notice of the paperback edition which quotes from **1287**.

1289. Sale, Roger. "The Realms of Gold." *Hudson Review*, 28 (Winter 1975/1976), 620–621 [616–628].

An omnibus review. This is a singular and fascinating book, but, as in most of Matthiessen's work, he never gets beyond a sense that he is forcing his material into a respectful special shape. He respects his characters and is absorbed in their lives. However, the book is excessively long. In attempting to inflate the story, he has attempted too much. The first and last one hundred pages are marvelous, but readers will be worn down by the overall length.

1290. Silvert, Conrad. "Boat Rotten, Mon, But de Book Not." *Literary Quarterly*, (May 15, 1975), 15.

This book of stark beauty and subtle, troubling undercurrents has the wholeness and grand scope of a major epic. The lilting rhythms of West Indian English are cannily and lovingly captured.

1291. Smith, Dave. *Library Journal*, 100 (April 15, 1975), 783.

Matthiessen risks trickery and confusion but boldly succeeds. It is a magnificent performance with enough truth "to fill the hearts of men for all their days."

1292. Stone, Robert. *New York Times Book Review*, 25 May 1975, pp. 1–2.

Matthiessen is "a unique and masterful visionary artist." The characters are, at times, a bit too obviously exotic constructs and a little too predictable, but his evocation of the Caribbean is uncanny. The book is "a singular experience."

1293. Weeks, Edward. "The Peripatetic Reviewer." *Atlantic*, 235 (June 1975), 92.

It is an exceptional novel whose tragedy drags at the heart. This notice is largely plot summary.

1294. Wolff, Geoffrey. "Modern Time, Mon." *New Times*, 4 (June 27, 1975), 64–65.

An admiring review. The book's great virtue is its "unique suitability to a fable about the sea." It makes no use of conceits of any kind, "relying on the found poetry derived from precise and necessary descriptions." Matthiessen reproduces the cadences of speech perfectly but mars his narrative by his "odd decision" to use dialect. The book is a lament for the "certain death of things still alive," and it provides a ceremony of remembrance for things and men now dead.

THE SNOW LEOPARD

1295. Adams, Phoebe-Lou. "PLA." *The Atlantic*, 242 (September 1978), 95.

An essentially descriptive notice of the book. Matthiessen's great skill as a writer allows the reader to share his vision.

1296. Adams, Robert M. "Blue Sheep Zen." *New York Review of Books*, 25 (September 28, 1975), 8–9 [8–12].

Reviewed with George B. Schaller's *Mountain Monarchs: Wild Sheep and Goats of the Himalya*. That part of the book which describes the expedition itself is "brilliantly and vividly written." When Matthiessen describes the landscape and wildlife, his prose is crisp and strongly appealing to the senses. His Zen reflections and discourses are comparatively "watery" and little new is revealed in his exposition of Buddhism. The trip seems a "bust" for Matthiessen in worldly or practical terms but a triumph from a Zen perspective.

The reviewer raises the question of whether the expedition and the book itself are not in conflict with the very Zen philosophy — of being in the moment and free from entangling worldly involvement — that Matthiessen seeks. A luke-warm endorsement of the book.

I297. "All About Me." *Book World* [*Washington Post*], 3 December 1978, p. E10.

A very brief notice is included among "The Books of Christmas." The book has vivid portraits of the people he travels with and those he meets.

I298. *Booklist*, 74 (June 15, 1978), 1594.

More than just an expertly told adventure story, Matthiessen's deeper reflections enlighten his physical and mental journey.

I299. Burger, Jack. "Himalayan Journey." *Backpacker*, 6 (December 1977/January 1978), 20.

Brief. The dual aspect of the journey is noted; there is plenty of introspection to accompany the descriptions of the Himalayas.

I300. Carroll, Jeffrey. *Hawaii Review*, 10 (Spring/Fall 1980), 183–185.

Matthiessen is unique among American writers in his considerable skills in both fiction and nonfiction. He has sustained the poetry of wonder in his nature writing. The book is a blending of memoir, poetry, zoology, and adventure fiction, with a careful explication of Zen Buddhism. He has merged motion with contemplation as well as anyone has, reconciling Western art and Eastern thought.

I301. Clapperton, Jane. "Cosmo Reads the New Books." *Cosmopolitan*, 185 (December 1978), 16.

A brief positive but inconsequential notice within a seasonal survey.

I302. *The Critic*, 37 (October 15, 1978), 8.

Brief. Matthiessen is a very good writer excelling at natural description and the explanation of Buddhist ideas. However, the tone of the book is too solemn and intense, and the reader may very well be bored before the end.

I303. Cross, Nigel. "Whore of Babylon." *New Statesman*, 100 (10 October 1980), 21 [21–22].

A brief assessment within an omnibus review of recent paperbacks. The book is a paean to Buddhism but is also interestingly digressive.

I304. Des Pres, Terrence. "Soul Searching in the Himalayas." *Book World* [*Washington Post*], 20 August 1978, pp. E1, E4.

A perceptive and admiring review. Matthiessen is not an adventurer or a man-against-the-elements explorer. He celebrates the virtues of lost cultures, praises the experience of life apart from life, and bears witness to creation vanishing. He is a visionary but hardminded too. This is a radiant book of extreme beauty; it is fiercely felt and magnificently written.

I305. "Expedition of the Spirit." *Horizon*, 21 (August 1978), 6.

Brief. This book is a fine addition to Matthiessen's canon. It is an extraordinarily rich book, distinguished by the interweaving of its various elements.

I306. "From a Far Plateau." *The Economist*, 271 (9 June 1979), 125–126.

This account is based on brilliant observation and description. His interior journey leads him to genuine insights into the spirit of the place as well as his own mind.

I307. Fuller, Edmund. "A Pilgrimage High Into the Himalayas." *Wall Street Journal*, 28 August 1978, p. 10.

Matthiessen writes a masterful evocation of places and sights. It is a book of poetic vision and exceptional beauty. It has a greater intensity than his earlier books.

I308. Gordon, John. "Toward the Still Center." *Inquiry*, 1 (November 27, 1978), 27–28.

Matthiessen's lyrical resources are only occasionally equal to the demand placed on them. He is a first rate prose writer but only a so-so poet. But because he has actually spent the time on the trek he has brought back an account both scrupulous and moving. No one could combine the two roles of Author and Mountaineer as well as he does. The book resists categories and is best as "dream travelogue" rather than "dream monologue." He has achieved "cultic status."

I309. Graham, Frank, Jr. "Worldviews." *Audubon*, 80 (November 1978), 8.

A review essay. This is "the genuine article in an era of ersatz wilderness travel books." Matthiessen is perhaps the "finest living writer on the natural world." Unfortunately, he has made the book into a tract on Eastern religions, and his discursiveness obscures things. His constant attempts to find cosmic messages in what he sees detracts from the book as a whole. When he frees himself from the "Himalayan holy men," he provides resonant passages that make the reader's spine tingle.

I310. Gray, Francine du Plessix. *Commonweal*, 105 (8 December 1978), 791–792.

In an admiring letter written to Matthiessen after reading the book, Gray praises its purity, its unwillingness to compromise, and its vigor. His language is unsurpassed in its precision and rightness. The book may well turn out to be a very great one.

I311. Hall, Donald. "From Death Unto Death." *National Review*, 30 (October 13, 1978), 1294–1295.

This is a serious book as few books are and a religious book which tells us how to live. The death of Matthiessen's second wife helps spin his "spirit out of its old path" and unlocks his tears (unshed in previous books). Through grief his unlocked spirit flows in a religious pilgrimage. It is this glimpse of loss which gives the rest of the book its profundity. This is his best book.

I312. Harrison, Jim. "10,000 Successive Octobers." *The Nation*, 227 (16 September 1978), 250–251.

Matthiessen "must be our most eccentric major writer" in terms of the eccentricities of thought. He writes cleanly and beautifully of his outward journey as well as his equally torturous inward journey. For the first time in his work, he is utterly candid. The book is also the best attempt at explicating Buddhist and Tantric terminology and hagiography. This is a magnificent book which provides a "map of the sacred for any man's journey."

Reprinted as "The Snow Leopard, by Peter Matthiessen" in I313.

I313. _____. "The Snow Leopard, by Peter Matthiessen." In his *Just Before Dark: Collected Nonfiction*. New York: Houghton Mifflin/Seymour Lawrence, 1991. Pp. [253]–256.

Reprint of I312.

I314. Hillaby, John. "Splendors and Miseries." *Quest/78*, 2 (November 1978), 71–72.

This book will outlive its author; it is a masterpiece.

I315. _____. "Truth in the Hills." *Observer*, 1 April 1979, p. 37.

It is a remarkable book — honest and outspoken — with a wide variety of themes.

I316. Hoagland, Edward. "Walking the Himalayas." *New York Times*, 13 August 1978, 264–268. [*New York Times* News Service wire during the strike period by Printing Pressmen in New York City].

This is "a radiant but rather fragile, flickering book." The interpolations concerning his wife do not fit into the narrative because of the falsity of their placement and carelessness. The Buddhist theology and history is "much too telescoped for a laymen," and Matthiessen's proselytizing is irritating. But no other so-called nature-travel writer has attempted a journey such as this, and he writes about the journey much better than anyone else. Matthiessen is undervalued as a writer; he is only getting better. This is his best nonfiction book.

Reprinted I317.

I317. _____. *New York Times Book Review*, 26 November 1978, pp. 3, 82.

Reprint of **I316**.

I318. "Holiday Reading." *Observer*, 15 July 1979, p. 37.

Very brief. Included in a list of "choice" books is this "beautifully contemplative work."

I319. *The Horn Book*, 54 (December 1978), 670–671.

Brief. This is a lyrical literary work. It is "wondrously evocative" of the Himalayas' natural grandeur as well as "sensitively tuned" to Matthiessen's own inner spiritual and worldly feelings.

I320. *Kirkus Reviews*, 46 (June 1, 1978), 624.

A brief positive assessment. Matthiessen's journal is numinous and a study in contrasts. He gathers the reader into his Buddhist consciousness.

See **I321**.

I321. _____. 46 (July 1, 1978), 700

Reprint of **I320**.

I322. *Kliatt*, 14 (Winter 1980), 38.

Brief. This book stands with the classic literary and spiritual pilgrimages. He records his spiritual journey with precision, honesty, and beauty.

I323. Lord, Nancy. "A Double Journey to Nepal." *Living Wilderness*, 42 (January 1979), 46.

An enthusiastic and admiring review of "a marvelous book." Matthiessen succeeds brilliantly in conveying the dual purpose of his journey. He brings to life the country and its people with lyrical prose. An important message on the need for wilderness, open space, and the preservation of "pure culture" is presented.

I324. Lynch, Dennis. *National Forum*, 60 (Fall 1980), 56–57.

This is an engrossing account in the classic tradition of quest books — a rousing adventure story and an intense philosophi-cal pilgrimage. Matthiessen combines a keen eye with a poetic grace of expression and maintains his sense of wonderment before nature. The book recounts a complex spiritual awakening, and it is to his credit that he maintains the reader's interest to the end, even after the journey's adventurous elements are completed.

I325. Lyon, Thomas J. *Western American Literature*, 14 (Spring 1979), 62–63.

Brief. Matthiessen's Buddhism gives the book dimension and vision beyond the immediacy and "unplanned-ness" of a great travel narrative. His descriptions are utterly clear and effortless.

I326. Michaels, Leonard. *New Republic*, 179 (23 September 1978), 33–34.

The book is an account into the wilderness of Matthiessen's mind as well as the wilderness of the Himalayas. It is a multifaceted work which is unified by the poetry of his vision, his intelligent simplicity, and his observation. It is a fascinating and beautiful book, which is ultimately, "a metamorphic death trip."

I327. "New in Paperback." *Nature*, 391 (5 February 1998), 551.

A very brief notice.

I328. Otness, Harold M. *Library Journal*, 103 (July 1978), 1397.

This book will please many tastes with its combination of adventure, anthropological, and nature writing, as well as its introspection.

I329. "Paperback Choice." *Observer*, 26 October 1980, p. 28.

Very brief. This is "an enjoyable combination of mountaineering and mysticism."

I330. "Paperbacks: New and Noteworthy." *New York Times Book Review*, 26 August 1979, p. 31.

A brief notice of "a beautifully told story."

I331. "The Post Recommends." *Saturday Evening Post*, 250 (October 1978), 87.

A brief inconsequential notice.

1332. Prescott, Peter. "Brave Journey." *Newsweek*, 92 (11 September 1978), 89B, 89C, 89E.

This is one of Matthiessen's most ambitious and most personal books. While there is a lot of fine material in it, a lot of the book does not work well. The exterior journey in the Himalayas is well described, but it is the more important interior journey which causes a problem. He tells us less than we need to know but more than his narrative can bear. It is a brave failure because Matthiessen must have been aware of the traditional failure of words to explain the Zen experience.

1333. Price, K. McCormick. *San Diego Magazine*, 30 (September 1978), 260–261.

An appreciative review. Matthiessen conveys a wide breadth of human experiences in this compelling account. The reader's internal and external landscapes of the mind's eye are vastly enriched.

1334. Priestland, Gerald. "Consciousness Raising — to 8,000 Feet." *Christian Science Monitor*, 26 October 1978, p. 19.

A cynical and skeptical assessment. High altitude revelations seldom maintain their significance at sea level. It is best to accept the book as a travel-diary and to dismiss the metaphysics, which are often self-indulgent. The writing is lucid and craftsman-like with an abundance of good description, but Matthiessen's journey was probably not necessary.

1335. *Publishers Weekly*, 213 (3 July 1978), 58.

Brief. A touch of the poet is brought to this account. The inner pilgrimage is as much an adventure as the actual trek through Nepal.

1336. _____. 216 (23 July 1979), 158.

A very brief notice of the paperback edition which draws from the original review, **1335.**

1337. Radford, Tim. "Playing the Great Game." *Guardian Weekly*, 120 (15 April 1979), 21.

Reviewed with John Keay's *The Gilgit Game*. This brief review gives no evidence of recognizing Matthiessen's true intentions in his journey and book. While recognizing that he "writes well," there is some disappointment that Matthiessen is too casual about the trip's hardships, that he doesn't provide enough detail about his equipment, and that he spends more time on Zen than on topography.

1338. Saunders, Bill. "Paperbacks." *Observer*, 15 February 1998, p. 16.

Brief. This book is irrepressibly cheerful. Matthiessen accepts the journey's highs and lows gracefully, without being "a drag."

1339. Schultheis, Rob. "'The Snow Leopard.'" *Outside*, 3 (November/December 1978), 103–104.

An admiring, although largely descriptive, review. He has produced the "Great Himalayan Book."

1340. Sheppard, R. Z. "Zen and the Art of Watching." *Time*, 112 (7 August 1978), 78, 81.

Matthiessen tries to juggle too many overlapping parts — natural description, geography, Zen discourses, intellectual history — and each seems to detract from another. The book needs a lightness of touch to succeed in dealing with its disparate elements, but it is lacking in the essential Zen element of wit.

1341. Sipper, Ralph B. "A Westerner Changes His Spots in 'Snow Leopard.'" *Los Angeles Times Book Review*, 10 September 1978, pp. 1, 10.

The book is informed with a keen sense of place and a fastidious eye for detail which illuminates. The descriptions of the journey's physicality provide the book's true power. It is a compelling, if not always comfortable, reading experience.

1342. Solomon, Charles. "Paperbacks." *Los Angeles Times Book Review*, 25 August 1996, p. 11.

While Matthiessen's descriptions of the local color of Nepal retain their interest, his "attempts to link mystical traditions ... into some all-encompassing whole seem superficial at best."

1343. Trevelyan, Raleigh. "On the Crystal Mountain." *The Listener*, 101 (12 April 1979), 528.

This is a strange, magical book of a quest for the snow leopard, for identity, and for recovery. The writing soars to poetic heights. It is very visual and almost every page contains a memorable image.

1344. True, Michael. "Journey Up the Himalayas." *The Progressive*, 42 (December 1978), 61.

A brief but overall positive review. The physical descriptions of the journey are superbly vivid, but Matthiessen's spiritual ruminations are cloudy.

1345. *Village Voice*, 19 June 1978, p. 82.

Very brief. He is "a luminous and captivating writer."

1346. Wolff, Geoffrey. "The Indescribable One: Still Undescribed." *New Times*, 11 (September 18, 1978), 68–69.

This book represents an exploration above all of the interior regions of Matthiessen's mind and faith. While he has undertaken on numerous occasions to directly and respectfully explain the unknown, to do so with Zen seems beyond the reach of his powers of imagination. Because of the intractability of language, attempts to share his experiences come dangerously close to parody. He makes a stubborn and courageous but doomed attempt to make his faith felt by others.

1347. Zweig, Paul. "Eastern Mountain Time." *Saturday Review*, 5 (August 1978), 44–45.

The didactic thread that ties the book together make it predictable and ultimately impersonal. Every event has its moral, and too often Matthiessen lapses into clichés of Zen psychology which detracts from his magnificent descriptive passages. When he allows his journey to speak for itself, it tingles with power. Those passages where the naturalist, the spiritual apprentice and the writer converge simply and dramatically, save the book and make it a vivid account.

SAND RIVERS

1348. Adams, Phoebe-Lou. *The Atlantic*, 247 (May 1981), 84.

Very brief. Matthiessen has successfully made a photographic safari on which nothing happened interesting.

1349. *Booklist*, 77 (January 1, 1981), 600.

This is a pungent book which displays Matthiessen's enthusiasm and intense power of observation.

1350. "Books." *Playboy*, 28 (April 1981), 30.

A very brief assessment: the book is a real treat.

1351. "Briefly Noted — Paperbacks." *Christian Science Monitor*, 9 April 1982, p. B11.

A brief descriptive notice.

1352. Dopp, Bonnie Jo. *Library Journal*, 106 (March 1, 1981), 567.

A brief, generally descriptive, notice. The book's first half is slow moving, but the account of the trip itself is absorbing.

1353. Drabelle, Dennis. *Smithsonian*, 12 (April 1981), 153–155.

There is an explicit political purpose to the book — increasing awareness of the need to save the Selous — but Matthiessen remains in control and never becomes sentious.

1354. Fuller, Edmund. "Ways of Looking at Afghanistan and Wild Africa." *Wall Street Journal*, 11 May 1981, p. 26.

One of three books discussed. It is a fine book that has engaged Matthiessen's best gifts and provides a ruefully beautiful account of the fading African wilderness.

1355. Gellhorn, Martha. "Scouring the Selous." *Times Literary Supplement*, no. 4099 (October 23, 1981), 1227.

This is a static, curiously earnest book. Its best part is Matthiessen's account of the foot safari at the end of the book. His reverence for Brian Nicholson is puzzling given his own credentials as a naturalist and traveler. It is hoped that Matthiessen will use his African experiences to produce a novel comparable to *At Play in the Fields of the Lord*.

I356. Harding, William Harry. "Books." *Westways*, 73 (September 1981), 68–69.

The book evokes an authentic sense of this special place. It is flawed by the lack of photographs from the foot safari and by Matthiessen's reluctant admiration for Brian Nicholson. Despite Nicholson's admirable administration of the Selous, he is an heir to "Old Africa." Matthiessen needed to comment more on his view of the future for "New Africa."

I357. Harrison, Jim. "Voice of the Wilderness." *New York Times Book Review*, 17 May 1981, pp. 1, 26.

This is a "strange, bittersweet, autumnal book" which "moves from natural history to the novel to some sort of majestic fable." Part of its fascination and charm is the result of the tensions between Brian Nicholson and Matthiessen. The prose exhibits a glittering, sculpted character. Like all of Matthiessen's work, the sense of beauty and mystery is indelible.

I358. Hayes, Harold. *New York Magazine*, 14 (27 April 1981), 79–80.

Matthiessen provides some interesting background information leading up to his foot safari, but the account of the actual trip is disappointing. Because of a lack of animals or interesting occurrences, he must sustain reader interest through a narrative theme revolving around Brian Nicholson. While Matthiessen's share of the book is lacking, the photographs are uniformly excellent.

I359. Hayward, Henry S. "An Unabashedly Sentimental Safari." *Christian Science Monitor*, 13 April 1981, "Monthly Book Review," pp. 1, 8.

A largely descriptive review. The Selous Reserve comes alive under Matthiessen's keen eye. He creates vivid word pictures that bring the animals to life.

I360. Gorman, James. *Discover*, 2 (April 1981), 88–89.

Matthiessen is a gifted writer who is touched with "the naturalist's zest and reverence for the world." The book is not a complete success because he is not able to draw together the two Africas he depicts: the one of wildlife and the other of man and human prejudices and deep feelings.

I361. Kastner, Joseph. "Safari to Save the Selous." *Book World* [*Washington Post*], 19 April 1981, p. 4.

Rather than the introspection of *The Snow Leopard*, this is an extroverted account of his journey to the Selous revealing his "special grace of perception and an understanding of nature made up in equal parts of love and learning." Matthiessen's prose is touched with a photographic immediacy; his story is richly and evenly told without sermonizing or any real climax.

I362. *Kirkus Reviews*, 49 (January 1, 1981), 62.

Intrinsically, this book does not equal his earlier work, but, helped by the photographs, it is a book of certain interest. Matthiessen's focus becomes the complex character of Brian Nicholson, the Selous's former warden.

I363. Luard, Nicholas. "Soft Zoology." *The Spectator*, 246 (13 June 1981), 18.

The text gives new meaning to "painful honesty." It may work as a field manual for the next expedition to the Selous, but minute detail overwhelms the reader. This is a pity since Matthiessen has an unaffected love for whatever is wild. In contrast, van Lawick's photographs provide a quick, luminous, and vivid portrait.

I364. Morris, Jan. "Visions in the Wilderness." *Saturday Review*, 8 (April 1981), 68–69.

While the review is not particularly well

conceived or presented, Morris sees the book as a kind of good, the bad, and the wild. It is a deceptive and remarkable book, and a far better book than it pretends. It begins slowly while Matthiessen assembles all of his characters and prepares for the safari. He creates an allegory among the conservative throwback Brian Nicholson as the devil's advocate, himself as progressive and ecologically minded, and nature in the raw.

1365. "Paperbacks: New and Noteworthy." *New York Times Book Review*, 14 February 1982, p. 35.

Very brief. The text renders the beauty and mystery of the area.

1366. Pickering, Samuel, Jr. "At the Beginning and the End of the Earth." *Georgia Review*, 35 (Winter 1981), 886–887 [883–888].

The book is a good one but not an extraordinary one. There are many interesting anecdotes and descriptions of animals. Matthiessen is an ascetic, and the stripping away generally leaves little of interest. Because he is a "true believer," his vision of life is sometimes clouded.

1367. Price, K. McCormick. *San Diego Magazine*, 33 (March 1981), 79.

Matthiessen's account of this African journey lacks the compelling involvement evoked by *The Snow Leopard*. He has an unparalleled gift for natural description; he seemingly misses nothing around him.

1368. *Publishers Weekly*, 219 (9 January 1981), 69.

A superb story of travel and adventure. Matthiessen's descriptions of the landscape and animals evoke a sense of wonder.

1369. _____. 221 (12 February 1982), 97.

A very brief notice of the paperback edition excerpted from **1368**.

1370. Rodman, Selden. "Books in Brief." *National Review*, 33 (October 30, 1981), 1288–1289.

Matthiessen seems to be running out of places wild enough to fully engage his talents. He is forced into anecdotal recreations of the Selous pioneers' experiences, which is often nothing more than dry reportage. However, he never fails to draw readers into his beguiling orbit, and his prose is capable of rising to poetry.

1371. Rensberger, Boyce. "The Wildest of All Wild Places." *Natural History*, 90 (June 1981), 76, 80–81.

This review-essay recounts much of the history of the Selous and its present condition rather than actually evaluating the book. Matthiessen gives a vivid and sometimes poetic diary of the foot safari. While in many ways the safari was a "publicity stunt" to raise awareness for the need to protect the Reserve, the book does not make a very strong case that the Selous is in grave danger at the present time. Despite the lack of hard evidence, Matthiessen allows his eloquence to serve the more pessimistic view of the Reserve's demise. He deliberately leaves many of his observations ambivalent and cryptic. If the book does rally support, it will assure that a piece of real Africa will always be there.

1372. Stacey, Michelle. "The Last Safari." *Outside*, 6 (June/July 1981), 98–99.

This book lacks the excitement of the inner crisis of *The Snow Leopard*, but it is successful in less cataclysmic terms. The prose paints a vivid picture of the romance of the bush. The first half is haunted by the absence of animals; the safari into the Selous is the book's climax.

1373. Strouse, Jean. "Call of the Wildlife." *Newsweek*, 97 (27 April 1981), 92.

A largely descriptive notice of the book. Matthiessen is in top form writing about the fauna and flora of the Selous. He teaches without being didactic. The book is the wild world's eloquent defense.

1374. Vaughan, Stephan. "The Wild Heart of Africa." *Observer*, 7 June 1981, p. 32.

Matthiessen has a superlative eye for beauty, but "for all the urgent message and the unlaid ghosts," the book suggests a "set curriculum" compared to *The Snow Leopard*.

1375. *Virginia Quarterly Review*, 58 (Spring 1982), 61.

A brief notice. This is a remarkable tale and a marvelous book. It is resonant in its description of the land's beauty and bittersweet in its frank account of the land's fragility.

1376. Wray, Wendell. *Best Sellers*, 41 (July 1981), 155.

Matthiessen remains sensitive to his total environment. The philosophical insights and humanistic judgments he offers rank him as a master of this genre.

1377. Young, Vernon. "Africa Addio." *Hudson Review*, 34 (Winter 1981/1982), 627–630 [625–630].

Matthiessen combines the exhaustive knowledge of the naturalist with a poet's response to exotic landscapes. The book is in the tradition of *journeys back* which have characterized trek literature for a hundred years. But the book also has political implications for the future of the Selous. Matthiessen is wonderful in his command of the color, sound and substance that captures the resonance of the wilderness.

IN THE SPIRIT
OF CRAZY HORSE

1378. Abley, Mark. "The Mandela of the Mid-West." *Times Literary Supplement*, no. 4659 (17 July 1992), 6.

A review-essay examining the American Indian Movement (AIM), Leonard Peltier's case, and Matthiessen's involvement with them which resulted in *In the Spirit of Crazy Horse*. The book is "long, tiring, [and] intermittently engrossing." Surprisingly, its most severe flaws are in the writing. Rather then his usual terse lyrical prose, the presentation is exhaustive and tedious. While the book honors Peltier's case, presenting a coherent defense of a wronged man, Matthiessen does not make clear his own attitude toward AIM and their political beliefs and demands.

1379. Biolsi, Thomas. *American Indian Culture and Research Journal*, 16 (no. 1, 1992), 180–182.

Matthiessen argues convincingly that Leonard Peltier was unjustly railroaded, and his epilogue adds "dramatic" material. He is less convincing in his larger argument that the F.B.I. oppression of the American Indian Movement was connected to corporate interests in developing the natural resources on Indian land. His presentation of Indians as one of two kinds, either good, traditional Indians or bad "'acculturated' BIA/tribal council" Indians, is simplistic. Still, this is an epic book which presents a "generally convincing analysis of a critical period and a dramatic series of events."

1380. *Booklist*, 79 (December 1, 1982), 467.

Matthiessen is able to advance his concerns and the Indians' cause despite the book's tedium in style and narrative flow.

1381. "Books." *Playboy*, 30 (March 1983), 25.

Very brief. This is a sad and detailed look at the wild west's unromantic part of its legacy.

1382. *The Bookwatch*, 12 (June 1991), 4.

Very brief. The book is a controversial and highly charged exposé.

1383. Bowden, Henry Warner. *Theology Today*, 40 (no. 2, 1983), 246–248.

Matthiessen's view is too simplistic in this "extended diatribe." All injustices are caused by whites while the Indians are characterized by complete innocence. This is an eloquent tract, but he mishandles the evidence and is therefore not trustworthy. The narrative is often confusing, and his argument lacks proper documentation. Even those sympathetic to the Indians' plight will find this overtly one-sided version detrimental.

1384. *Chicago Tribune Books*, 15 March 1992, p. 8

A notice of the paperback reissue.

I385. *Choice*, 20 (July/August 1983), 1654.

This is a well written, exhaustive, detailed account of the shootout at Pine Ridge Reservation. Matthiessen's reconstruction of the events appears fair and competent. His portrayal of the American Indian Movement (AIM) leaders is romanticized, and Leonard Peltier is portrayed as almost larger than life. Unaware readers will be misled into believing that AIM is alone in its defense of traditional Indian interests.

I386. Cosgrave, Mary Silva. "Outlook Tower." *The Horn Book*, 59 (October 1983), 610–611.

Brief. It is a powerful and provocative book, although at times his lengthy report on the government's Indian relations and the rise of the American Indian Movement is repetitious.

I387. Dershowitz, Alan M. "Agents and Indians." *New York Times Book Review*, 6 March 1983, pp. 1, 26–27.

An interesting, contentious, and important evaluation of the book. Matthiessen "admirably dramatizes" the plight of the Indians, and this is one of those rare books that "permanently change one's consciousness about important … facets of history." He is at his best when discussing the complex moral issues surrounding the violence at Pine Ridge but at his worst when he becomes "a polemicist for his journalistic clients." At times he becomes unconvincing and "embarrassingly sophomoric" pleading the legal innocence of individual criminals. On the question of Leonard Peltier having been framed by the F.B.I., Matthiessen is not only unconvincing, but he actually makes a case for Peltier's guilt. He offers no proof beyond the self-serving claims of the alleged victims. He is a "good-hearted naif" who has been taken in by the usual nonsense that every convicted murderer attempts. The book documents the imperfection of the American legal system but also the destructive quality of many leaders of the American Indian Movement who exploit their heritage for their own personal ends. The real tragedy of the book is Matthiessen's failure to realize that his heroes did not act in the selfless spirit of Crazy Horse.

See **C71.**

I388. Dwyer, Victoria. "Echoes of Murder." *Maclean's*, 104 (22 July 1991), 41–43.

On the re-release of the book, a review of its publishing and legal history is given along with the events surrounding the Leonard Peltier case. The book is a flawed but captivating account. Matthiessen allows his anger to sometimes lead him into questionable assessments and, at times, the book "takes on the air of a conspiracy theory." While argumentative and unabashedly one-sided, the book is also thought-provoking and riveting.

I389. Erickson, Kai. "New Indian Wars." *Vanity Fair*, 46 (March 1983), 97–98.

The book is an able, thorough, important, and exhaustive piece of investigative journalism. There is a certain nobility in Matthiessen's recounting of the "long shadow of the white man" on Indian history, but the book suffers from his obsession with detail. While individual sentences exhibit Matthiessen's handsome craftsmanship, the book as a whole seems assembled rather than composed. There is much that is offered in the book, so one hopes the reader's level of interest is sustained over the expanse of words.

I390. Farrell, Bill. "The Haunted Plains." *Newsday*, 5 May 1991, "Fanfare," pp. 42–43.

The reissuing of the book is a major political, legal, and literary event. Matthiessen is honest in admitting his bias but is not uncritical of American Indian Movement members and their supporters. The book offers an essential view of the Lakotas' current struggles.

I391. Graeber, Laurel. "New & Noteworthy." *New York Times Book Review*, 22 March 1992, p. 28.

A brief notice of the new edition.

I392. Hamburger, Susan. *Library Journal*, 108 (January 15, 1983), 120.

Very brief. This is a "powerful and compelling book."

1393. *Kirkus Reviews*, 50 (December 15, 1982), 1380.

Matthiessen builds a persuasive case for a new and fair trial for Leonard Peltier. He compellingly tells a complex and grim story, providing a comprehensive and impassioned account of American Indian activism.

1394. _____. 51 (January 1, 1983), 10.

Reprint of **1393**.

1395. Klausler, Alfred P. "Books." *Christian Century*, 100 (August 3–10, 1983), 721–722.

The review provides a brief account of the Leonard Peltier case rather than an evaluation of the book itself, other than to note its long and sometimes convoluted narrative. Matthiessen has produced an explosive book.

1396. Kuhlman, Thomas A. *Best Sellers*, 43 (May 1983), 64.

The book is a diatribe, with sometimes libelous accusations, which will not contribute to correcting the wrongs perpetuated on the Indians. Matthiessen has little objectivity, and he clumsily adds ancient grievances and personal prejudices into his mass of arguments. The result is a book that is chiefly an attack on the F.B.I. and that is difficult to respect.

1397. Lehmann-Haupt, Christopher. "The Troubled Indians." *New York Times*, 5 March 1983, p. 17.

While Matthiessen makes a persuasive case that Leonard Peltier deserves a new trial and he documents injustices that need rectifying, there is little new or of interest in this particular case. The story is all very familiar, and he seems to have lost his perspective and gone on too far about people and events that do not deserve his attention. He presents his story as too black and white in its portrayal of the good guys and bad guys. The reader grows bored and loses his capacity for outrage.

1398. Mackey, Mary. "Long Wait for Banned Book." *San Francisco Chronicle*, 21 July 1991, "Sunday Review," p. 1.

A brief report on the legal history behind the book, its reissuing, and the revelation of "X" in the epilogue.

1399. McAllester, David P. *Parabola*, 8 (August 1983), 106–108, 110–111.

Reviewed with *Now That the Buffalo's Gone* by Alvin M. Josephy, Jr. The majority of this review is concerned with Josephy's book and comparatively little attention is given to Matthiessen's work. His involvement seems to have overwhelmed his artistic judgment. The reader is buried in the sheer quantity of the material presented. He clearly portrays the F.B.I. as the bad guys and the Indians as the heroic warriors.

1400. McQuaig, Linda. "A Bitter Historic Legacy." *Maclean's*, 96 (21 March 1983), 56.

In this "startling" book, Matthiessen presents a stinging indictment of the United States authorities. He painstakingly dissects the events that occurred at Pine Ridge and their consequences.

1401. Montrose, David. "Still Biting the Dust." *The Spectator*, 268 (23 May 1992), 34.

Reviewed with *Stolen Continents: The Indian Story* by Ronald Wright. Matthiessen is tougher-minded than those who accept that Leonard Peltier may have been framed but is not innocent. He insists on due process. This review is not evaluative; it provides brief background information on the case and Matthiessen's position concerning it.

1402. *New Yorker*, 59 (11 April 1983), 136.

A brief positive assessment. While his sympathies are apparent, Matthiessen is not gullible or uncritical.

1403. Nordell, Roderick. "Eloquent Recital of Wrongs to Lakota People and Efforts to Right Them." *Christian Science Monitor*, 11 March 1983, p. 17.

Matthiessen's considerable literary skills perhaps undercut the persuasiveness of his case. The unadorned facts may have provided the strongest presentation of Leonard Peltier's case. Matthiessen does not overlook anybody's human flaws, but he also immerses the reader in Lakota life and lore and conveys a sense of their achievements, disappointments, and spiritual yearnings.

1404. Ortiz, Rozanne Dunbar. "Review Essay: In the Spirit of Crazy Horse." *Social Justice*, 9 (Summer 1992), 87–94.

The legal history of the book's publication is briefly reviewed. The essay is essentially a summarization of the relations between the Sioux and the federal government, the development of the American Indian Movement, and the involvement of Leonard Peltier as Matthiessen presents them. Little evaluative comment on the book is given, although at the conclusion of the essay it is stated that the book will "live on as a work of literature and a late–20th-century documentation" of Peltier's and the Indians' journey toward justice and sovereignty.

1405. Prescott, Peter S. "Peltier's Last Stand." *Newsweek*, 101 (28 March 1983), 70–71.

Matthiessen's cause is important, but his book is "damn near unreadable." It is far too long, and Leonard Peltier case is finally not interesting enough to warrant the extent of Matthiessen's presentation. While Matthiessen doesn't know what happened at Pine Ridge, he does argue convincingly that Peltier was railroaded into an illegal conviction.

Prescott, however, cavalierly states that Peltier, as a victim of injustice, is not very unique or uncommon. And Matthiessen's concern with his possible unlawful persecution is unwarranted because Peltier is "not necessarily [a] good [guy]."

1406. *Publishers Weekly*, 223 (21 January 1983), 76.

This gripping, exciting and controversial work provides a comprehensive background on Indian activism. It is a powerful

story with more detail than any recent book on the subject.

1407. _____. 239 (24 February 1992), 52.

A very brief notice of the new edition.

1408. Reed, J. D. "Black Hills." *Time*, 121 (28 March 1983), 70.

The plight of the Indians demands something more than the inflamed and patronizing words of Matthiessen's polemic. In his partiality and "angry righteousness," he has ignored his usual gifts for observation and organization. His could have been the voice that helped clear the air; instead, he only adds to the confusion.

1409. Rogers, Michael. "Classic Returns." *Library Journal*, 116 (June 1, 1991), 202.

The reissued edition remains a powerful and compelling book.

1410. See, Carolyn. *Los Angeles Times Book Review*, 6 March 1983, pp. 1, 7.

This is "a giant of a book, comparable in intent if not in structure to *War and Peace*." It is long, indescribably touching, and extraordinarily intelligent. When the Dickensian personal histories of Denis Banks and Leonard Peltier are recounted, the book is almost too powerful to read. Still, the question of what is to be done remains unanswered.

1411. Shafer, Jack. "The New Indian Wars?" *Inquiry*, 6 (June 1983), 34–36.

A good portion of this review-essay is devoted to recounting the events that led to the book. The despair of modern Indian life seems to have affected Matthiessen. He does little to advance the Indian cause because his obvious partisanship weakens the skepticism the Peltier–AIM case deserves. His attempt to construct a government conspiracy against the Indians collapses under its own weight. While the book makes a good case for a retrial for Peltier, it also casts deep suspicion on his innocence.

1412. Sherman, Marlon. "Another White Explorer." *American Book Review*, 14 (December 1992/January 1993), 7, 11.

While well intentioned, Matthiessen is firmly established within the "condescending traditional-Indian-as-environmentalist-versus-mixed-blood-as-sellout mode of reportage." He unconsciously manifests a romanticized view of Indians. The focus of the book is the loss of the Lakota Nation, but Matthiessen sacrifices that for developing a portrait of a single Lakota, Leonard Peltier. By focusing solely on Peltier and his case, Matthiessen ignores the variety of problems confronting Indians today. His insensitivity to tribal controversies is also evident in *Indian Country*; he is willing to ignore concerns of the Indians to advance his own agenda.

1413. Sherrill, Robert. "A Warrior's Legacy." *The Atlantic*, 251 (March 1983), 112, 114–116.

After a review of the circumstances surrounding the events at Pine Ridge, Sherrill finds the book to be evidence of a profound change in Matthiessen. He is losing confidence in mankind and perhaps in himself. The book does not share the hope seen in Matthiessen's last book of social issues, *Sal Si Puedes*. He has lost, if only temporarily, his "touch of poetry." The violence, victimization, and death of this story has only hardened rather than inspired him.

1414. Specktor, Mordecai. "An Indian Activist's Struggle Continues." *National Catholic Reporter*, 20 (May 4, 1984), 18.

This is an excellent work which provides a thorough investigation of the shoot-out at Pine Ridge and its aftermath.

1415. Stegner, Page. *California*, 8 (April 1983), 130–131.

The book is a powerful and angry indictment of contemporary American Indian policy. It demonstrates that Leonard Peltier's guilt is "highly suspect" and that he has been victimized by "a racially biased judicial system."
See also **1416–1417** for other reviews by Stegner.

1416. ____. "Reds." *New York Review of Books*, 30 (April 14, 1983), 21–24, 31.

In this powerfully unsettling book, Matthiessen tells the story which slowly clarifies "what probably happened" at Pine Ridge Reservation. Those events are the means by which Matthiessen can explain the large questions which concern him regarding the plight of the American Indians and the national Indian policy. A summary of the history of Indian militancy and the incidents at Pine Ridge is given. Matthiessen makes no case for mitigating responsibility for the murders of the F.B.I. agents but questions why the numerous violent deaths of Indians went largely ignored. This superb book is "one of the most dramatic demonstrations of endemic American racism that has yet been written."
See also **1415** and **1417** for other reviews by Stegner.

1417. ____. "The Secrets of Wounded Knee." *New Republic*, 188 (7 March 1983), 31–34.

This is more of a recounting of the circumstances leading to the Pine Ridge Reservation shoot-out and the interrelationships and machinations of the American Indian Movement, the Bureau of Indian Affairs, and the F.B.I. than a review of this "important and angry book." Matthiessen has written an urgent book, painstakingly and carefully reconstructing the incidents at Pine Ridge.
See also **1415–1416** for other reviews by Stegner.

1418. Weidman, Bette S. "Other Voices, Other Americas." *Commonweal*, 110 (20 May 1983), 305–307.

Matthiessen is writing in the tradition of the European-American counterpart to the American Indian tradition of powerful oratory. This is a tradition of great truth and shows the way. The authorial "I" of this book is immensely important because it is an artist's voice, and its reporting is graced with imaginative understanding.

1419. Weyler, Rex. "Drastic Means to Quell Dissent." *New Age*, 9 (May 1983), 72–73.

Matthiessen has approached the story

with the zeal of an ace crime reporter and his usual exceptional story-telling skills. In the most complete and credible investigation to date, he proves beyond a shadow of a doubt that Leonard Peltier was set up. This is a shocking story by a great writer.

INDIAN COUNTRY

1420. Abley, Mark. "Custer's Revenges." *Times Literary Supplement*, no. 4329 (March 21, 1986), 299.

Reviewed with *The Papers of Chief John Ross* (vols. 1 & 2) by Gary E. Moulton. These essays are a polemical appeal for change, but Matthiessen realizes that they are unlikely to have much effect. Matthiessen's cool, factual prose sometimes buries too much of his artistic talent. He is a brave and articulate journalist and essayist, but his personal ambivalence occasionally detracts from his work.

1421. Adams, Phoebe-Lou. "Brief Reviews." *The Atlantic*, 253 (June 1984), 124.

This is a depressing account but worthwhile in both a social and an ecological context. The writing is graceful and unhurried.

1422. Brady, Hugh. "Their Country." *Guardian Weekly*, 2 February 1986, p. 21.

An admiring notice. Although it is not a rhetorical or polemical book, it is a remarkably powerful one which will not leave the reader unmoved.

1423. Brown, Dee. "Red and White Confrontations." *Natural History*, 93 (April 1984), 82, 84–85.

What Matthiessen reveals the government is doing to the Indians is being done to all Americans. He methodically assembles the data of one outrage after another across the United States by the federal government in conjunction with giant corporations and the interests of energy consortiums. If the book finds the audience it should, its impact could be comparable to that of Rachel Carson's *Silent Spring*.

1424. *Christian Century*, 101 (29 August 1984), 809.

A brief positive review. The book is travelogue-cum-ideology but also a subtle, deft and patient listening to the ways and world of the Native Americans. He hints at what may still be based on what opportunities we have already missed.

1425. Clow, Richmond L. *Minnesota History*, 49 (Fall 1984), 119–120.

Matthiessen is unable to separate myth from reality and is tied to industrial society's "noble savage" stereotype of Native Americans. He is clearly biased toward traditionalist viewpoints and contemporary conflicts. The book's serious faults include a lack of analysis and clear understanding of tribal factionalism. This is an emotional presentation of traditionalism and should be read with caution.

1426. Derosier, Arthur H., Jr. *American Academy of Political and Social Sciences Annal*, 480 (July 1985), 194.

Matthiessen is a masterful writer who evokes the reader's shame and anger, but he provides no answers to the questions he raises. While the argument is persuasive and biased, it is also one-dimensional. In his advocation of traditionalism and vilification of everything else, Matthiessen offers anger without options.

1427. Hamburger, Susan. *Library Journal*, 109 (March 1, 1984), 477.

A brief notice of a forceful, eloquent account.

1428. *Harvard Law Review*, 98 (March 1985), 1104–1108.

This review is an insightful, fair-minded evaluation of the book and the problems that generated it. While Matthiessen is understandably militant and even strident at times in his calls for justice, he meticulously chronicles the efforts by Indians to maintain their traditional way of life and protect their sovereignty and land against governmental encroachment. His interest in the "Indian way" is motivated by his hope that they will provide the means and vision by which the land will be better cared for and protected. A reverence for the earth is the potential common standard for the cultures of the Indians and the whites.

1429. Hauhart, Robert C. *American Indian Quarterly*, 9 (Spring 1995), 198–199.

The majority of this review is a summary of Matthiessen's account of the history of the Seminoles, particularly the Miccosukee group in his essay, "The Long River." While admiring Matthiessen's intent of purpose and eloquence of execution, Hauhart finds fault with his failure to provide any analysis for an understanding of the social and political circumstances which allowed the injustices against the Indians to occur or a prescription for their rectification.

1430. Hofkins, Diane. "Paper Backs." *Times Educational Supplement*, no. 3706 (July 10, 1987), 23.

This book is an eloquent catalog of injustices and an attempt to show what can still be learned by a more "natural" way of life.

1431. *Kirkus Reviews*, 52 (January 15, 1984), 86.

This is a powerful, more depressing "quick sequel" to *In the Spirit of Crazy Horse*. It combines expressive nature writing with openly partisan reportage.

1432. Livingston, Ruth. *Best Sellers*, 44 (August 1984), 197–198.

Matthiessen has rendered an invaluable service with this book. He speaks eloquently, spreading the Indian gospel. If he is heard, much can still be saved.

1433. Longyear, John M. *Science Books*, 20 (January/February 1985), 131.

The book contains a message for Indians and non–Indians alike. These essays are of limited scope, however, and the problem they reflect is enormously complicated and important. Matthiessen's strong bias is evident in his simplistic depiction of all traditional Indians as being noble children of nature and their enemies as heartless money-grabbing corporations and unscrupulous government officials.

1434. Montrose, David. "Lamentations." *New Statesman*, 111 (10 January 1986), 26.

While calling it a "fine book," this review is primarily a summary of and an agreement with the case Matthiessen makes against big business and the federal government and his support of the "traditionals." It is not an evaluation of the book itself.

1435. Morton, Brian. "America's Shame." *Times Educational Supplement*, no. 3637 (14 March 1986), 26.

Most of this review is not about the book but rather the status of the Indians and Matthiessen's work. The book is a precise and detailed account. Its value is in presenting the Indians as genuinely modern political constituents rather than as mythological abstractions.

1436. Nabokov, Peter. "Return to the Native." *New York Review of Books*, 31 (September 27, 1984), 44–45.

Matthiessen presents a mystical romanticism concerning the Indian. He views most whites as exploiters and non-traditional Indians as sell-outs. The major failing of the book is the perpetuation of the "monolithic stereotype" of "the" Indian. He has a pervasive certainty as to what Indianness means. He is victimized by lapses into "purest sentimentality" and unwittingly perpetuates "the oldest image that whites have used to turn Indians into symbols of their own deepest longings." The book is most powerful in its depiction of environmental ruin rather than human misery.

1437. *New Yorker*, 60 (4 June 1984), 134–135.

Brief. The book is a well organized and integrated collection which presents a plea for ecological sanity. Matthiessen conveys an intense feeling for the natural beauty and variety of the wilderness.

1438. *Publishers Weekly*, 225 (10 February 1984), 184.

A brief descriptive notice.

1439. _____. 239 (24 February 1992), 52.

A very brief notice of the Penguin paperback edition.

1440. *Quill & Quire*, 50 (August 1984), 37.

Brief. While his partisanship occasionally blinds him to the significance of the serious division within the Indian community, Matthiessen still makes a good case for their cause. It is a well written, passionate, and controversial defense of endangered peoples.

1441. R. M. "Books Encountered." *Encounter*, 67 (June 1986), [57].

Brief. This is an angry and eloquent book that documents the savage evils of "progress."

1442. Rice, Julian C. *Western American Literature*, 20 (Spring 1985), 59–60.

Matthiessen's presentation of these urgent but little known environmental battles should alarm the majority of readers into complete attention. He brings the skills of a polished fiction writer to this book, identifying the monster so that it can be stopped.

1443. Sanders, Scott R. "Indian Betrayal." *The Progressive*, 48 (September 1984), 43–44.

The review is concerned more with the issues Matthiessen raises than his presentation of them. He reveals a pattern of economic, religious, and political exploitation of Indians that parallels the country's treatment of Third World nations.

1444. Sherwood, Michael R. "Harsh and Angry Words." *Sierra*, 69 (November/December 1984), [86]–89.

This review recounts many of the issues raised in the book. While Matthiessen's historical sketches are poignant, the most memorable and touching parts of the book are his descriptions of his personal contacts and relationships with the Indians. It is a profoundly moving book which tells a shameful story in often angry language.

1445. Swann, Brian. *The Amicus Journal*, 6 (Winter 1985), 41–42.

This book is a call to arms on behalf of our own self-interest. Matthiessen is a brave man to face matters so fully and openly because the overall picture he presents in this powerful book is very grim. It is spectacular reporting, bringing attitudes and beliefs alive.

1446. Wagoner, David. "'Somebody's Got to Hang On.'" *New York Times Book Review*, 29 July 1984, p. 9.

The book is an eloquent and painful look at the Indian situation in the United States, past and present. Its importance lies in Matthiessen's attempt to impart a sense of immediate urgency. His deepest insights are limited to the preface, epilogue, and brief passages through the book, although the entire work is infused with his "openly lyrical and passionate voice." This will be a sourcebook for future Indian leaders and the wiser of the whites as well.

1447. "Western Books in Brief." *American West*, 20 (September 1983), 58.

A brief descriptive notice.

1448. Wordsworth, Christopher. "Land of the Free?" *Observer*, 23 March 1986, p. 27.

A brief review that focuses more upon the plight of the Indian than upon the book itself.

1449. Zweig, Paul. "Vanishing Tribes." *New Republic*, 190 (4 June 1984), 36–38.

There are two subjects to this book: the destruction of the last open land in the United States by industry and the struggle of the last people of this land to preserve it and their traditions which are linked to it. Matthiessen writes movingly of an utterly sad story and of the complex relationships among Indians themselves. He is an accomplished elegist for a vanishing world.

MIDNIGHT TURNING GRAY

1450. *Booklist*, 81 (November 1, 1984), 343.

A brief review. These are traditional

stories in the adventure/outdoors vein. Matthiessen writes in big, bold sentences, eschewing understated short fiction.

NINE-HEADED DRAGON RIVER

1451. *Booklist*, 82 (March 15, 1986), 1055.

An informative discourse on the transformation of Zen through western culture is coupled with the highlights of a personal pilgrimage toward enlightenment. The book occasionally meanders and contains a number of questionable attitudes from a psychological standpoint, but its deeper philosophical truths are refreshing.

1452. Fields, Rick. *Parabola*, 11 (November 1986), 113–114, 116, 118–119.

In many ways these journals sum up the history of American Zen so far. Matthiessen is an inspired amateur in the best sense of the word. He provides clear and useful accounts of the philosophical rationale for *zazen* and Buddhist practice, but he comes most alive for the reader as a naturalist rather than as a philosopher or scholar. In his observation of and participation in nature, he comes closest to expressing the fundamentally inexpressible experience of Zen. His naturalist and *zazen* trained eye give rise to a prose style of Zen realism.

1453. *Kirkus Reviews*, 54 (March 1, 1986), 373–374.

This is Matthiessen's most intimate book. It is distinguished and lyrical, and filled with fierce pain.

1454. *The Listener*, 118 (5 November 1987), 31.

The book is a highly personalized voyage of the spirit. It is hard going at times and lacks the kind of immediate energy one might expect from so charged a subject.

1455. "New in Paperback." *Book World* [*Washington Post*], 16 August 1987, p. 12.

Brief. *The Snow Leopard* showed Matthiessen to be one of the few authors capable of holding the non-believer's interest on religious topics. Of particular appeal is his account of "a major Zen scandal," the publication of the purported answers to classic Zen koans.

1456. *New Yorker*, 62 (21 April 1986), 125–126.

Brief. The journals speak candidly and personally. They provide a broad picture of Japanese history, Zen masters, and Zen traditions.

1457. Nixon, C. Robert. *Library Journal*, 111 (March 15, 1986), 67.

This is a well written book, full of memorable incidents and impressions. It contains "fascinating thoughts on Japanese culture and history from a Zen perspective."

1458. *Publishers Weekly*, 229 (14 March 1986), 90.

This is a moving and highly personal story. He excels at detailed descriptions of inner mental states.

1459. Pye, Michael. "Inner Voyage." *Times Literary Supplement*, no. 4398 (July 17, 1987), 777.

This is "a travelogue of the spirit." Beneath the description, personal encounters, poems, and historical information is the story of Matthiessen himself. He achieves a heightened awareness of things as they are and discovers his own original humanity.

1460. Scott, Victoria. *Los Angeles Times Book Review*, 18 May 1986, p. 11.

The book is an ambitious but incomplete work. It is compellingly written only in the first part; the writing here is the most personal and rawest. Matthiessen attempts to tackle the subject that escaped him in *The Snow Leopard*: what an enlightened state of mind is and how to attain it. Despite its faults, the book provides important insights into the process of seeking enlightenment in twentieth century America.

1461. Spencer, Duncan. "Zen and the Art of Fishing." *Book World* [*Washington Post*], 29 June 1986, p. 5.

A laudatory review including *Men's Lives*. The review is more of a paean to Matthiessen rather than specifically about either book. Matthiessen has the knowledge to write with confidence about subjects not well known; he lets his subjects speak in a strong, pure prose. He is one of the American prose poets. With apparent ease he writes the most beautiful, flexible and simple descriptive passages. He uses language musically and combines its beauty with something important to say.

1462. Wetering, Janwillem van de. *New York Times Book Review*, 6 April 1986, p. 23.

A brief, mocking, sarcastic response to the book. Too many fools show off throughout the book. The holy men abuse our silliness as well as their own.

MEN'S LIVES

1463. Adams, Phoebe-Lou. "Brief Reviews." *The Atlantic*, 258 (September 1986), 104.

Matthiessen has brilliantly recorded a way of life not likely to survive. This is a knowledgeable and sympathetic portrait.

1464. *Booklist*, 82 (15 May 1986), 1343.

The book is a gentle, reflective cultural history. It combines anecdotes, reminiscences, and salty tales into a vivid and poignant portrait.

1465. Boucher, Norman. "Tales of Nature's Resiliency and Hope." *New Age Journal*, 2 (July 1986), 58–59 [58–60].

An omnibus review. The book's power derives from Matthiessen's deep feelings for his subjects, and his affection and nostalgia permeate the book. Rarely has he been this relaxed in a work. The palpable sense of loss in the book is indicative of his more openly political stance in his recent books and is representative of today's nature writing developing a more explicit political element.

1466. Calder, Angus. "Collected Works." *London Review of Books*, 11 (5 January 1989), 15–16 [13–16].

A largely descriptive notice within an omnibus review-essay. Thanks to Matthiessen's brief period of work as a commercial fisherman, he can tell this story from a position both close and objective. His ability to build personal nostalgia into his account is one of the book's many virtues.

1467. Catling, Patrick Skene. "Fishing for More than Complements." *The Spectator*, 261 (20 August 1988), 26.

The review is a sympathetic assessment of a "macho lament for communal disinheritance." Matthiessen's story is sadly and inevitably a defeatist account. The local story of Long Island fishermen offers the "universal, perennial tragedy of obsolescence."

1468. Clemons, Walter. "The Last Catch for the Fisherman." *Newsweek*, 108 (11 August 1986), 57.

This quiet, angry book has a biting eloquence that no outsider could command.

1469. Dunn, Douglas. "Oceans Away." *The Listener*, 120 (18 August 1988), 24–25.

Reviewed with *Whale Nation* by Heathcote Williams. Matthiessen is one of the best observers of the natural world. His prose is clean and crisp, and the book is a lively amalgam of autobiography, local history, sociology, and oral history. He uses clever and affectionate gifts of description to enliven a potentially boring subject, bringing it to life.

1470. Dutton, Joy. "Heroes and Humanity." *World Magazine*, no. 26 (June 1989), 89 [88–89].

A brief review of the Collins Harvill paperback edition of *The Cloud Forest* and *Men's Lives*. The latter presents an epic vision and a "powerfully documented" story.

1471. Fletcher, Janet, Francine Fialkoff, and Barbara Hoffert. "The Best Books of 1986." *Library Journal*, 112 (January 1987), 57 [53–59].

Brief. Matthiessen has provided a clear understanding of the fishermen's struggle.

The book is filled with "salty detail and deep affection."

1472. Hughes, Robert. "Something Fishy in the Hamptons." *New York Review of Books*, 33 (October 23, 1986), 21–22, 24.

Matthiessen has presented the baymen's story with "great care and decent anger." It is "a precise and distinguished social history" which shares two virtues with *Far Tortuga*: a precise and respectful ear for spoken dialect and a sensitivity of eye, the descriptions of Long Island are unsurpassed. Much of this review/essay is a recounting of the story of the baymen and surfmen that Matthiessen tells.

1473. Johnson, George. "New & Noteworthy." *New York Times Book Review*, 31 January 1988, p. 34.

A brief notice of the Vintage paperback edition.

1474. *Kirkus Reviews*, 54 (April 1, 1986), 526.

The book would have benefited from a stronger editorial hand. Still, it is a remarkable evocation of the fishermen of Long Island's South Fork. There is a sense of guilt that underlies the book, and Matthiessen believes that the cause is lost, thus creating an elegy for those he used to work among.

1475. Lehmann-Haupt, Christopher. "Books of the Times." *New York Times*, 19 June 1986, p. C24.

In this "haunting documentary record" and tribute to a way of life, Matthiessen has written a local history. It is haphazardly organized and meandering, but the text in combination with the photographs is extraordinary. It is the photographs which give the book its special power.

1476. Livingston, Kathryn. "Men and the Sea." *American Photographer*, 17 (November 1986), 34, 36.

The focus of this review is the photographs and the photographers of the single volume and the two volume deluxe set. The work of Dan Budnik picks up the delicate grace of the fishermen that their own

words and Matthiessen's barely approach. The text is "lyrically historical" and magnificently, if at times excruciatingly, thorough.

1477. Lowe, Ed. "A Writer Pays Tribute to the Last of the Fishermen." *Newsday*, 22 June 1986, "Ideas," pp. 20, 17.

An effusive review. The book is well-documented, well-reported, eloquent, and subtly impassioned. It is rewarding, informative, beautiful, inspirational, and, ultimately, poignantly sad.

1478. Norman, Geoffrey. *Outside*, 11 (July 1986), 107–108.

This is a rich and complex book graced throughout by Matthiessen's keen eye and restrained yet compassionate prose style.

1479. "Notes on Current Books." *Virginia Quarterly Review*, 63 (Winter 1987), 29.

Brief. This moving lament combines history and sociology with a healthy dash of nostalgia.

1480. Person, Roland. *Library Journal*, 111 (May 1, 1986), 112.

A freely written, somewhat melancholy portrait of "frontier characters bowing to modernism." It is "a masterful celebration of craft, of pride in one's work, of community, of endurance."

1481. Pitts, Denis. "Fisherman's Friend." *Punch*, 295 (2 September 1988), 52–53.

A brief notice of a "remarkable book" prefaced by a personal anecdote of greater length than the appreciative review.

1482. Pollack, Sandra. "'Men's Lives' is Rich in Flavor but Falls Short on Documentation." *National Fisherman*, 67 (November 1986), 134–135.

This is a good book overall; it is well written and interesting , and it fairly represents the concerns of the baymen. It conveys a real sense of the people and place; as such it is strongest when Matthiessen writes about his own fishing experience or when he lets the people of the fishing community speak for themselves. The book is not entirely successful, however. It relies too much on single-source documentation of history. Matthiessen occasionally has difficulty moving beyond a romanticized view of the baymen. He doesn't acknowledge their sophistication or calculatedness. He fails to adequately discuss the forces responsible for their predicament concerning striped bass.

1483. *Publishers Weekly*, 229 (28 March 1986), 44–45.

Brief. This affectionate portrait is a unique piece of Americana.

1484. Raban, Jonathan. "This Is the Way a World Ends." *New York Times Book Review*, 22 June 1986, pp. 1, 30–31.

This remarkable book is fired, as all of Matthiessen's best work is, by equal parts of love and indignation. He is a tough and knowledgeable craftsman and also a very fine and equally professional writer. He has transformed a village chronicle into a case study of the systematic destruction of a community and a way of life.

1485. Richardson, Nan. *Aperture*, no. 108 (Fall 1987), 74–76.

The book displays a powerful passion for both the people and the place. His prose is taut, athletic and graceful, but his story is incomplete without the story of the women's lives. There is a confusing and patronizing sense of social reform about the book. It comes too late to awake awareness and interest in the baymen's plight. The book too quickly presents an elegy for the people rather than confronting the political challenge it was meant to. It creates no energy for the next generation. This book is destined for the homes of the very people who have displaced the Bonackers of Long Island's East End.

1486. Rose, Peter I. "Documenting the End of an Era." *Christian Science Monitor*, 5 August 1986, p. 23.

A largely descriptive notice of this "sensitive portrait" of the South Fork. The book is evidence of Matthiessen's uncanny ability to capture the moods of nature, the

essence of place, and the everyday drama of human life.
See **1487**.

1487. _____. *Los Angeles Times Book Review*, 24 August 1986, p. 9.

Reprint of **1486**.

1488. Scott, Joanna. *Afterimage*, 14 (December 1986), 21.

Both the text and photographs sentimentalize the fishermen's struggle. While Matthiessen has written a dramatic defense of the fishermen and their lives, his generalizations are inadequate.

1489. Spencer, Duncan. "Zen and the Art of Fishing." *Book World* [*Washington Post*], 29 June 1986, p. 5.

Reviewed with *Nine-Headed Dragon River. See* **1461** for annotation.

1490. "Summer Reading." *Time*, 128 (7 July 1986), 63 [60–63].

Brief. This is a handsome and passionate volume which presents an admiring and absorbing elegy for a dying breed.

1491. Thompson, Paul. "The Fishermen's Tales." *New Statesman & Society*, 1 (12 August 1988), 32–33.

This is a hybrid book — a loose, novelistic depiction of marine nature, oral history, and a polemic in defense of the baymen. Although the book has been well received in the United States, Matthiessen's message doesn't travel particularly well. While it is artfully presented, it is not straightforwardly presented, and the message becomes "irritatingly obscure."

1492. Tisdale, Sallie. *Whole Earth Review*, 55 (Fall 1987), 99.

A brief notice of the book is followed by three brief excerpts. The book is a flawless and sorrowful narrative presenting both history and memoir.

1493. Wright, Ronald. "Baymen versus Laymen." *Times Literary Supplement*, no. 4, 455 (19 August 1988), 902.

The conflict between the baymen and the sport anglers is a serious one, but Matthiessen pays too much attention to it to the detriment of the more serious issue of pollution. His preoccupation with this conflict, though, is a testament to his integrity as an observer since it is exactly this issue which obsesses the baymen. The book brightens with his lucent prose in passages of description, but he has deferred his own voice to the voices of the men he admires.

ON THE RIVER STYX

1494. Blom, J. M. and L. R. Leavis. *English Studies*, 71 (October 1990), 436–437.

A brief notice. The stories show the influence of Faulkner, Hemingway, Poe and Updike. The first two influences produce the greatest effects.

1495. Budd, John. *Library Journal*, 114 (April 1, 1989), 113.

A brief, harsh review. While recognizing that most of these works are early stories by a young writer, if they are any indication of Matthiessen's ability as a fiction writer, he should continue to focus upon non-fiction. Little here is successful. The stories read like the unsuccessful exercises of an unpolished writer.

1496. Clute, John. "We Are for the Dark." *The Listener*, 122 (19 October 1989), 30–31.

These are hard stories that do not flinch from the difficult message that we have reached the end of using up our world. It is a "deeply readable , furious, icy, wise" book, a lesson for the new age.

1497. Donavin, Denise Perry. *Booklist*, 85 (March 1, 1989), 1050.

Very brief. This emotionally powerful collection demonstrates remarkable diversity.

1498. Dubus, Andre, III. *America*, 161 (25 November 1989), 383–385.

This is a fine collection with a wide thematic and textual range. The title story

alone — one of the most sophisticated in structure and scope — is worth the price of the book.

1499. Edwards, Thomas R. "Failed Journeys to the Wrong Place." *New York Times Book Review*, 14 May 1989, pp. 11–12.

The stories are a good reflection of the progress of Matthiessen's career; they grow more expansive socially, geographically, and imaginatively. These are stories of departures and ambiguous returns which suggest some of his splendid imagination.

1500. Hoffman, Eva. "Surmounting the Confines of Short Stories." *New York Times*, 3 May 1989, p. C25.

Despite the rarity of his forays into the genre, Matthiessen has a masterly control of it. His seriousness and vision surmount the confines of the form. *On the River Styx* and *Sadie* leave the reader discomforted and suspicious of his intentions, but the other stories are marked by classical or old-fashioned qualities like gravitas, grandeur, and beauty. The prose is sharp, lean, and precise. He almost always treats his characters with a stoic, unsentimental compassion. This is a saturnine collection of accomplished art.

1501. Johnson, George. "New & Noteworthy." *New York Times Book Review*, 18 August 1991, p. 28.

A very brief notice of the paperback edition.

1502. Jones, Louis B. "Scree at the Foot of Mount Matthiessen." *Los Angeles Times Book Review*, 14 May 1989, pp. 2, 11.

Despite the book's feel of raked-together scree, it is remarkable how good all the stories are. There are a few mistakes among the earlier stories, but they are peopled by imperfect mutations who will become the great characters of the later fiction.

1503. *Kliatt*, 26 (January 1992), 11.

Very brief. Each story dazzles with Matthiessen's ability to consistently create a tension and an unspoken dimension of uneasiness.

I504. *Kirkus Reviews*, 57 (February 15, 1989), 241.

Little new ground is broken in this collection, but the tone is somberly compelling. The stories may lack the moral outrage of his recent work, but they provide, instead, a dispassionate evocation of a world dying because people do not know how to live.

I505. Medcalf, Stephan. "Longing Hearts." *Times Literary Supplement*, no. 4512 (22 September 1989), 1023.

The unity of tone, style and concerns is extraordinary given the time period over which these stories were written. This is a taut, vivid collection which is superbly written.

I506. *New Yorker*, 65 (3 July 1989), 95.

Brief. This is a surprisingly consistent collection considering the range of years represented by the stories. Matthiessen is at his best when he writes as what he is: a well educated professional traveler. All the stories reflect his coming-of-age, revealing the influence of Faulkner and Steinbeck and the "unquestionable virtue" of "manliness."

I507. *Publishers Weekly*, 235 (17 February 1989), 68.

This is a book of "powerful stories" that "objectively explore the lack of communication between husbands and wives, between races and cultures."

I508. _____. 238 (25 July 1991), 49.

A brief notice of the Vintage paperback edition.

I509. Rea, Paul W. *Bloomsbury Review*, 10 (May/June 1990), 22–23.

One leaves these stories impressed with Matthiessen's gifts for fiction. They reveal his uncanny talent for evoking places and despite their range of years they are thematically linked by death and violence (both threatened and realized) sometimes marked by racial conflict. *Travelin Man*, in particular, is an "extraordinary" story.

I510. Wilhelmus, Tom. "Various Pairs." *Hudson Review*, 43 (Spring 1990), 152–153 [147–154].

Part of an omnibus review. The early stories are interesting for what they suggest of the growth of Matthiessen as a writer and for revealing the origins of his style in Hemingway and Faulkner. The best of the collection are two later stories: *On the River Styx* and *Lumumba Lives*.

KILLING MISTER WATSON

I511. Becker, Elizabeth L. *Kliatt*, 26 (January 1992), 10–11.

A brief, generally complimentary notice, although the violence is deemed "very strong" and the book is not easy.

I512. Bemrose, John. "Memories of Murder." *Maclean's*, 103 (13 August 1990), 59.

An admiring review. This is a superb book, albeit a pessimistic one. It portrays a people wedded to violence and the resultant slaughter of both humans and wildlife. Watson becomes a complex symbol of American society itself.

I513. "Briefly Noted." *New Yorker*, 66 (17 September 1990), 108.

There are heartbreakingly acute descriptions of the destruction of wildlife and the loss of Indian families, but the various narrative accounts fail to make Watson a compelling character and never transform the historical raw material into myth.

I514. Brosnahan, John. *Booklist*, 86 (April 15, 1990), 1585.

Matthiessen has created a docudrama out of Edgar Watson's life. The book does not hold together; its episodic impressions and contradictory evidence create confusion rather than resolution. The climax is gained not by a powerful conclusion but by exhausted relief.

I515. Clark, Susan L. *Armchair Detective*, 24 (Summer 1991), 350–351.

Much of this review is descriptive rather than evaluative, but the concluding paragraph holds high praise for Matthiessen's outstanding and perceptive writing. The book is "an astounding combination" of, among other things, history, true crime, travelogue, and human nature. It will make the reader laugh, cry and reexamine his own life.

I516. Clute, John. "Preying on the Planet." *Times Literary Supplement*, no. 4561 (31 August 1990), 916.

There is little in this review of an evaluative nature concerning this "compelling meditation on the fragile labyrinth of south Florida." It is difficult to distinguish one narrative voice from another.

I517. Duffy, Martha. "'The Wild Tread of God.'" *Time*, 136 (16 July 1990), 82.

The mythologizing of Watson partially undermines the book's larger, tougher themes, but Matthiessen can write like an avenging angel. His moral anguish and human sympathy are inescapable.

I518. Hansen, Ron. "Larger Than Life, Deader Than Dead." *New York Times Book Review*, 24 June 1990, p. 7.

A laudatory review. This is a marvel of invention and Matthiessen's most impressive novel to date. The different narrative voices are fascinating and "beautifully idiomatic." The book is a virtuoso performance "attuned to the necessary preservation of the heart and soul of the world."

I519. Hiassen, Carl. "On Civilization's Edge." *Chicago Tribune Books*, 24 June 1990, pp. 1, 5.

Matthiessen richly brings Watson to life in this wonderful and tantalizing story. He has an affectionate ear for dialect and a perfect instinct for how Southern stories get passed around. His words dazzle even if the narrative voices sometimes blend together.

I520. Johnson, George. "New & Noteworthy." *New York Times Book Review*, 18 August 1991, p. 28.

A brief notice of the Vintage paperback edition.

I521. Jones, Malcolm, Jr. "A Murder in Paradise." *Newsweek*, 115 (11 June 1990), 63–64.

See **H107.**

I522. *Kirkus Reviews*, 58 (April 15, 1990), 526.

Matthiessen never lets the reader make up his own mind about Watson. But this is an elegiac tour de force that masterfully evokes the Florida wilderness.

I523. Klinkenborg, Verlyn. "Moral Swamp." *New Republic*, 203 (5 November 1990), 43–45.

The book is placed within the context of Matthiessen's career as a fiction writer. All of his fiction seems to raise the same questions: Am I my brother's keeper? How am I to know my brother? He creates one memorable voice after another and the texture of speech is the novel's most enjoyable aspect. However, the very lack of consensus among the narrative voices leads to the ambiguity of Watson's story at the novel's end. None of the questions raised are answered. There is a surprising emptiness at the novel's heart. The amorality of the world depicted sets this book apart from the rest of Matthiessen's fiction. He has produced "a good, dark story," but he hasn't raised it to the tragic tale it might have been.

I524. Knight, Lynn. "Heart of Darkness and Eyes of Light." *Observer*, 2 September 1990, p. 62.

In this intricately meshed story, Matthiessen combines anthropological precision with a command of the vernacular. While the documentary approach is occasionally overwhelming, the scale of the story is impressive. He maintains a tight hold on the material.

I525. Koenig, Rhoda. "Darkness Visible." *New York*, 23 (18 June 1990), 60.

A mostly descriptive rather than evaluative review. Matthiessen knows the territory well, and it's a "fascinating, eerie voyage," although one in which the "jungle atmosphere" sometimes overwhelms the characters and action.

1526. Lemon, Lee. *Prairie Schooner*, 65 (Summer 1991), 130 [129–134].

An omnibus review. This is a rare novel that does a number of difficult things superbly. Matthiessen tells the story with fine control; his characters' unthinking acceptance of the horrors of racial bigotry is more effective than overt condemnation would be.

1527. Matousek, Mark. "Call of the Wild." *Harper's Bazaar*, 123 (July 1990), 18, 22.

See **H108.**

1528. McNulty, Tim. "A Life Reimagined." *The Bloomsbury Review*, 10 (September/October 1990), 22, 24.

This is a remarkable novel; it brings together in a vivid and compelling way the very best elements of Matthiessen's unique vision. The story is a deeply historic narrative that touches the very roots of our culture's attitudes toward the land, the native people who dwelled there, and the rich tapestry of life that once graced it.

1529. Mendelsohn, Jane. "Swamp and Circumstance." *Village Voice Literary Supplement*, 12 June 1990, p. 20.

A decidedly mixed review. The narrative is a virtuoso performance, and Matthiessen has ingeniously recreated the dialects. He has taken the strange absence of necessity in his earlier novels and made it his theme here. Edgar Watson becomes a figure for Matthiessen's own detached, unmotivated fictions. A portrait of Watson himself is never developed. The work comes to life in its descriptive passages, giving a voice to place more so than to the characters. It is a chilling corpse of a book, victimized by Matthiessen's too generous, uncritical love.

1530. Mitgang, Herbert. "The Wild West in the Everglades." *New York Times*, 7 July 1990, p. 16.

An appreciative but essentially non-evaluative review. It is more concerned with the background of Watson and Matthiessen's penchant for those people who live close to the land. His imagination has successfully fixed another place in time forever.

1531. "New in Paperback." *Book World* [*Washington Post*], 11 August 1991, p. 12.

A brief descriptive notice.

1532. Oates, Joyce Carol. "One Mean Customer." *Book World* [*Washington Post*], 24 June 1990, p. 5.

This novel, typical of Matthiessen's other works, is an enterprise of obsession and, ultimately, his obsessions become the reader's. It is "a nightmare of a novel, intricately structured, richly documented, utterly convincing."

1533. "Paperbacks." *Observer*, 5 January 1992, p. 41.

Very brief. This is a slow-burning novel short on variety of style and irony but long on moral intensity and epic sweep.

1534. *Publishers Weekly*, 237 (27 April 1990), 52.

This is a curious hybrid of re-imagination based upon fact. It presents "an imaginative and haunting evocation of a time and place."

1535. _____. 238 (25 July 1991), 49.

A brief notice of the Vintage paperback edition.

1536. Quinn, Anthony. "King of the Wild Frontier." *Listener*, 124 (August 9, 1990), 33.

An admiring notice of this "considerable achievement." Most of the review is a summary of the novel's action but Matthiessen's "deft arrangement of conflicting accounts" and vividly pictorial prose are duly noted.

1537. Robertson, William. "A Haunting, Compelling Story of Florida." *Miami Herald*, 24 June 1990, "Viewpoint," p. 1C.

This is the most original and compelling story to emerge from Florida. It is a haunting and resonant novel that confirms Matthiessen's position in the forefront of American fiction. Much of the review is a summary of Edgar Watson's story as Matthiessen presents it.

1538. Rose, Peter I. "An Ingenious Rashomon in the Everglades." *Newsday*, 18 June 1990, Part II, p. 6.

The novel is a master work. It is a multi-layered story of artistry and ingenuity, whose theme is the vagaries of the human condition.

1539. *Roundup Quarterly*, 3 (Fall 1990), 47.

A brief inconsequential notice.

1540. St. John, Edward B. *Library Journal*, 115 (June 1, 1990), 182.

A brief, mostly descriptive notice of "an important and provocative book."

1541. Skenazy, Paul. "Harsh Justice of the Florida Frontier." *San Francisco Chronicle*, 15 July 1990, "Sunday Review," p. 1.

The book is a stunning, imaginative feat despite some flat moments resulting from repetition of incidents and less interesting characters. Matthiessen has created a kaleidoscopic account, an almost Cubist portrait, of Watson and the ways he attained eminence in the Florida frontier. Beyond that, he also presents a compelling vision of the place and time.

1542. Sokoll, Judy. *School Library Journal*, 36 (November 1990), 150.

Brief. The book has a demanding format but it presents a study rich in history, social studies, ecology and nature.

1543. Storace, Patricia. "Betrayals." *New York Review of Books*, 38 (January 31, 1991), 18–20 [18–21].

The novel's problem is that Matthiessen overloads the character of Watson with mythological weight. He is too far removed from the other characters in the story, and there is no real sense of a community in which they are a part. Since all of the narrators are inferior to Watson, none of them can really bring him to life. Watson remains static, and the other characters simply evaporate in the effort to transform him into

legend. The book is, however, a brilliant display of Matthiessen's gifts for creating a sense of place.

1544. Tomb, Eric. "Hearing Voices." *San Francisco Review of Books*, 15 (Summer 1990), 31–32.

This book is "as precision-crafted and as haunting as anything [Matthiessen's] ever done." The land and water provide the strongest voice in the novel. The story plods a lot; there is no real climax and only a few of the characters really come alive. His short story, *On the River Styx*, works more efficiently and economically while creating an equally strong sense of place.

1545. Wiggins, Marianne. "Of Justice and a Good Night's Sleep." *Los Angeles Times Book Review*, 8 July 1990, pp. 1, 5.

Although the book suffers from being too long, Matthiessen has produced a first-rate philosophical study of "the duality of human-and all-nature." It is also a stunning political allegory. The work will stand in a historical sense among the best literature America has produced. If nothing else, it should be read for the simple beauty of its "Florida cracker's life and talk."

1546. Wilhelmus, Tom. "Visionary Historians." *Hudson Review*, 44 (Spring 1991), 125–126 [125–132].

An omnibus review. An appreciative if not an evaluative notice. Similarities are suggested between the novel and Joseph Conrad's work in the handling and presentation of the story.

AFRICAN SILENCES

1547. Abeel, Erica. "From Serengeti to Cape May." *New Woman*, 21 (August 1991), 26.

An inconsequential notice of a book of "mesmerizing beauty."

1548. Adams, Phoebe-Lou. "Brief Reviews." *The Atlantic*, 268 (August 1991), 104.

This is not the kind of travel book that makes you want to visit the area. Matthiessen's depiction of the understaffed and underfunded national wildlife parks is depressing.

1549. Bierman, John. "The Last of the Wild Things." *Los Angeles Times Book Review*, 28 July 1991, p. 4.

While Matthiessen is not at his celebrated best in this book, he is still more worth reading than many of his contemporaries at their best. The book offers few fresh insights or new information but contains some characteristically fine descriptive passages.

1550. *The Bookwatch*, 12 (October 1991), 10–11.

Very brief. The book is a moving account notable for its focus on the interactions between natives and wildlife.

1551. Brosnahan, John. *Booklist*, 87 (April 1, 1991), 1530.

The book has a patched together quality and lacks the consistent examination and details of his best work. The concluding section of the book is by far the most successful.

1552. Chettle, Judith. "A Continent Adrift." *The World & I*, 6 (September 1991), 386–391.

A long, favorable review/essay of a sympathetic but unsentimental appreciation of Africa's plight. Matthiessen offers a realistic assessment of some hope for Africa's wildlife. He understands that animals and man are not natural antagonists but partners and that there is a need to reconcile the conflicting needs of each. There must be an equilibrium in man's relationship with the environment rather than the arbitrary action of overzealous environmentalists.

1553. *Chicago Tribune Books*, 16 August 1992, p. 2.

A very brief notice drawn from the original review.
See **1567**.

1554. Clewis, Beth. *Library Journal*, 116 (June 15, 1991), 100.

This is a grim message about the fates of the people and wildlife of Africa. Matthiessen's disgust and pessimism make for uncomfortable reading. His account of his trip to Central Africa to survey the forest elephant and visit the Mbuti pygmies is particularly engrossing.

1555. Cryer, Dan. "In the Absence of Elephants." *Newsday*, 14 July 1991, "Fanfare," p. 35.

This work is not as inspired as his best, but, nonetheless, it is consistently absorbing. The book's biggest disappointment is its relative silence about people; they rarely come to life in these pages. It really begins to work when Matthiessen joins Dr. David Western for the forest elephant census.

1556. Gould, Stephen Jay. "The Last Chance Continent." *New York Times Book Review*, 18 August 1991, pp. 3, 29.

This book is a long and powerful argument for the position that the African wildlife and environment can only be saved if long-term economic and social benefits accrue to the African people for the effort. Matthiessen is "our greatest modern nature writer in the lyrical tradition" but the subject here cannot inspire his best writing.

1557. Graeber, Laurel. "New & Noteworthy." *New York Times Book Review*, 16 August 1992, p. 32.

Brief notice of the paperback edition.

1558. Holyoke, T. C. *Antioch Review*, 50 (Summer 1992), 586–587.

This is primarily a descriptive rather than evaluative notice. Matthiessen has provided an entertaining and informative travelogue as well as a scientific discussion of the biology and ecology of the area.

1559. Kinder, Marjorie. "Sounding Off for African Wildlife." *Animals*, 124 (November/December 1991), 33.

A largely descriptive notice. The book does continue in the tradition Matthiessen has established as "an eminent naturalist, explorer, and writer." It provides insightful reading.

1560. *Kirkus Reviews*, 59 (April 15, 1991), 529–521.

The book is vintage Matthiessen. He offers a moving, yet never sentimental, evocation of loss. His prose is lucid, and he informs his account with sympathy and realism.

1561. Koenig, Rhoda. "Monkey Business." *New York Magazine*, 24 (22 July 1991), 50.

Matthiessen's vivid and emphatic descriptions are a great pleasure, but the book is marred by some "flaccid travelogue writing" and "cozy, flimsy sketches" of his travelling companions.

1562. Lewin, Roger. "Lament for a Wounded Continent." *Book World* [*Washington Post*], 14 July 1991, p. 1.

No matter how inadequate or inaccurate the term is to describe them, Matthiessen's works are among the most evocative and perceptive examples of travel writing. Rather than a shrill proselytizer, he acts as an observer who allows the force of his story to carry a message. The prose has his characteristic grace and perfectly distilled passion.

1563. Lyon, Thomas J. "Reviews." *Sierra*, 77 (January/February 1992), 141.

Brief. It is a rich and disturbing book.

1564. Mackey, Mary. "A Silent Continent." *San Francisco Chronicle*, 21 July 1991, "Sunday Review," p. 1.

Matthiessen has produced what may be "the most exciting piece of travel writing to appear since the death of Bruce Chatwin." He delivers an important message of conservation and environmental concern.

1565. Miller, David. "In the Company of the Universe." *Sewanee Review*, 103 (Fall 1995), 616–617 [613–620].

An omnibus review. There is no better guide and interpreter than Matthiessen. His purpose is not to conquer or to transcend but "to pay attention, to learn, to report, truly, and if possible to help."

1566. New, William. "Last Page." *Canadian Literature*, no. 133 (Summer 1992), 215 [214–216].

An extremely brief notice within an omnibus review/essay. Matthiessen's conservationist agenda gets in the way of both style and detail.

1567. North, James. "Protecting Elephants from a Hostile World." *Chicago Tribune Books*, 28 July 1991, pp. 6–7.

A largely descriptive review of this "adroit account."

1568. Pace, Eric. "The Dark Fate of Africa's Elephants." *New York Times*, 22 August 1991, p. C18.

While the book's reporting has its crotchets and longueurs, it is leavened and reinforced by the travel writing, which is often exciting and cheerful. Much of the reportage is stunningly sad and contains many powerful scenes. The book is significant and, at times, fascinating, if not exactly new.

1569. Page, Betty B. *Kliatt*, 26 (November 1992), 43.

A brief, positive descriptive notice.

1570. *Publishers Weekly*, 238 (17 May 1991), 49.

The book offers "a superb vicarious experience." It is a dazzling, albeit dismaying, account.

1571. _____. 239 (1 June 1992), 59.

A very brief quoting from the original review.
See **1570**.

1572. Ramsey, Marie. *Book Report*, 10 (January/February 1992), 64.

A descriptive notice.

1573. Solomon, Charles. "Paperbacks." *Los Angeles Times Book Review*, 16 August 1992, p. 9.

Brief notice. It is a sobering book.

1574. Tidrick, Kathryn. "Who's to Blame?" *London Review of Books*, 15 (25 February 1993), 20 [19–20].

Part of an omnibus review. Matthiessen can be eloquent and some of his observations, if they came from others, would be banal. His specialty is to "articulate the sense of innocent wonder at the natural world usually assumed to be the prerogative of primitive people." But the question remaining is whether there is justification for the invasion of a whole continent by outside observers.

BAIKAL: SACRED SEA OF SIBERIA

1575. Andrews, Colman. "A Conservationist's Paen to Siberia's 'Sacred Sea.'" *Los Angeles Times*, 8 November 1992, p. L9.

The text is fashioned with Matthiessen's usual grace and informed with his usual awareness of environmental issues. It is also "scattered with his usual New Age–ish sentiments."

1576. Hoelterhoff, Manuela. "Christmas Books: A Holiday Sampler." *Wall Street Journal*, 1 December 1992, p. A14.

A brief, curious notice. The only comment regarding Matthiessen is that "the aging nature" writer was winded from climbing the Baikal ridge.

1577. J. M. *The Bloomsbury Review*, 12 (December 1992), 17.

A brief notice with *Nowhere Is a Place* by Bruce Chatwin and Paul Theroux. Matthiessen's essay is brilliant. These works represent the finest format nature books of our time.

1578. Krist, Gary. "Travel." *New York Times Book Review*, 6 December 1992, 52 [9, 52].

Brief. This is typical of Matthiessen's travel writing, which tends to be pompous, but his message concerning the need to save Lake Baikal is irreproachable.

1579. McNamee, Gregory. *Outside*, 17 (December 1992), [126].

A very brief notice of *Baikal* and *Shadows of Africa*. Both books are evidence of Matthiessen's "extraordinary talent for exhaustive research and vivid narrative."

1580. "Neat Stuff." *Sea Frontiers*, 40 (August 1994), [58].

A very brief notice. The text and photographs provide "a clear look" at the lake.

1581. Person, Roland. *Library Journal*, 117 (November 15, 1992), 98.

A brief descriptive notice.

1582. *Publishers Weekly*, 239 (14 September 1992), [92].

Matthiessen's brief text combined with the photographs make an eloquent pleas for the lake's preservation.

1583. *Reference and Research Book News*, 8 (February 1993), 6.

Very brief. The illustrious Matthiessen's journal forms the heart of the book.

1584. Schoen, Sarah. "Traveling Tales." *Condé Nast's Traveler*, 27 (October 1992), 120 [119–120].

Brief. A more descriptive than evaluative notice of this "moving" book.

1585. Seaman, Donna. "A Sense of Place." *Booklist*, 89 (November 1, 1992), 482.

A brief omnibus review.

1586. "Top New Titles." *Russian Life*, 41 (no. 4, 1998), A1.

Very brief. This portrait of Baikal is without compare. While the essay is a personal account of his discovery of Baikal, it is also full of history, local flavor, and literary allusions.

SHADOWS OF AFRICA

1587. "Books." *Science News*, 142 (7 November 1992), 306.

Brief notice.

1588. Gold, Tracy M. "Spotlight on Africa." *Travel & Leisure*, 22 (September 1992), 22.

A very brief notice of "a surpassingly beautiful book."

1589. Marschall, Laurence A. "Where the Wildebeests Roamed." *The Sciences*, 33 (January/Febvruary 1993), 43.

This is a splendidly produced book. Matthiessen's language is luxuriant with sensation, and his writing resounds with a sheer auditory intensity. The contrast between his rich prose and Frank's spare art is striking and disturbing.

1590. McNamee, Gregory. *Outside*, 17 (December 1992), [126].

Reviewed with *Baikal. See* **1579.**

1591. Merriam, Dena. "Africa Discovered." *Sculpture Review*, 41 (no. 2/3, 1992), 67.

The focus of these comments is more upon Mary Frank's art than Matthiessen's text. His "poetic narrative" gains great power and beauty from her drawings.

1592. Phillips, Jonathan. *American Ceramics*, 11 (no. 1, 1993), 48–49.

The book is a rare successful collaboration between art and literature where each component exists successfully on its own but complements the other immeasurably. Although the art work is the review's central concern, Matthiessen's "poetic prose" is admiringly noted. It is an enjoyable work as a book, a prose poem, or as a visual notebook.

1593. Phillips, Patricia L. *Artforum*, 31 (December 1992), 85–86.

This is not a long-rehearsed collaboration between Frank and Matthiessen but "an improvisational duet." His observations are "laconic, poetic, and often disquieting," capturing "the sweeping scale and regional textures of Africa in visceral detail."

1594. *Publishers Weekly*, 239 (7 September 1992), 87.

A brief notice of this "unusual and rich book." The prose is sparkling, and Matthiessen's knowledge is deep.

1595. *Reference and Research Book News*, 8 (June 1993), 43.

A very brief inconsequential notice.

1596. Rorabeck, Dick. *Los Angeles Times Book Review*, 6 December 1992, p. 36.

Matthiessen has a wondrous, almost primordial, sense of Africa. The book provides adventure, lamentation, crankiness, and mesmerization.

EAST OF LO MONTHANG

1597. Gorra, Michael. "Travel." *New York Times Book Review*, 3 December 1995, 49 [7, 49–50].

Brief comments within an omnibus review. The book is coupled with Clara Marullo's *The Last Forbidden Kingdom*. While the text cannot match the brilliance of *The Snow Leopard*, it is still "richly elegiac." The photographs convey the full grandeur of Mustang but are too sumptuous in some ways.

1598. Nino, Raul. *Booklist*, 92 (January 1–15, 1996), 779.

Brief. This is a superb report of detached compassion. The clarity of the photographs equals the clarity of the prose.

LOST MAN'S RIVER

1599. *Books Magazine*, 12 (Summer 1998), 22.

Very brief. The book is a powerful sequel.

1600. "Briefly Noted." *New Yorker*, 73 (22–29 December 1997), 136.

Although Matthiessen's skills as a naturalist and as a journalist are in evidence, this is an uneven novel.

1601. Burroway, Janet. "Still Looking for Mr. Watson." *New York Times Book Review*, 23 November 1997, pp. 16, 18.

This review provides more of a summary of the story than an evaluation of the book. The convolution of characters and their contradictory and intertwining narrations are hard on the reader. The novel does not entirely entice readers to want to follow through the maze.

1602. Catling, Patrick Skene. "The Redneck Riviera." *The Spectator*, 281 (18 July 1998), 35.

Matthiessen's attempt to construct a massive memorial to the vanishing wilderness of the Florida Everglades is going well. His dialogue is "marvelously convincing" and there are passages of quiet lyricism and sharp relevance throughout the book.

1603. Diehl, Digby. *Modern Maturity*, 41 (January 1998), 31.

A very brief notice.

1604. Fichtner, Margaria. "A Saga of Regret, Shattered Lives in Old Florida." *Miami Herald*, 2 November 1997, "Viewpoint," p. 1L.

This is a much more deeply textured and demanding story than *Killing Mister Watson*. Matthiessen has an eye and an ear for detail, and he uses the oral-history monologue to consistent effectiveness. There are some problems, such as his references to serial killer Ted Bundy and the occasional annoying blurring of the peripheral characters.

1605. Gorra, Michael. "Following the Trail of Edgar Watson." *Times Literary Supplement*, no. 4966 (5 June 1998), 23.

The lack of a coherent compelling plot is lamentable given that *Killing Mister Watson* was one the finest novels of the 1990s. Rather than keep Lucius's character in steady focus and produce a dark, moody tale, Matthiessen has allowed the narrative to drift away from the story into the backwaters of Florida history — adding not to the story itself but only to its length.

1606. Harvey, Miles. "Season's Gleanings." *Outside*, 22 (November 1997), 176.

The chorus of conflicting voices will give readers a sense of being lost at times, but this is part of "a monumental portrait of a ruinous time and a nearly ruined place."

1607. *Kirkus Reviews*, 65 (September 15, 1997), 1409.

This large vivid work is one of the best novels of recent years. It provides a powerful portrait of life in the Everglades at the turn of the twentieth century. Matthiessen skillfully interweaves a lament for the wilderness, a persuasive character study, and a powerful meditation on the sources of American violence.

1608. Kloszewski, Marc A. *Library Journal*, 122 (October 15, 1997), 142.

The book's large cast and leisurely tone make for slow reading. This is a labor of love, but readers will benefit from perusing the more succinct *Killing Mister Watson* before "tackling" it.

1609. Levi, Jonathan. "'Watson' Continues With Son's Quest." *Los Angeles Times*, 8 December 1997, p. E4.

Matthiessen has produced a powerful "triple-breed parable ... part history, part novel and part prolegomenon to some future ecological manifesto."

1610. Mars-Jones, Adam. "Welcome to the Everglades, Home of the Strangled Quonk." *Observer*, 10 May 1998, p. 17.

A persistently unfavorable review. Watson doesn't emerge as a vivid presence and doesn't seem to merit the status Matthiessen accords him. Lucius's quest for him is undramatic. Only one episode in the novel is a properly worked scene. The book is repetitious and its characters indistinct. The descriptions of nature are consistently strained and mystical. There are no certain chronological markers in the text, and Matthiessen isn't able to consistently establish the book's interior time.

1611. Mewshaw, Michael. "Mired in the Everglades." *Book World* [*Washington Post*], 8 February 1998, p. 9.

The book is a repetitious rap sheet of felonies that don't advance the story's plot or the reader's understanding. The overall effect is of a writer who has lost his selectivity. The characters are undermined by their proclivity to spout ecological cant, and by Matthiessen's failure to give them individual voices. Too often the story grinds to a halt with mini-lectures on crops or the weather. *Far Tortuga* or *The Snow Leopard* are far better examples of Matthiessen's talent.

1612. "Notable Books of the Year 1997." *New York Times Book Review*, 7 December 1997, p. 62.

Included on the list of the year's best fiction.

1613. "A Noteworthy Collection." *New York Times Book Review*, 6 December 1998, p. 97.

The book is included among those so considered by the title.

1614. Pastan, Rachel. *Salon*, 11 November 1997. <http://www.salon1999.com/books/sneaks/1997/11/11review.html>. (18 June 1999).

The characters and their interviews are too much alike. Matthiessen has lost a potentially strong, irresistible story to an intricate, mosaic meditation on the meaning of legend and history. His characters provide his historical research rather than create a story.

1615. Perrick, Penny. "Warning Belles." *The Times* [London], 9 May 1998, "Metro," p. 16.

Matthiessen may wear the reader down at times with his tenaciousness and repetition and the endless entrances and exits of characters, but he can enthrall with a quick and luminous phrase. He writes with a mournful bitterness of the woeful effects of modernity. Lucius is a masterful creation.

1616. P. K. *Rapport*, 20 (no. 5, 1998), 29.

Despite the initial difficulty of becoming involved in the story, Matthiessen has written "an extraordinary novel." The characters are drawn with great precision. This is not an easy read, but it is an immensely rewarding one.

1617. *Publishers Weekly*, 244 (13 October 1997), 56.

The trilogy "will stand as a monument to the brutal and densely layered history" of southwestern Florida. While the Faulknerian soliloquies may at first seem a contrivance, they ultimately are a "testament to both the insidious and the cathartic power of storytelling."

1618. "PW's Best Books '97." *Publishers Weekly*, 244 (3 November 1997), 52 [50–60].

Lost Man's River is among the 32 best fiction books of 1997. It is an intoxicating sequel. Matthiessen's powers as a storyteller and a naturalist combine to provide a haunting lamentation for the region's ecological and cultural depredation.

1619. Schudel, Matt. "Lost in the Swamps." *Brightleaf*, 1 (March/April 1998). <http:// www.brightleaf-review .com/Mar98/schudel.html>. (15 April 1999).

The fact of Watson is far more compelling than Matthiessen's fiction. The story bogs down in the fragmentary accounts of Watson's life and the use of dialect. It is not a persuasive work as either history or fiction.

1620. Scott, A. O. "Sins of the Father." *Newsday*, 21 December 1997, "Currents & Books," p. B9.

This is a large, flawed novel that demonstrates Matthiessen's sense of place and brilliant eye for detail. It is an example of the rare novel whose story is less interesting, and less surely handled, than its themes of the passing of a landscape and the resulting loss of a way of life attached to it. The overall narrative incoherence is masked by Matthiessen's gifts as a writer. He tells the story more truthfully and fully than most authors who attempt it.

1621. Segedin, Benjamin. *Booklist*, 94 (September 15, 1997), 180–181.

Brief. Matthiessen shows the inexactitude of history. His depictions of the families of southwest Florida are colorful. The book should appeal to those who enjoyed Cormac McCarthy's *All the Pretty Horses.*

1622. Skow, John. "Been There, Done That." *Time,* 150 (24 November 1997), [106–107].

While Matthiessen excels at writing nonfiction, he seems uncomfortable inventing "the outrageous lies" that keep novels afloat. He is at his best in his "loving descriptions" of the human and animal swamp dwellers and the natural environment. The trilogy has perhaps two books too many.

1623. Veale, Scott. "New & Noteworthy Paperbacks." *New York Times Book Review,* 4 October 1998, p. 36.

Brief. A notice of a new edition.

BONE BY BONE

1624. "Annual 1999 Bookwatcher's Guide." *Christian Science Monitor,* 18 November 1999, 13 [11–14].

Within a listing of sixteen "Noteworthy" fiction titles, *Bone by Bone* is included and briefly recommended as a brutal story and a remarkable look at the Southern frontier.

1625. Birkerts, Sven, "Heart of the Swamp." *New York Times Book Review,* 11 April 1999, pp. 8–9.

An ambivalent review. The early sections are "by far the most vivid" of the Watson trilogy, but Matthiessen's use of the Jack Watson character as a motif becomes heavy-handed. While the naturalist in him crowds the book with passages of keenly observed detail and poetic evocations, ultimately the story of Edgar Watson is too monumental. Matthiessen long ago moved from documentation to artistic redundancy. Conrad accomplished no less in *Heart of Darkness* in a fraction of the space. Still, this is a work of genuine dignity.

1626. Brett, Brian. "Matthiessen Walks on the Dark Side." *Globe & Mail* [Toronto], 17 April 1999, p. D10.

Matthiessen is a true observer whose obsessive witnessing has gradually injected a deep, pessimistic note into his recent work. He is also a troubling writer; his brilliance shines on every page but he fails often, everywhere, and magnificently. His greatest weakness is his lack of empathy toward his characters. He refuses to become emotionally involved; they are all observed from a distance. *Killing Mister Watson* is awesome and reads like a long elegiac poem, but it is marred by the similarity of voices among the minor characters and the sheer number of characters. *Lost Man's River* is the most human volume and provides a good preamble for *Bone by Bone,* but it ends with an improbable chain of events. The final volume ties the trilogy together beautifully, despite its "grinding haul to closure." The trilogy is a "tough read" by a gutsy writer, a work of flawed and uncommon genius.

1627. Camuto, Christopher. "Fiction, Forests, and Mountain Lions." *Audubon,* 101 (July/August 1999), 124.

Brief. Matthiessen writes in the company of Faulkner and Melville, embodying profound and troubling truths in his fiction. In this conclusion to a remarkable trilogy, Watson is portrayed with a passionate clarity. Matthiessen is among a very few novelists who can embed their characters so deeply in the American landscape.

1628. Charles, Ron. "The Heart of a Murderer Searching for Its Reasons." *Christian Science Monitor,* 15 April 1999, p. 17.

A very favorable notice, although one that is more descriptive than evaluative. The story is raised to the level of classic tragedy and provides a fascinating history of the southeast. Matthiessen "conveys the kind of Shakespearean insight into human nature that outstrips what nonfiction can do."

1629. Drabelle, Dennis. "Return to Chokoloskee Key." *Book World* [*Washington Post*], 16 May 1999, p. X5.

This is more of an evaluation of the trilogy than the individual book. Matthiessen is a skilled storyteller, and there is much in the trilogy to admire and savor. However, it sinks under its own weight. The repetitive stories do not always provide depth and richness but rather stupefication. *Lost Man's River* is far inferior to both *Killing Mister Watson* and *Bone by Bone*. The middle book should not be read unless the other two leave one hungry for more.

1630. "Editors Choice 1999." *Booklist*, 96 (January 1, 2000), 817 [812–829].

Brief. Watson is an utterly compelling character, and the trilogy is a magnificent epic.

1631. Fichtner, Margaria. "Trouble Comes Hunting for Mister Watson." *Miami Herald*, 11 April 1999, "Arts," p. 16I.

Although the prose is dense at times and there is an unwieldy number of secondary characters, Matthiessen has saved his best for last in this big and compelling conclusion to his trilogy.

1632. Filkins, Peter. "The Dark Side of Paradise." *The World & I*, 14 (October 1999), 276–281.

An extensive and perceptive review/essay. Matthiessen has used Watson's life "to construct an extended meditation on the relationship between truth and fiction, the ways in which the past conjures the present, and the special role of violence in shaping the frontier mentality that governs American society to this day." At the heart of the trilogy is the question of whether man is responsible for his actions or if external conditions largely control individual lives. Matthiessen's "clunky notion" of the Dr. Jekyll and Mr. Hyde idea concerning the question of Watson side-steps the answer. But it is indicative of the different approaches to the interpretation of individual experience that grapple for control of the book. The urge to regenerate oneself and the freedom to do so are at the core of both the American spirit as well as Matthiessen's ambitious effort to capture that spirit.

1633. Flynn, Gillian. *Entertainment Weekly*, 7 May 1999, p. 59.

Brief. This is a dense, mesmerizing novel that will leave the reader stunned.

1634. Gathman, Roger. *Salon*, 13 April 1999. <http://www.salon.com/books/review/1999/04/13/matthiessen>. (18 June 1999).

The reader of the previous two books will sometimes feel as if he is trudging through old business or that Matthiessen is just piling up events for their own sake. Watson's language never has the "artless plaintiveness of the first book." Only in the latter half does the story shift back to the "eerie energy" of *Killing Mister Watson*.

1635. Gilpin, Sam. "Swamp Memories." *Times Literary Supplement*, no. 5025 (23 July 1999), 21.

In Edgar Watson, Matthiessen has created a strongly realized presence and a convincing multifaceted character. This book as well as the entire complex and significant trilogy confirms Matthiessen to be a novelist of impressive range and power. It is ambitious in scale as well as in its thematic concerns.

1636. Gogola, Tom. "Our Outlaws, Ourselves." *Newsday*, 9 May 1999, "Currents & Books," p. B13.

This is a triumphant conclusion to the Watson trilogy. Watson's experiences throughout the three books are an allegory for the internal tensions taking place in late nineteenth-century America. Watson is the quintessential American outlaw and his story presents a vital understanding of the outlaw life. Matthiessen "brilliantly contextualizes" Watson, revealing both his good and bad sides to highlight his essential, albeit shortsighted, humanity.

1637. *Kirkus Reviews*, 67 (March 1, 1999), 323–324.

This is Matthiessen's *Absalom, Absalom!*. It is richly imagined and compulsively readable. Watson comes stunningly alive in a brilliant character which also serves as a provocative commentary on the "capitalist energies" that built America.

1638. Levi, Jonathan. "Last in Trilogy Navigates Legend and Life." *Los Angeles Times*, 15 April 1999, p. 4.

A favorable, although largely descriptive, review. The story of Watson's life is an allegory for the quest for life's meaning.

1639. Mastrogiorgio, Tony. "A Violent Man's Fate Fulfilled." *San Francisco Examiner*, 16 May 1999, "Book Review," p. 5.

An extremely positive assessment. The voice of Edgar Watson is an artistic triumph. He is a vividly realized character whose articulate complexity brilliantly justifies the entire trilogy. The story has an almost Brechtian sense of tragedy. It may well be a classic.

1640. McCay, Mary A. "Mister Watson, We Exhume." *New Orleans Times Picayune*, 16 May 1999, "Travel," p. D6.

A positive but not explicitly evaluative review. Generally, it provides a sense of Watson's story and his milieu and the larger achievements of the trilogy rather than the specific book.

1641. McNamara, Mary. "Author's Creation Is Larger Than Life." *Calgary Herald*, 18 July 1999, "Entertainment," p. D7.

The final book of the Watson trilogy is its heart. It answers the questions raised by the first two books. The scope, detail, and ambition of the trilogy is unmatched by any of Matthiessen's previous work.

1642. "Notable Books." *New York Times Book Review*, 5 December 1999, p. 66.

Bone by Bone is named in the "Fiction & Poetry" listing.

1643. O'Briant, Don. "Mr. Watson Has His Say." *The Atlanta Journal-Constitution*, 25 April 1999, "Arts," p. L10.

Matthiessen completes his brilliant trilogy with a searing portrait of frontier Florida and Edgar Watson. It is a sprawling tale that eloquently recreates the last years of the American frontier. He presents the tragedy of Watson in meticulous detail, but he is more interested in the greater tragedy of the plundering of the natural environment. In Watson he has presented the American capitalist spirit at its best and worst.

1644. Pearson, Ian. "Final Days of Mister Watson." *Edmonton Journal*, 20 June 1999, "Books & Authors," p. F6.

Reprint of **1645**.

1645. ____. "Mr. Watson's Unquiet Grave." *Ottawa Citizen*, 30 May 1999, "The Citizen's Weekly: Books," p. C14.

It is questionable whether most readers will share Matthiessen's obsession with Edgar Watson. The trilogy is an endurance test which is taxing at times, although ultimately worthwhile. The book is not an easy one to read, and a reading of *Killing Mister Watson* is essential to make the reader care about this voice. Too often Watson's descriptions of the natural environment are too close to Matthiessen's own nature writing. Matthiessen creates a great sense of impending doom in the last hundred pages. The brutality and potential of evil in Watson's story remain pertinent in understanding America and the American character.

Reprinted in **1644**.

1646. *Publishers Weekly*, 246 (15 March 1999), 47.

Edgar J. Watson is "a monumental creation." Matthiessen has "created an unforgettable slice of deeply true and resonant American history."

1647. "PW's Best Books 99." *Publishers Weekly*, 246 (1 November 1999), 46 [44–58].

This is one of the twenty-five best fiction books of the year. It is a triumph of characterization and historical recreation. Watson's complex character gives the novel the status of a classic.

1648. Segedin, Benjamin. *Booklist*, 95 (February 15, 1999), 1004.

This is a magnificent tour de force and a worthy companion to Wallace Stegner and Cormac McCarthy's work.

1649. Skow, John. "Lost Man's Tale." *Time*, 153 (17 May 1999), [89].

The quirky Watson trilogy is composed of three dense, fascinating novels. It is brilliant, obsessive, panoramic and probably two novels too long. The Watson character does not reach heroic stature, and the essential truth of his character ultimately does not require three long books of explication.

1650. "Summer Reading." *New York Times Book Review*, 6 June 1999, p. 34.

The book is one of the suggested "high points" in the year's fiction.

1651. Taylor, D. J. "A Question of Upbringing." *The Spectator*, 282 (29 May 1999), 34–35.

Matthiessen is an American novelist of the very top rank; this book is never less than absorbing and occasionally is breathtakingly good. It bristles with unrestrained passions. Matthiessen, as do most American novelists, easily surpasses the majority of contemporary British novelists, but he also makes a good many "modern American giants," like John Updike and Norman Mailer, look pretty feeble as well.

1652. Vaill, Amanda. "American Anti-Hero." *Chicago Tribune*, 16 May 1999, "Books," p. 4.

This is a largely descriptive notice of the book and the character of Edgar Watson. It was Watson's life force which generates the novel's raw power. He is a real American anti-hero.

1653. Vidimos, Robin. "A Last Look at Mister Watson." *Denver Post*, 25 April 1999, p. G5.

This book provides an unexpected show of force and a stunning conclusion to the trilogy. The three Watson books are unique in that there is not the sense that Matthiessen has gone on too long, despite the fact that he is retelling the same story. The novel is a haunting work that breathes realism.

1654. Wolfe, Peter. "Hard Life Gets Harder in the Never Cozy Climate of Everglades." *St. Louis Post Dispatch*, 2 May 1999, "Everyday Magazine," p. C5.

Matthiessen's alert, textured style and his decision to make Watson his narrator pro-

vide the character's evolution, or degradation, with a "whacking authority." This is an honest, gripping novel about our national origins. Matthiessen has described the pioneer sinew and grit needed to survive on a lawless frontier.

1655. Zug, James. "Eyewitnesses." *Outside*, 24 (April 1999), 177 [176–177].

Brief. The Watson saga doesn't have the scope and drama to sustain a vast trilogy, but this work is "a grand achievement" in itself. Matthiessen has created "an all-too-human character."

THE PETER MATTHIESSEN READER

1656. Harris, Hope. "A Guide to The Natural." *The Sag Harbor Reader*, Autumn 1999, p. 10.

The selections from the various books reveal the commonality of his subject matter through the years. Matthiessen has lived his life as a mission to document the vanishing ways of life, and he writes with an inherently melancholy voice.

1657. Hightower, Elizabeth. *Outside*, 25 (January 2000), 97.

A descriptive notice. The excerpts support Matthiessen's "towering stature as a writer on contemporary environmental and geographical exploration."

1658. Howard, Jennifer. "Paperbacks." *Book World* [*Washington Post*], 27 February 2000, p. X10.

In his nonfiction work, Matthiessen has repeatedly faced the same problem: how to capture a beauty that is already compromised or threatened as he encounters it. As a result, some of his finest writing is simultaneously love song and lament. While the book covers a lot of territory, his best work may still be his first nonfiction book, *Wildlife in America*.

1659. *Kirkus Reviews*, 67 (December 1, 1999), 1865.

The book is a "tasting menu" of Matthiessen's nonfiction. This collection reaffirms his "unshakable conviction that the earth's beauty and mystery are not to be trifled or tinkered with to gratify our greed or hubris."

1660. *Publishers Weekly,* 246 (20 December 1999), 75.

Brief notice. It is difficult to go wrong when compiling a selection from an author as capable as Matthiessen.

1661. Samson, Sue. *Library Journal,* 125 (January 2000), 108.

Brief. This book is a wonderful introduction and reintroduction to Matthiessen's nonfiction. These excerpts are prime examples of the literary excellence to be found in his nonfiction.

1662. Sims, Michael. *BookPage,* February 2000. <http://www.bookpage.com/0002 bp/nonfiction/peter_matthiessen_reader. html>. (2 May 2000).

Brief. This broad sampling demonstrates that Matthiessen possesses "an artistry denied to most naturalists and an expertise few literary writers ever attain."

TIGERS IN THE SNOW

1663. Abbott, Elizabeth. "Cat's Decline Is a Warning." *The Gazette* [Montreal], 26 February 2000, "Books and the Visual Arts," p. J4.

This is a dramatic, poignant and compelling book that is presented in exquisite and measured prose. It is a work about the interconnectedness of everything—about human need, greed, and the environment. The review summarizes Matthiessen's analysis of the tiger's status.

1664. Anderson, John. "Burning Bright?" *Newsday,* 20 February 2000, "Currents & Books," pp. B9, B11.

This is a passionate, gorgeous and sad elegiac defense of the Siberian tiger. Matthiessen captures the animal's nobility particularly well.

1665. Bent, Nancy. *Booklist,* 96 (December 1, 1999), 660.

Brief. Matthiessen creates an immediacy in his narrative that produces in the reader an awe of the Amur tiger. His lyrical eye provides an evocative account.

1666. Carver, Robert. "Men to Go Tiger-Shooting With?" *Times Literary Supplement,* no. 5060 (24 March 2000), 35.

The book is an easy-to-read guide to tigers, particularly the Siberian. Its tone is jovial, even jocular, popularism—a tigers for Everyman. The book is part of "conservation politics" as Matthiessen is espousing "his way" as opposed to other conservation efforts, particularly Project Tiger. The review compares the efforts of the Siberian Tiger Project to the American approach to the Vietnam War. The program is flawed, and despite its noble scientific intentions, at its heart is a desire to control, discipline, and punish. This is a deeply depressing book for reasons beyond the wild tigers doomed to extinction.

1667. *Choice,* 37 (July/August 2000), 2005.

This is a well written, well researched, thought-provoking and often exciting book. Much of this brief review is pointlessly concerned with the fact that the work is not like *The Snow Leopard.*

1668. Croke, Vicki. "In His Latest, Peter Matthiessen Has 'Tigers' by the Tale." *Boston Globe,* 17 March 2000, "Living," p. C18.

Matthiessen and tigers is a sure-fire pairing. He provides a lively primer on the tigers of the world. Although the book's real joy begins when he nears his destination, it is "low-key" Matthiessen. Still, a fine read, it never achieves "that combustible combination of evocative prose and deep understanding of all things natural" that one finds in *The Snow Leopard* and *African Silences.*

1669. Franscell, Ron. "Eyeing the Tiger's Decline." *Atlanta Journal and Constitution,* 30 January 2000, p. 12L.

Same as **1670.**

1670. ____. "Saving the Vanishing Tiger." *Chicago Sun-Times*, 30 January 2000, p. 17.

Matthiessen is one of the most intuitive nature writers of our time. He makes an eloquent case for desperate efforts to save the tiger and for enlightened coexistence between humans and tigers. This work is more analytical and less lyrical than *The Snow Leopard*; it is comparable to *African Silences* in its sobering account.

Also appears **1669, 1671–1672**.

1671. ____. "Of Siberian Tigers ..." *The Moscow Times*, 4 March 2000.

Reprint of **1670**.

1672. ____. "Vanishing Tigers." *Denver Post*, 6 February 2000, "Books," p. G1.

Reprint of **1670**.

1673. Gardner, Dan. "Thy Fearful Symmetry: Peter Matthiessen Captures the Elusive Siberian Tiger." *The Ottawa Citizen*, 27 February 2000, "The Citizen's Weekly: Books," p. C16.

This is an elegant and important book in which Matthiessen merges his "compendious scientific knowledge" with a deep feeling for the tiger. An immediate sense of the tiger's "spectral and elusive nature" is produced by the text and photographs.

1674. Gillen, Francis. "Plight of Siberian Tiger May be Test of Human's Ability to Survive." *Tampa Tribune*, 6 February 2000, "Commentary," p. 4.

This review is mostly a discussion of the tiger's status in Asia. The book is balanced, engaging, and quietly passionate. It is a "must" read for any naturalist and presents a "significantly enlightening journey" for everyone else.

1675. Goodheart, Adam. "Rough Beast." *New York Times Book Review*, 19 March 2000, p. 12.

The review is mostly a summary of the status of the Amur tiger. The book is distinctly low-key Matthiessen. It pales in comparison to *The Snow Leopard*. While the

prose is always lucid and often sad and affecting, it is less frequently poetic.

1676. Grossman, Elizabeth. "'Tiger' is Eloquent Tale of Great Beast's Plight." *Seattle Times*, 2 April 2000, "Books," p. N9.

Most of the review explains the plight of the Amur tiger and the efforts to save it. Matthiessen's call for conservation is direct. He offers his usual eloquence and depth of understanding.

1677. Hertsgaard, Mark. "Wild Things." *Book World* [*Washington Post*], 23 April 2000, p. X1.

This review is primarily a discussion of the efforts to save the tiger. The book is beautiful and urgent, written in a stately prose. Its great value is to awaken the reader to the need to act now to save the tiger.

1678. Kirkland, Bruce. "When Nature Calls ..." *Toronto Sun*, 19 March 2000, "Comment," p. C8.

An omnibus review. Matthiessen provides compelling reading. He has become "a collaborator, a historian and a convincing advocate for the tiger's survival."

1679. *Kirkus Reviews*, 67 (December 1, 1999), 1865.

Matthiessen has successfully captured this magnificent animal in an erudite profile filled with a keen anger, which makes it as much weapon as book.

1680. Lanham, Fritz. "The Cry of the Tiger." *Houston Chronicle*, 6 February 2000, "Zest," p. 14.

The book is both a brief primer on the tiger and a report on efforts to save it. It is not comparable to *The Snow Leopard*; it is "Matthiessen lite"—brief and somewhat meandering but still filled with fervor.

1681. MacDougall, Carl. *The Herald* [Glasgow, Scotland], 9 May 2000, p. 18.

A descriptive notice of the book, briefly commenting on the plight of the Siberian tiger.

1682. *Natural History*, 109 (March 2000), 82–83.

A very brief non-evaluative notice.

1683. *Publishers Weekly*, 247 (10 January 2000), 57.

The book is an eloquent and marvelously effective report on the tiger's fate. Matthiessen combines compact reportage and natural history with poetic meditation on the tiger's significance and majestry.

1684. Reynolds, Susan Salter. "Discoveries." *Los Angeles Times Book Review*, 30 January 2000, p. 11.

Brief. The book is written in a clear diplomatic, scientific tone. The concern is as much with the habitat as with the tigers.

1685. Robertson, James. "Earning Your Stripes." *Scotland on Sunday*, 19 March 2000, p. 15.

Like the tiger, Matthiessen is an endangered species, "a writer of great integrity, who lives the life he writes." His scathing critique of the all-consuming, all-exploiting society is realistic. Much of the book, which highlights the successes and disappointments of the Siberian Tiger Project, is depressing reading.

1686. Schaefer, Edell Marie. *Library Journal*, 125 (January 2000), 152.

Brief. The book is engaging and very readable.

1687. Shechner, Mark. "Matthiessen Pleads for the Wild Tiger in Splendid, Gloomy Book." *The Buffalo News*, 30 January 2000, "Book Reviews," p. 6F.

This is a tribute to Matthiessen as well as a strong recommendation of the book. The status of the tiger and the work of the Siberian Tiger Project is discussed. Matthiessen is "a writer of deep sympathies and a firm and controlled intelligence." "He is the master of the half-captured splendor, the instant that suddenly catches fire."

1688. _____. "Wanted: A World Safe for Tigers." *Jerusalem Post*, 11 February 2000, "Books," p. 12B.

Reprint of **1687**.

1689. Volkmer, Fred. "Matthiessen's Warning Cry For Big Cats." *Southampton Press*, 11 May 2000, p. B1.

It is as a nature writer that Matthiessen truly shines. This work is highly readable and informative, despite being occasionally slipshod. It lacks *The Snow Leopard*'s profundity and resonance, but Matthiessen's heart is in the right place.

1690. Wingfield, Andrew. "Tigers in the Snow." *The Amicus Journal*, 22 (Fall 2000), 35–37.

This book is another coup for Matthiessen, who once again demonstrates himself to be a distinguished eyewitness reporter, first-rate travel writer, and skilled naturalist. His approach here is a holistic one which considers the tiger's natural history along with its lore.

EDITED WORKS
NORTH AMERICAN INDIANS

1691. *American West*, 27 (April 1990), 9.

A very brief, non-evaluative notice with no mention of Matthiessen's contributions.

1692. Horwell, Veronica. "Fate's Portrait From the Prairies." *Guardian Weekly*, 21 October 1990, p. 26.

A brief appreciative assessment of Catlin as a painter and writer within an omnibus review. No comment concerning Matthiessen is made.

1693. Hymes, Dell. "Indian Identities." *Times Literary Supplement*, no. 4662 (7 August 1992), 3–4.

An omnibus review of works related to Native Americans. The Matthiessen edited volume of Catlin's work is discussed but Matthiessen is not.

J. Dissertations

1979

J1. Ladin, Sharon. "Spirit Warriors: The Samurai Figure in Current American Fiction." University of California, Santa Cruz. 218 p.

The "heroes" of four novels, Ken Kesey's *One Flew Over the Cuckoo's Nest* and *Sometimes a Great Notion*, Robert Stone's *Dog Soldiers*, and *At Play in the Fields of the Lord*, are examined and compared to don Juan's warrior in Carlos Castaneda's works. These spirit warriors are professional fighters who have a mystical predilection and a commitment to personal power. In chapter III, "Peter Matthiessen: A Lost Reality," Lewis Moon's quest for personal power and renewal is examined in relationship to Casteneda. The origin of Moon's character in the man called Picquet from *The Cloud Forest* is also discussed. The relationship between Moon's search for identity and release from "life-fear" and Matthiessen's work in *The Snow Leopard* is examined.

1980

J2. Gaines, David Jeffrey. "The Sun Also Sets: American Writers in Paris After the Second World War." University of Texas at Austin. 266 p.

Three distinct groups of writers in Paris during the post World War II years are examined: black authors, the Beats, and those associated with the various little magazines of the period. Chapter Four, "Little Magazines, Bluebloods, and Pornographers: Enterprise in the Service of Art and Self," discusses the inception and development of *The Paris Review* in comparison to other little magazines of the time, such as *Merlin* and *Points*. The cadre of writers surrounding *The Paris Review* is examined, particu-

larly George Plimpton, William Styron, Donald Hall, and Matthiessen. Matthiessen's first three novels are briefly discussed. The American writers in Paris, as a group, were "other-directed, self-advertising, and more interested in popular writing than in traditional high culture."

1981

J3. Aton, James Martin. "'Sons and Daughters of Thoreau': The Spiritual Quest in Three Contemporary Nature Writers." Ohio University. 154 p.

Edward Abbey's *Desert Solitaire*, Annie Dillard's *Pilgrim at Tinker's Creek*, and *The Snow Leopard* are examined for the thematic and formal influence of Thoreau's *Walden* upon them. *The Snow Leopard* is the quintessential twentieth-century *Walden* because it captures the spirit of its age. *Walden*'s strong influence on Matthiessen is seen in his use of "Eastern ways" to spiritual oneness. Like Thoreau, he is an explorer of the self, and nature functions as the primary vehicle for the transcendence he seeks to achieve. Matthiessen uses the snow leopard as his generative symbol, much like Thoreau uses Walden Pond. They are the central symbols of the transcending self, representing everything about the inner world that the authors want to explore. The differences among Abbey, Dillard, and Matthiessen's relationships with *Walden* are also discussed.

1987

J4. McClay, Eileen Taylor. "Images of Latin America in Contemporary U. S. Literature." George Washington University. 264 p.

The works of Joan Didion, Robert Stone, Carolyn Forché, and Matthiessen are examined for the recurring themes, use, and portrayals of Latin America. In the chapter, "Peter Matthiessen: Adam's Continuing Quest," *At Play in the Fields of the Lord* is discussed in terms of its interweaving of two traditions, the search for identity and the "heart of darkness atmosphere," with the moral tale. Matthiessen uses the jungle for its symbolic weight. It can be either heaven or hell, and evil can flourish with moral ambivalence.

1989

J5. Raglon, Rebecca Sue. "American Nature Writing in the Age of Ecology: Changing Perceptions, Changing Forms." Queen's University, Kingston, Ontario. 215 p.

Nature writing that emerged from the "age of ecology" includes three fundamental features: a growing awareness of the separation between man and nature, an expressed need to find a way to regain an entry into nature, and a perception that "self" must be defined in terms which include the world. The works of Annie Dillard, Barry Lopez, Edward Abbey, and Matthiessen demonstrate these concerns and have expanded the narrow definition of nature writing. In chapter V, "Fact and Fiction: The Development of Ecological Form in the Works of Peter Matthiessen," the way in which his life-long concern with natural history blended with his Zen Buddhist training, particularly in *Far Tortuga*, is examined. Matthiessen's career can be divided into a period of imitations and

explorations prior to his discovery of Zen (1970) and than a post–Zen period of greater spiritual and emotional journeying in his works. In *Far Tortuga* Zen provided a way of looking at the world which helped heal the division between man and nature. This work most profoundly exhibits Matthiessen's ecological philosophy of the profound sense of the inter-connectedness of all things and the need to search for new ways to be reconnected with the world around us.

1993

J6. Hovell, Laurie L. "Horizons Lost and Found: Travel, Writing, and Tibet in the Age of Imperialism." Syracuse University. 423 p.

The primary intent of this work is an examination of the British texts of travel (c. 1773–1933) to trace the idea of travel to Tibet as a means of transformation. In chapter 8, "Arrivals and Departures," the legacy of this paradigmatic structure is examined in James Hilton's *Lost Horizons*, as well as Frank Capra's film adaptation of it, and *The Snow Leopard*. Hovell finds Matthiessen's book both seductive and problematic, and attempts to work out a new approach or understanding of it. Matthiessen acknowledges the "linguistic and cultural baggage" he carries and tries to free himself of it, but he can only be partially successful. *The Snow Leopard* is a very western text in its adherence to particular ideologues, its concept of travel, and its adherence to the structure of epiphany.

K. Reviews of Sound Recordings

AT PLAY IN THE FIELDS OF THE LORD

K1. *The Bookwatch*, 13 (December 1992), 3.

A very brief review. This recording is a dramatic rendering that covers the novel's "high points."

PETER MATTHIESSEN AND GARY SNYDER

K2. Winslow, Colwell. *Whole Earth Review*, no. 89 (Spring), 75.

This tape of Snyder and Matthiessen at the Herbst Theatre in San Francisco is a good introduction to their resounding minds. They share a planetary affection and warm banter.

KILLING MISTER WATSON

K3. *The Bookwatch*, 13 (April), 10.

A brief review. The collaboration of four strong narrators provides the recording with both interest and variety.

K4. Fetherolf, Shirley. *Kliatt*, 26 (September), 58.

The reading is skillfully done, and the readers provide a variety of voices and accents for the "odd characters" who tell the story.

K5. Hoffman, Preston. *Library Journal*, 117 (March 1), 138.

The unusual narrative structure of *Killing Mister Watson* presents a problem for an audiobook, but the result is unique and challenging.

THE NATURALISTS

K6. Keppler, Joseph. *Booklist*, 90 (September 15), 170.

This is a brief review, which notes that the tape is informative.

NO BOUNDARIES

K7. *Publishers Weekly*, 240 (6 December), 37.

No Boundaries is an expansive, Zen-infused monologue. Matthiessen's "good-natured musings are contagiously appealing."

K8. Hoffman, Preston. "Books Sounds." *Wilson Library Bulletin*, 69 (February), 86 [85–86].

A brief review. This recording is an "excellent literary memoir."

L. Reviews of Videos

LOST MAN'S RIVER

L1. Cohen, Martha. *Library Journal*, 115 (September 15, 1990), 111.

This is a rambling, meditative journey with Matthiessen into the depths of the Everglades. The pace of the video is sluggish and the photography is mildly interesting but not unexpected given the subject. What makes the film worthwhile is Matthiessen himself. He is fascinating — mellow and articulate, with a lively sense of humor.

L2. Rea, Paul W. *Bloomsbury Review*, 10 (September/October 1990), 22.

The video provides a charming portrait of Matthiessen and a vivid rendering of the Everglades. It is an engaging and varied film.

L3. "Video: Videosyncrasies." *Playboy*, 37 (December 1990), 26.

Very brief. This is a Huck Finn–style journey in which Matthiessen waxes poetic.

M. Miscellany

1980

M1. Krementz, Jill. *The Writer's Image.* Preface by Kurt Vonnegut. Introduction by Trudy Butner Krisher. Boston: David R. Godine, Inc., p. [68].

A photograph of Matthiessen surf-casting at Sagaponack, Long Island, in 1975.

1997

M2. Planz, Allen. "Turtle" (For Peter). In his *Dune Heath: Selected Poems.* Sag Harbor, NY: Canio's Editions, pp. 74–79.

Poem

Index

with Patsy Southgate C72,
H192, H199; and writing
D11, D18, D23, H88, H92,
H154; and Zen D11, D17–
D18, D23, H47, H59, H88,
H92, H115, H131, H146,
H152, J5; see also *Nine-
Headed Dragon River*
"Matthiessen, Peter (May 22,
1927–)" H139
"Matthiessen, Peter, 1927–"
H13, H18, H20, H36,
H73–H74, H177, H208
Matthiessen, Rue A8
"Matthiessen and Updike" I149
"Matthiessen, Innes, Jones"
I120
"Matthiessen on Africa" H49
"Matthiessen Pleads for the
Wild Tiger in Splendid,
Gloomy Book" I687
"Matthiessen Takes Audience
on a Wildlife Adventure"
H196
"Matthiessen Walks on the
Dark Side" I626
"Matthiessen's Voyages on the
River Styx: Deathly Waters,
Endangered People" H149
"Matthiessen's Warning: Cry
For Big Cats" I689
Matthieussent, Brice A6, A9
Maxwell, Frederic Alan H162
Mayne, Richard I59
Mayoux, Suzanne A8
M. B. 184
McAllester, David P. I399
McCandless, Bruce H209
McCarthy, Cormac I621
McCay, Mary A. I640
McClay, Eileen Taylor J4
McCue, Helga P. H131
McDonald, William J. H109,
H193
McLaughlin, Richard I10, I60
McLellan, Joseph I240, I280
McLucas, Katharine H116
McMullan, James C40
McNamara, Mary H210, I641
McNamee, Gregory H134,
I579, I590
McNulty, Tim I528
McNutt, Robert J. H172
McQuaig, Linda I400
"Mean Spirit" C130
Medcalf, Stephan I505
*Meeting the Buddha: On Pil-
grimage In Buddhist India*
C131
"*Mehti* and Snow Leopard"
A32

Melville, Herman I627
"Memories of Murder" I512
"Men and the Sea" I476
*Men of Courage: True Stories of
Present Day Adventures in
Danger and Death* C36
"Men to Go Tiger-Shooting
With?" I666
Mendelsohn, Jane I529
Mendelson, Phyllis Carmel
H20
Mengel, Robert M. I169
Menil, Adelaide de A27
"Men's Lives" H75
Men's Lives A27, A33, C50,
C78, C127, C149, C155, F3,
H69, H71, H75, H84,
H123, H178, H200, H203,
I461, I463–I493
"'Men's Lives' is Rich in Flavor
but Short on Documenta-
tion" I482
Merlin J2
Merriam, Dena I591
"Mesas" A25
"Messrs Universe" I59
Metraux, Rhoda I106
Mewshaw, Michael I281, I611
"Mexican Americans I191
Mexican Life 184
Miami Herald A25, C63,
H111–H112, H122, H182,
I279, I537, I604, I631
Miccosukee Indians C63
Michaels, Leonard I326
Michalson, Greg H183
"Midnight Turning Gray"
A7–A8, B12
Midnight Turning Gray A7,
I450
Miller, David I565
Miller, Stuart H7
Mills, Nicolaus I191
Milton, John A11
"Mindful of Unity" C146
"Miniatures of Ourselves" I101
Minnesota History I425
"Mired in the Everglades" I611
"Misguided Advocacy Journal-
ism Twists Facts" H125
The Missouri Review H88
"Mr. Cook Replies" H6
"Mister Watson Author Plans
to Revisit Character" H122
"Mr. Watson Has His Say" I643
"Mister Watson, We Exhume"
I640
"Mr. Watson's Unquiet Grave"
I645
Mitchell, John G. C24
Mitgang, Herbert I530

"Mixed Up Generation" I8
Miyamoto, Kenneth A6
Moby-Dick H151, 1269
Model, F. Peter H84
Modern Maturity I603
"A Modern Quest" I21
"Modern Time, Mon" I294
"Modern Times" A27
Mohawk, John C. C105
Molloy, Robert I11
"A Moment with Peter Matthi-
essen" H142
Mongolia C111
"Mongoose Story" D11
"Monkey Business" I561
Monsieur Watson Doit Mourir
A9
Montgomery, Ruth H5
Montherlant, Henry de G1
"Monthly Book Review" I359
Montrose, David I401, I434
Moore, Marianne A21
Moore, Terrence C100
Moore, Tui De Roy C58
"Moral Swamp" I523
"More Big 1967 Books" I171
Morgan, Speer H183
Moritsch, Marc A34
Mörling, Mikael A20
Morris, Jan I364
Morrison, Philip H158
Morrison, Phyllis H158
Morse, J. Mitchell I143
Mortiz, Charles H19
Morton, Brian I435
Morton, Robert A31
The Moscow Times I671
Moseley, Charles W. H116
"Mostly Top-Notch" I57
Mother Jones H80, I43
Moulton, Gary E. I420
*Mountain Monarchs: Wild
Sheep and Goats of the
Himalya* I296
"Moving East of Eden" I139
Ms H117
Muench, Josef A24
Munos, Jose Luis Lopez A4
"A Murder in Paradise" H107,
I521
"Murdered Ink" H147
Murray, John J. I282
Murray, Michelle I241
Muste, John M. H130
"My Face (before my parents
were born)" G6
Myers, Norman I224, I234,
I242, I250
"The Mystic and the Myth:
Thoughts on *The Snow
Leopard*" H48